T012347

MY EXPERIENCE
CLIMBING OUT THE HOLE

The views expressed in this work are solely those of the author and do not necessarily reflect the views of the publisher, and the publisher hereby disclaims any responsibility for them.

iUniverse books may be ordered through booksellers or by contacting:

iUniverse
1663 Liberty Drive
Bloomington, IN 47403
www.iuniverse.com
1-800-Authors (1-800-288-4677)

Because of the dynamic nature of the Internet, any web addresses or links contained in this book may have changed since publication and may no longer be valid. The views expressed in this work are solely those of the author and do not necessarily reflect the views of the publisher, and the publisher hereby disclaims any responsibility for them.

ISBN: 978-1-5320-3391-9 (sc)
ISBN: 978-1-5320-3390-2 (e)

Library of Congress Control Number: 2017917459

Print information available on the last page.

iUniverse rev. date: 12/14/2017

My Experience

Climbing Out the Hole

Andrew Marshall (Drew M)

Contents

Intro

ey!!!

So, I guess the reasoning behind why I wanted to write a book and this book specifically is because well...why not!? I consider myself an opinionated person, plus this is a book where I decided to talk about my life so who best to tell the story about certain parts of my life than myself, right?

People have many reasons for why they do things and straight up I'm doing this to get and make some good money off this fuckin' book, make people laugh, and to help those who read my book in the process.

My life is pretty funny, and I am pretty interesting for someone who was deemed as a fuck up by society, but they can't stop me or people similar to myself!

There are many, MANY people out there who would love to read or hear about different life subjects from an individual who is a bit different from them and I consider myself to be that guy. So, sit back, read and enjoy this book while I take you for a ride!

I also would like to point out that this book is also for people who deal with some sort of mental health related issue/s, as well as people who are dealing with a hell of a lot feeling isolated not knowing what to do. Coming from a guy who wanted to jump subway train tracks and bridges, trust me "YOU/WE" can get better.

You are not alone.

My name is Andrew Marshall and I have many nicknames for the social circles I find myself mixed in. I grew up within the central part of Toronto (North York). People called me Biggs or Biggie since I looked similar to Biggie Smalls.

One of my close childhood friends who is now an extremely talented and successful artist used to call me "Drew Bot" along with another close childhood friend Mr. Beow who used to come down to the city on the weekends to chill since we all liked to head downtown for comic books and records for DJ'ing.

People called me Drew once in a while, but I didn't start calling myself Drew until I was in my early twenties. I now refer to myself as Drew M since it sounds cool and if I were to pick up a girl it sounds smooth.

While I was growing up I was fun and loving. I think I am still fun and loving because of my sister who was very protective of me. She was also bossy, but I guess she just wanted the best for me.

I love my moms, but when it comes to being raised in the city my sister taught me what I needed to know since she herself was learning firsthand how to live in the city since we were first generation Canadians born to Jamaican parents.

With all that being said, I have always been somewhat of a sensitive person for whatever reason, and I really felt as if I could sense and feel what others were going through, kind of like picking up on good, or, bad, energy.

I also naturally did things in an inverted way, and did things differently from other people.

When I was in the fourth grade at this school in my area which is now a private academy, my teacher, who was this strict East African, favoured girls and was very strict on the dudes for whatever reason.

One month we gave out chocolate bars for charity and then had weekly draws to see who would win whichever toy they were giving away that week! On this particular week, he was giving away this pod that would light up once you pressed the bottom platform it was connected to and flew vertically. When I saw that I knew right away I had to have that!

We had to write our names on little pieces of square paper, and fold it up until it was small enough to throw in a box so our teacher could shake it to do a draw. Maybe it's twisted, sick, or me just knowing early in life how people worked, but before I threw my name in the box I took a pencil and shaded my folded piece of paper all over to the point it was dark and shiny!

Once the draw started and my teacher sifted his hands through the box my name was called. I was eight years old then and knew what I did and my teachers face stayed looking puzzled, knowing damn well he wanted to give the prize to a girl instead.

That was back in nineteen-eighty-nine or so. Back then I was more happy and loved life, but something kept happening to me...I kept getting anxious and for the slightest reasons! I never knew why and I don't know how it all started, but for me all I've known up until recently (two-thousand-and-fifteen) is anxiousness! And I figured everyone for the most part was just like me.

From as early as five years old, I remember going to school feeling anxious and as I got older in age going into grade after grade my anxiety became worse. When having breakfast in the morning my stomach would feel so fragile. Then once I went to the front door? Bam! I felt like my world was about to be over! Looking outside seemed like hell, and looked like something I couldn't deal with. I guess that was the start to what would be known as my troubled life.

While at school, once gym time came, I would hide or didn't wanna be a part of the activities at all. I used to leave and hide somewhere or take off, especially when we played volleyball.

At that early of an age I didn't get or care why a lot of people cared to "win" at a game they weren't getting paid for. I didn't like the pressure either so it all seemed pointless to me.

My school experience from a very early age was far from normal. I was put into special education classes since the third grade and since that time found it very hard to break free from their clutches once I was in their system. Slowly, the more I was attending my special education classes the more I was missing out on the actual curriculum. I was falling further and further behind, and this is the main thing that kept me in the special education system for quite a while.

By the time I got to the sixth grade my anxiety got even worse so, I really didn't give a fuck about school in any sense of the word by that point. I was into cutting and hurting myself, and didn't care much about anything and figured EVERYTHING was my fault. I would hit my head until I had a pounding headache or to the point of being dizzy. I would recite the phrase "I hate myself" and that's how I lived my life.

By this point I was extremely far removed from what school was about so I found it very easy to disengage from school and the only reason for why I would get up in the morning was to find loose change so I could play video games at the convenience store on my way to school. This type of pattern carried on until I was in high school and I find it funny how I reached high school in the first place since I hardly attended any of my classes.

Once in high school, skipping was like my version of school by this point and I did it with flying colours! As time went on I felt more alienated because I was in a place that had nothing to do with my daily life and I wondered why I even came to school in the first place. I think I might have done grade nine over two and a half times. My heart was never really into it because I truly felt like I would gain nothing from finishing school.

Around this time, I always used my imagination to help me execute ideas and knew how to put them together, which is what I still do to this day, and since I developed a love for good music since my dad was always playing it I decided that I wanted to be a DJ at the age of fourteen.

The more events and experiences I kept having in life the more I realized my path had nothing to do with me going to school, so I just went with the flow and did what I loved. Aside from entertaining you and making you laugh, this book was also written to show love, understanding, and courage. I believe we are all special, but we just need a reminder of that.

Throughout my chaotic fuckup of a life I started to realize that whatever made logic to me is all I needed to worry about and stopped listening to outside sources as much as I used to. There is no "normal" way when it comes down to it and there definitely isn't a right way to do things because guess what? Although we are all the same in a lot of ways we also have had different and unique experiences which make us all process the world the way that we do!

My experience and story is a testament to that, and I want to let people know and realize there is more than one way of how to be or go about things in this huge world of ours, and really there is no standard way. Whether you find yourselves like me, or slightly different from me, don't worry. Hold your head up regardless! There's a reason for why you are the way you are.

CHAPTER 2

Before I Got Help

I was always anxious and an extreme over thinker.

In nineteen-eighty-seven, at the age of seven, I remember always playing outside running around with my sister, my neighbour who is pretty much like my second sister, and one of my other childhood friends. We lived right off a major intersection that bordered two neighbouring boroughs, North York and Scarborough. We played in the front yard running around trying to catch each other. While we played, I remember everything seemed fine, then out of nowhere time seemed to slow down in a sense.

When this happened, it was as if I stepped out of my body and watched everything happening around me, everyone was having fun, smiles, and cars passed up and down the street and as I watched this? The main thought that I had was "we're all gonna die one day and that this very moment will just be a memory, a period in time, then, nothingness is what's after."

Once I somewhat snapped back into the present, I freaked out and started to run. Just run as if I was trying to get away from those thoughts and the feelings of nothingness and sure sudden death being right around the corner in the near future. Things like that would happen to me repeatedly throughout my life.

I remember playing Nintendo one time, playing a game I borrowed from my friend in the house over (*Little Nemo: Dream Master*). I was playing on a weekday, it might have been on a Wednesday, then "Bam" everything slowed down, I stepped out of my body, but everything was still happening as I watched it.

I kept playing the Dream Master game, but said to myself that it would all be a sweet memory that will fade into grey since we're all going to die. That's when I stopped the game, well paused it since that's all we could do back then, and just RAN. I ran to my mom's room and saw her and my dad talking like everything was okay. I looked at them and thought fuck, they're gonna be dead too!

I don't know how I recovered or managed to cope with this constantly happening to me, but I somehow seemed to carry on with life. While stuff like that was going on, I remember being at home with Mom sometimes and would run up to her, holding her, freaking out thinking I was going to die, then... it would all stop! As fast as it happened, is as fast it would not happen. Heh, I guess that's the start of what developing panic attacks is supposed to feel like...

By the time it was nineteen-ninety, I was in the sixth grade and I remember not liking the change and transition from elementary school to middle school since it was different. New faces, new people, but at least I was connected back with some of my boys that were a grade higher than me. In the earlier stages of elementary school I was known as a big guy not to mess with, but that slowly started to change as I got into higher grades and different schools. I guess we all meet our match sooner or later.

In sixth grade, I remember seeing a lot of the grade seven and eight kids. They usually tried to intimidate the grade six kids a bit because we didn't really know what the hell was going on. Luckily for me it wasn't too crazy because a lot of the people I knew in and around my neighborhood knew me so it wasn't nothing I couldn't really handle.

As time went on while being stuck in this grade I remember increasingly not liking it! I mean sure, most kids don't like school, but I already had an early head start hatred for it. On Sundays, especially at night, I remember not being able to eat and kept thinking about how school would turn out the following day. I played video games, but wasn't fully aware or paid attention because I was thinking about school and for some reason all I can remember is me eating curry goat and the taste reminded me of death and trouble.

I also had a short temper and couldn't handle or control myself if something went wrong. I always felt as if I did things the wrong way, so always looked forward to punishing myself for it. I always felt like I had to be perfect.

So now I'm melting down with panic and have anger issues that come and go, and I'm not doing any school work. One night I had a parent and teacher meeting and my mom came, so the teacher explained to her how I was behaving. She told my mother that I wrote

"I hate myself" in big letters in my binder. They talked about me while I was sitting a few desks away from them, then they called me over to join them.

"Andrew? Why did you write I hate myself in your binder?" my teacher asked. Once I heard that, I was in shock and kind of embarrassed at the fact she brought it up, so, like any other kid around the age of ten I did what kids do best— I lied. I made up this bullshit story about how my friends and I created a game called "I hate myself" with a ruler spinning and whoever it ended up pointing to had to say they hate themselves.

I gave them details and was very descriptive with how the game worked, but looking back at it now, I doubt either of them bought my bullshit story since no grown woman would believe that! But at the time I figured I was hiding my issues well. Then what do you know? A couple of weeks after this "meeting" my teacher asked me, along with this other girl in my class to stay after school to discuss placing us both in special education. "Fuck" I said to myself, not again! I got very defensive with my teacher and said, "I don't wanna go in." She then said, "Oh, you can try it out for a week and see how you like it." We both agreed, but really do kids have any authority or say so? Hardly!

After about a week of being in special education with this butch-like female teacher that tried to hide or downplay her sexuality since she might have feared being judged or feared losing her job, we stayed after school once again to speak with our main homeroom teacher about how we liked spending some time in this new class. I immediately said, "I don't like it" thinking that's all it would take to get me out of that class. That's when my homeroom teacher went on to say, "Oh, well I don't think you're giving it a fair chance."

Back into Special Ed I go…

I fell so far behind in my regular school curriculum where all my other friends were to the point I hardly knew what was going on, but by this time I put little to no significance on school so this made it that much easier to skip. To kill time, I used to walk the hallways a lot and didn't care much unless it was music class and that in its self was bullshit! I played the clarinet in music class, but the teacher switched me to the drums and at the time I was happy about it. But really? Looking back, she might have done that to make things easier on herself and maybe me, but little did she know I programmed drum arrangements at home on my sister's keyboard, and always thought of patterns in my head.

In class, I ended up playing the same repetitive snare hits over and over and over and OVER again in class. Yeah, it bothered me too. One time while in class I played the *Smells Like Teen Spirit* drum pattern by *Nirvana* then everyone stopped to come over, so then I stopped as people started to crowd around.

When seventh grade came around I was…beyond lost. I was basically a walking body with no soul, so any chance or opportunity I got to sneak off to leave I did! When school spring dances came around I viewed that as the perfect time to be gone, heading to the mall or I would dip out with one of my boys who had one of those chill type of dads who was okay with everything. He also had a thing for black women and LOVED them!

Me and this kid used to play video games at the mall during lunch or even after lunch. He was like me in many ways and didn't give two shits about school either. It's funny because out of all my middle school friends he was among some of the coolest! Since his dad always hooked him up with more than enough money for lunch he'd ALWAYS lookout for whoever was around him and shared whatever he bought just so long as you were a part of the crew. He had a built-in smile on his face and had a goofy laugh with little to no care in the world.

During sixth and seventh grade is when I also discovered porn and was hooked from day one! Books, movies you name it I tried to experience it then after a while I decided "shoot, why not sell this?" I sold books and movies to my close friends in middle school to make them happy and I loved being the "go-to" guy. This one Filipino friend of mine started to call me Mr. X and I loved the title. I figured that if I was going to be at school I might as well make it worth my while, and eighth grade was no different really.

During this time, I started to notice I became a bit more avoidant, especially around the morning rush but didn't understand why. And getting slapped into special education was just the cycle, which they refused to understand.

Starting in high school with more of my friends and my sister being there was perfect, I thought. But half way through grade nine I disliked it. The new people, the lockers, and I just wasn't into the school lifestyle since it had nothing to do with me, and my feelings of anxiety developed into something even more extreme than what I experienced before, so I avoided everything.

Since I had issues with conforming and settling into places, I did what I seemed to do best — withdraw — so that's when I took my skipping profession to a whole new level and I loved it! I'd leave school to go hang out at another school since some of my middle school friends went there, but little did I know life would gradually take its course so people I once knew naturally grew apart and made new friends. I stopped going over as much, and if I happened to see someone it would be a quick greet of hi, and then bye as we kept it movin'.

Life-changing events, such as changing schools, friends, and different situations were a shock to my system and something that was hard to get used to. Like many other male kids hitting puberty I started becoming VERY uncomfortable around girls and stopped functioning. So between the school hallways and now me not being able to function around girls I slept in the washrooms or hung out until it was time to head home. Slowly, my routine became sleeping in until the afternoon then I would hang out with the older guys in my area. Now that was fun! And I learned a lot more about life from them than any form of school.

Because of my absence from school and all my other issues, Children's Aid and Social Services tried to get involved. I used to see cars parked outside of my house. I didn't know if they were undercovers checking up on our house from time to time, or trying to spy on nearby friends. While writing this I also did a mental count of how many therapists I have seen in my life, and the count comes up to around eight or so! Ha! The first one I saw was this black dude who had an office with dimmed lights, which made the place look pretty cool. Me, my mom, and my dad were at this session as he asked them what I would do. My mom said I screamed a lot and got hyper out of the blue and would hit and hurt myself when mad. They were just looking for answers and I don't even remember how I even ended up seeing him.

Then when I was fourteen or fifteen we headed to Sick Children's Hospital located in downtown Toronto so I could see a child psychologist. I remember waiting outside in the hallway with my sister joking around while our parents were inside talking with the doctor. It all seemed to take so long and all I remember is I was bored and just wanted to leave.

The door finally opened, and then I was invited to come into the room. I don't quite remember all of what happened, but me, my parents, and the doctor were there talking until I was left in the room with just the doctor and him asking me to draw a picture of myself. I drew a picture of myself with a big fro (afro) decked out in nice clothes looking cool! Or so I thought. I think my drawing even had a screw face.

After our interaction with me doing some tests, my parents were called back into join. My sister must have been in the room at some point, but I just remember it being me and my parents in the room near the end of the session. Based off our interaction, this doctor diagnosed me with having ADHD then we left the psychiatric section of the hospital and headed back down towards the main floor to leave. I remember I asked for a chocolate Danish with butter cream in the middle since that's what I saw as we walked past this food section since I was hungry. Then my sister said, "You can't have that." Then my mom said, "Andrew, remember what the doctor said, you can't have sugary things anymore because it'll make you hyper." I begged for it and they eventually got it for me then we left.

Once we got home I headed over to my boy's house next to me to laugh and joke about what happened at the hospital. He loved sweets, well sour sweets, and bought some. At first I didn't get any sweets, but I think I ended up buying a pack of some M&Ms saying to myself, "Fuck it." Sometimes when people get diagnosed with having something they fall into these certain categories. Some wear it like a badge of honour; others are simply relieved they finally know what's going on, and for others it makes them want to isolate, which makes them worse! As for myself, I think I rejected the whole ADHD theory and continued to live life.

The Third was a double team pair of psychiatrists at Scarborough General Hospital in east end Toronto. I remember being scared walking through that hospital and their hallways, but excited and alive at the same time. We walked through the hospital then went out of these doors then up, crossed through this strange little playground to get to another children's psychiatric unit. As a family, we all waited for a bit until we were finally called in to sit with this pair of doctors. They looked like a comedy duo instead of actual doctors, but as some may already know doctors can sometimes be more fucked than we actually are!

We all introduced ourselves, but the main reason for why we were there was because of me. After talking to us one by one, the doctors started asking my parents about how they got along with each other. That was one of the first times I heard my parents express emotions for each other that deeply. It also shed some light on MORE issues that were lurking within our household, and the doctors pointed out that sometimes all it takes is for one child to act up inside the home to let you know there might be other issues going on. That child is usually classified as the "identified child" they went on to say.

My sister was sweet and cute as usual and said her piece about FAM, herself, and left it at that. By the time it got to me, I started talking about school, hallways, anxiousness, anger and really let out how I felt about life and myself. I ended up going back to see those doctors a few more times, but sessions just with me and them. In and around this time I was also prescribed Prozac and Ritalin and never wanted to take it, but what kid likes medication?

Pop is something I loved, just like any other kid, but I wasn't allowed to have it whenever I wanted it. My dad started giving me pop after a while and usually at night, and I was more than willing to take it, but I never understood why he kept giving it to me. The top of my drink always seemed to look white, but I thought nothing of it, that is until I put two and two together and I said "wait." If I'm not supposed to have this then why is my dad giving it to me? After a while I realized that my medications were being mixed in my drinks!! I was probably pissed about it, but my dad probably just wanted to "fix" this situation and didn't know what else to do.

I chased my dad around the house once with a knife until I got him downstairs where he locked himself in one of the rooms then called the police on me. Four police came, and the oldest one dragged me outside of the house in just my robe. My dad told them the story, then they (the police) followed me to my room and demanded I take my Ritalin. I put it in my mouth, but faked that I swallowed it.

There was this very attractive and sexy female out of the four of them who watched to see if I swallowed my meds, and the whole time while they were in my room all I kept thinking about was is them not going under my mattress since my hardcore porn mags were there, plus that's where I hid the knife. Since I faked taking my medication they just left after as if nothing happened.

I was barely going to school at this point and even if I did go I never stayed long and I usually headed back home to watch *Jerry Springer* back when it was HOT! Digging into my skin with my nails to feel the pain and banging my head into walls hoping I would blackout or get knocked out was VERY normal by now. On one of my last visits with those comedic doctors at Scarb General, my dad told them how I dug into my skin and I was forced to show them. I felt embarrassed about it and even more so since a female student was present doing her placement for social work.

The last family session we had with these doctors started and ended with one of them saying, "I'm sorry I can't work under these conditions!" Then he flung his hands up and walked off. I purposely made sure we were late since I didn't cooperate when we had to leave the house to go. That was one of the last times we saw them and one of the last times we were at Scarborough General Hospital. This was nineteen-ninety-five.

As a few years passed, my mom found an African doctor instead of the Chinese doctor I had for a couple of years. I was glad too because that crazy fuck had it out for me. He never seemed to like me or my sister very much and he tried his hardest to try and put me away in a mad house! This new doctor was in the heart of Scarborough near Kennedy Station. My mom told him all about what was going on with the family and with me. Based off what he heard he quickly replied and said, "Your child doesn't need medication. He's just acting up as kids do! He's fine!" Hearing that kind of made me feel better and I took a liking to him because he actually listened to me when I would speak about my problems.

My parents finally took me off the medications I was taking, but it didn't really matter as much because it wasn't like I was taking them on a regular basis, but it at least felt good knowing that war was over. I saw this doctor from, ninety-seven all the way into two-thousand-and-one.

Victoria Park and Ellesmere is where I was born and raised, but we eventually left in November nineteen-ninety-nine. It happened so fast to the point I never really got the chance to tell some of my friends, and this was another shock to the system, being away from friends and being in a whole new area.

Around this time, I was going to an alternative school named Scarborough Centre for Alternative Studies and crossed paths with old friends ironically. This school was like the final destination or landing spot for dysfunctional youth who schools gave up on. It was a pretty neat system, though, because it helped everyone go at their own pace. It was like a school within a school with different sectors and all.

For the most part, I loved the SCAS system. I was at home with others who were similar to me and there was this cute girl I kept seeing around school. Let's call her Lesia. Lesia was very cute and shy, which is probably why I liked her. I wasn't the only one that did, though. Being who I am and always figuring out a way to get what I want, I told myself that I would say "What's up?" to her the next time I ran into her. Then it just so happened we ended up in the same classes together, so I eventually straight up told her I liked her and wanted her number. She was in shock at first then agreed to give it to me, then we started talking.

We had three or so sweet conversations on the phone until one evening while we were on the phone her personality shifted a bit and she started acting bitchy. I guess everyone has an "intro" personality then once they feel it's time to bring out the true them they do it. I thought she was joking with me at first, but she kept saying "Yup, this is me." I mean, she was still nice and cute and all, but she was more... expressive. She eventually told me most of the details about her life, one of them being that she was molested by her father and stepbrother. She ended up talking A LOT about that and to me it seemed like she was reliving her past every day! She kept telling me not to feel sorry for her whenever she would talk about it, but the more I heard her stories the more fucked up they became.

One thing I learned from that situation is if you're someone with issues who can't confront your issues they'll plague you for years and it's tough for you to move on. Rape and molestation are hard to deal with and some people who deal with that live it every day, even down to the sex. Which is when, where, and why she wanted me to fuck her "rape style" or else she wouldn't give it up she said. Though we fooled around and stuff, I never did anything relating to rape style at all because it was straight up too disturbing to me. That situation caused me to become a bit obsessive and compulsive with having scary obsessive thoughts such as:

- Forgetting how to talk
- Having my mind being reduced to the intelligence of a small child
- Becoming Schizophrenic
- Turning Gay
- Turning Crazy

I had rituals, or maybe I should say compulsions I would do. Checking, checking and MORE checking! I for sure thought I was batshit by this point and was depressed about it all, and figured there was no going back. I made an appointment with my doctor to talk to him about how I was feeling, and also slipped it in that I was concerned about my dick size. The African doctor I had progressively started to hear more and more of my concerns and I guess because of all that I was sayin' it led him to quickly say, "You have issues" then he gave me a referral to go see a psychiatrist at Scarborough General Hospital. I never wanted to go back to Scarborough Gen and feared I would run into someone I knew, so we chose another location, and I specifically requested I see a Black doctor this time so he made it happen.

It was year two-thousand-and-one, and by this point I desperately wanted a psychiatrist since while at my friend/brothers house a Paxil commercial came on talking about people not feeling comfortable in social situations. This same commercial also mentioned the words "Social Anxiety" so I became a bit uncomfortable, and although I had no idea what Social Anxiety was at the time, the commercial made PERFECT sense to me, so I told myself that when I get home I might have to research online more about what it all meant.

I remember it like it happened yesterday. I was in my basement and typed in the phrase thinking nothing important would come up at all, but to my surprise the net was littered with anxiety stuff. Being excited and overwhelmed, I clicked on every link after the other until I had over twenty tabs opened. When I read up on the description for what Social Anxiety means and how it affects people, I knew without a doubt that I had it and I didn't deny it. This is another reason for why I obviously wanted to see a psychiatrist too.

The doctor's office wasn't too far from where my actual family doctor was and not too far from where I lived, so that was a good thing. I showed up and sat in the waiting room with some other people who didn't look like they were in good shape. I felt uncomfortable in the room so I had my head down looking at the floor half the time until my name was finally called, then I went upstairs to the doctor's office.

When I got upstairs I was greeted by this very old doctor that had an unkempt office that looked like an attic. I told him that I think I have Social Anxiety Disorder and that I looked it up on the internet and related to half the symptoms, but then he abruptly stopped me and told me that I had Generalized Anxiety so I reacted back saying, "No I don't! I have Social Anxiety!"

Our session slowly turned into an arguing match over who was right, so near the end he got mad and we both stopped talking only for me to get booked to see him again the next week. When I went back to see him he didn't even want to debate; he just wrote me up a prescription for Lorazepam then told me I had Generalized Anxiety and sent me on my way.

Before and after seeing this doctor, I researched a bit about Mood and Anxiety medications and figured they would save me. I also took heed to the fact that some could also become very addictive, but I highly doubted it.

I was one month into school by this point since I enrolled into a private college and finally got my prescription for the Benzodiazepine Lorazepam filled. Fuck, the first time I put them things under my tongue I was in heaven by the time it dissolved! "Yes! I did it! I'm cured!" I said to myself. I was walking around without a care in the world I felt so free! I was prescribed to take three pills a day, but once the medications effect wore off I found myself needing more! And found myself becoming addicted.

My life went further downhill, although I got good grades. I slowly stopped going to school (what a surprise) and started getting sick to my stomach because of all the stress. I changed doctors around this period so that I had a doctor who was closer to my area. I also started becoming very isolated around this point.

It's crazy what the mind can and will do to you, feeling physically and mentally tired from life after heading back home on the bus from a visit from my new doctor, which was closer to home. As soon as I stepped out of the doors of this bus I actually remember making up my mind right there and said, "This is the last bus ride I'm gonna take." From that point on the insides of my house would be all I would mostly see until two-thousand-and-six, when I slowly tried to get myself back into the flow of shit!

In two-thousand-and-three to two-thousand-and-five I saw two other psychiatrists at another hospital in Scarborough, which was closer to me. The first was this short woman who seemed like she was out of her damn mind!

As usual, I waited uncomfortably in the waiting room with everyone else who was there and it killed me! I was so fragile by this point that simply thinking about any kind of doctor visit and waiting rooms had me awake for the whole night, and with me having thoughts of slitting my wrists.

"Andrew, are you incompetent? You must be if you can no longer take the bus," she said to me after I told her my situation and why I didn't go anywhere. I was mad at her so I remained silent and then she said, "Andrew, I sense that you are mad. Tell you what, this is what we will do." She wrote me up a prescription for another Benzodiazepine then said, "Sure, you might lose some of your memory after a while, but who cares you'll live better. Sounds good?" Our time was up and I don't think I said much to her beyond that point and left.

Still not giving up on myself, I called that same hospital back and told them I wanted a good doctor that wasn't burnt out who deals with people who have Social Anxiety, so the secretary set me up with another doctor ASAP. The second doctor at this same hospital was a bit better. I told him my deal and why I'm so screwed up. He said to me. "Okay, I want you here Tuesday at eight a.m." He did this for me so I wouldn't have to deal with the waiting rooms and so I could have more time with him. He was an interesting doc to say the least, and had an "I don't give a fuck" attitude about things and helped me out as much as he could at times too.

He recommended certain books to me pertaining to Anxiety Disorders and wanted me to write Cognitive Behavioral Thought Records (CBT) so that I could keep track of my distorted thoughts, so that I could change them.

When I came to see him in the morning he'd always be on the phone trading stock like an asshole then tried to get me into it. It was cool seeing him but after a while he seemed to only care about one thing... "Money!" Making, selling and buying money.

By the end of two-thousand-and-five I was still in the same situation and I wasn't getting out unless it was to go with my sister shopping or hangin' out with my boy here and there. I institutionalized myself to hell, and if I wasn't inside I didn't feel safe. Picture that, being inside so long you've forgotten the smell of natural air to the point you've lost most of your social skills. Then being so paranoid to go into your room fearing people can see you from outside because your lights are on and that everyone is watching you.

Your whole block is making fun of you because everyone looks at you as Mr. FUCK UP and everyone knows, you've been inside so long to the point you've literally lost the ability to open the door to go outside. Only those who have gone through this cycle know how that feels, but I say this...don't worry yourselves; you will get better because you are alive and are breathing. If you can picture a healthier version of yourself then that person is right around the corner waiting for you.

My sister would run errands here and there, and tried to get me out whenever she could. I used to create a lot of outlandish excuses for why I couldn't, which only made sense to me. My sister and people that support just like her deserve awards, though, because she helped me during my darkest periods, so for that I am always thankful.

I remember my sister kept asking me to go outside and I kept saying I'm not ready, but out of nowhere she said to me, "Drew, you're never gonna be ready, you just have to go." Hearing that hit me pretty hard and made me say, "Damn, my sis is right. I'll never be READY...I just have to go!" So, I tried to seize the day.

My sister was going to school for journalism and always wanted to intern at one of our local news stations and eventually did! She started working at Global News, a station here in Toronto. In the fall of two-thousand-and-five, close to Christmas heading into December, my sister randomly gave me a call. "Drew, they're doing a special at Global News about people who have Mood and Anxiety Disorders. I know you always wanted to share your story, so would you be interested in doing this? They have been looking for someone to feature on a special they would like to air about all this stuff."

Freaked out, scared, and on the verge of shitting my pants, I said "yes." This was my opportunity to speak my mind and let people know more about Mood and Anxiety and other Mental Health related issues such as Social Anxiety Disorder, which was wrecking my life. I really had NO idea what I was getting myself into, but that's how I was. Even though there were certain things that scared and freaked me out I always seemed to want to do them and passion was overriding my fear I guess.

My sister got off the phone with me to tell her crew she knew of someone who would be willing to talk about Anxiety related issues. She then called me back within ten minutes and told me everything was a go and that I'd meet up with a reporter a week or two from then, and I couldn't wait.

Within a week and a half, I finally met up with the reporter who was assigned to do the feature on me along with her cameraman. They came directly to my house, so I made sure I was ready beforehand.

The reporter was average height white with dirty blonde hair. She looked beautiful and I sensed she was very compassionate as soon as I laid eyes on her and as we started to communicate. The cameraman was a white, brown-haired, husky dude around my height with a beard. We talked for a bit before heading out and talked about how individuals with Anxiety issues deal with being outside and at the mall.

They put a heart monitor on me to rate how my heart would react once leaving my house. I figured it wouldn't show or do much, but it did in fact start going all crazy once I stepped foot outside, but we all dismissed it. When we finally arrived, and ended up at this mall in another area away from where I lived, a mall called Pickering Town Centre, the reporter asked to see my heart monitor, so I showed it and the reading jumped up again so they were in shock and so was I. I chose this mall since I didn't want many people within my area to see what I was doing.

We walked into the mall as the cameraman filmed me, and if there was anytime that I felt like people were watching me it would obviously have to be now! I walked and people started looking and wondering what the fuck could be going on. And in a sick and twisted way, I loved the attention since I felt like I was doing a service to others like me who weren't willing to put themselves out there to tell their story.

The way I saw it? This story had to be told and I was right there on the frontlines to explain it all. After it was all done I remember the reporter asked me if I wanted anything to eat, but I said no since so many of my rusty social skills made me think I couldn't eat out in the public, and that I had to be perfect like everyone else.

We sat and talked as they ate, then we ended up talking about Social Anxiety and the cameraman out of the blue said, "You know, I feel like that sometimes," then the beautiful reporter gave him a look as if to say "c'mon, you gotta be kidding me? You do not deal with that fool." But you never know...

Once they were finished eating, we did two more shots before leaving the mall and wrapping up the segment. Now before or after all of this we filmed at my house, they talked to my mom, my sister then me. It kind of gave me relief to see my mom talk and express herself about what it is I was going through since I never heard her talk about my situation the way that she did.

After it was all said and done, they told me all of what we filmed would be edited and aired by the evening, then they thanked me and left! I never fully knew the power of editing video, but in less than a couple of hours it was on air and I remember I emailed a few of my friends to let them know that I would be on TV. By the time it aired, I was at my friend's house watching the repeat of it with his family. I don't know what they thought of it since no one really addressed it since it was touchy, but I suspected his brother might be dealing with what I deal with, but never asked.

By the time I got home, a lot of my friends were hitting me up via email and on the phone. One of my close friends at the time, and someone I still love, Te-Te, called me and said, "Aww, I'm so proud of you, Jewels." That was one of my many nicknames. Then she went on to say, "There's so many mans in the city getting shot up and here you are as this guy talkin' about how you can't leave your house though?" I found it funny, but didn't find it funny. My situation was pretty real! And at that moment there were a lot of people getting shot in Toronto, especially in my area since people from my area weren't getting along with people south of my area and niggas were getting dropped every week if not every two weeks. That raised my Anxiety up even more and made me not wanna head out since I didn't know what was going on.

Although I loved doing the feature and felt like I was doing people similar to me justice when the actual feature was shown, HALF of what

I said was cut out and they only focused on Panic Attacks (a form of Anxiety Disorder). Here I was this guy thinking Social Anxiety would get talked about, but the segment was turned into an issue about Panic while going Christmas shopping. A few days right after the feature was aired I was notified that this doctor who was also a part of the same feature wanted to help me with all that I was going through, since he not only understood my issues, but he wanted to treat them as well.

After getting myself processed into his clinic I finally got a chance to see him and then I was set up to see a therapist at this same clinic. "This is it, this is what I've been waiting for," I said to myself. I felt like all the other doctors I went to didn't quite get me or what I was going through enough to fully help me, so it seemed like I struck gold with this doctor and this new clinic, so yeah, this is how I found and started seeing my eighth doctor, which I am still currently seeing to this day.

CHAPTER 3

Feeling Discouraged

*I*t was two-thousand-and-six and I was finally getting the help I thought I needed. I started going to this new clinic where my new psychiatrist and therapist were at. My therapist was a drop-dead beautiful Indian woman who I felt very uncomfortable around at first and I remember I had a dream about her the day right after she introduced herself to me for the first time. In the first stages, I saw her every Wednesday in the afternoon and it was pretty tough just to get there.

My routine after a while turned into me seeing her three times a week and walking around. She walked around with me, then gave me certain tasks to do on my own. My sister helped me to get to the clinic by driving me down and helped me with taxi fare after a while.

In the beginning when I started going down with my sister I could hardly walk the streets on my own since my body just went into shock and then I'd start shaking. So, she sometimes parked her car and accompanied me on my way to the clinic. Then gradually she parked her car a block away from the clinic and encouraged me to walk down the street until I got there (Yonge and College).

At first I thought she was insane for thinking I could manage and do it, but she kept assuring me that I would be okay and forced me somehow. My self-esteem and self-confidence was beyond what low actually is. Fuck, I think I was close to feeling subhuman, but not far enough down to the point I wanted to cancel myself out, or maybe I was…I saw my therapist three times a week for three weeks and during this time we did a lot of social experiments. Well, she basically brought me back outside, socializing me back into society. Going to the mall, walking down the street, staying in big shopping stores and EATING in public at the food court! It was Behavioral Therapy at its finest!

Whenever we were at this nearby food court close to the clinic she asked me to walk around the food court three times! I felt stupid doing it, thinking everyone around me must be watching, thinking I was this dumb, strange guy. Then after that we sat in the middle of the food court a couple of times while eating poutine (something she kind of introduced me to that I'm still addicted to). If we happened to go to the mall or a store during our sessions she would walk with me, then after she would tell me to do it on my own now. Then, before I knew it she vanished!

I felt like a kid, a child reduced to nothingness and doing all these activities on my own felt as if I was walking on a tightrope. Out of touch with the outside world and feeling calmer when someone was around me. I remember once after having a session one too many, she made me walk around as usual, but by myself in order to "condition" me back into the outside world. But I felt like shit and ended up heading back to her office not feeling as good about myself. I told her how I felt and then our session was over.

Whenever my sessions with her were over I would leave her office then would wait at the corner of the intersection for a taxi to pick me up so I could head back home. While waiting I usually thought about how my life ended up the way it did and asked myself, "How did I get myself in all this mess?"

During this time, I also looked and observed everyone as they passed by and they all seemed so happy while I felt invisible and not part of their society, which made me feel even more detached. Everyone, for the most part, looked dressed up, in groups, and were socializing and laughing while I looked on and envied them until my taxi came.

By the time the next week came around I told (let's call her Alicia) what happened the week before and how much I envied all the people out on the street because they seemed to be WAY more functional than myself. After telling her how I felt, she decided to give me twenty dollars and told me to go shopping for her with a list of tasks and things to get, and she specifically wanted me to go and treat myself to something. Within this task, the mall I had to go to was the Eaton Centre located in the heart of Toronto's downtown, and I remember the first reaction I had was "ah... I can't handle that" since like I was saying before my self-confidence was beyond low at this point and it really felt like a suicide mission!

So, once Alicia talked me into doing this "exposure" I just went along with it since I didn't think I had much say into the matter at all anyhow. I reluctantly walked out of the office with her twenty dollars and headed downstairs to the lobby and just went! I remember saying to her that I don't even know my way around that mall, so how could I possibly pick anything up for her and come back. "You'll figure it out," she said, and out of the both of us she was the only one that believed in me.

When it came time to travel there I don't remember if I walked or took the subway train to The Eaton Centre, but I somehow managed to get there. But once I finally got there and walked around, I remember feeling lightheaded and spaced out since I wasn't used to seeing so many people walking around all at one time. I walked around a bit more, then asked this mother that was with her daughter where or how I could find a certain store. She was just as confused as me though, and said "I'm looking too. I have no idea where to go." So that's when I went into saving mode since I didn't want the both of us to be clueless, and it's funny how seeing someone else in need can do that to you.

I looked around and observed my surroundings, then my instincts clicked in and I decided to look at the mall directory and map, which showed me my current location and where everything else within the mall was. I asked the woman where she needed to be, found it, and gave her the directions, then I also headed along my way. As I walked, everything felt so unnatural to me since I was living, doing, and acting how regular people act like. Then I managed to find the stores I needed.

First on the list was getting a Butterscotch Lollipop, which is what I got and I remember feeling stupid and being afraid that someone would assume I was gay for wanting that, but this goes to show you how extreme and out of the park a person's anxious thoughts can be for them. The last thing on my list to get was a treat for myself, so I ended up getting this little small Buzz Lightyear action figure with arms and legs you could mangle around anyway you wanted. I couldn't find anything else in and around that was cheap so I decided to get a random toy.

Walking through the mall and out felt good, and I started to feel like an actual person again since I had shopping bags, which helped to make me feel like I was like them and included back into society. On my way back to Alicia's office, my confidence levels were up and I felt like no one could fuck with me. By the time I arrived, I sat down and gave her everything she asked for. She laughed at the Buzz Lightyear toy, though, and asked me, "Why did you get that?" So, I said, "That's all I could afford."

After that and about three or so weeks of exposures three times a week I did start to feel pretty DIFFERENT outside and I was learning how to integrate myself into social situations. "You're cured!" Alicia said, but I figured she was damn crazy for saying that since before all that I was suffering a hell of a lot and still felt like this newborn baby in an unfamiliar world that seemed to change quite a bit once I stopped going out as much.

Our sessions dropped down to once a week, then I started doing group sessions during the week which she facilitated. Groups can be a funny experience though, since you can sometimes feel one or two ways towards them: you either A) don't feel like you belong, or B) you feel right at home and just "get it" and can relate to half of what others are saying.

For this particular group, though, I put myself in category A, and couldn't really relate to most of the people in my group since they seemed "light year/s" better than myself, and a lot of their concerns made me feel like I was either too fucked up or they were putting on an act. For the most part this became my routine for a while, though, and it eventually made me feel like I was stuck in a rut since nothing made much sense again. Sit around and do nothing, sleep, then, get ready for group depending on the day, and I either felt very proud of myself for attending or questioned myself on why I even went in the first place.

Around this time, I looked around for anything that would help me cope. Most times in group I voiced what was bothering me, but most didn't get it, and the other fifty percent of the time? I was a joker saying fucked up jokes making others laugh, but sometimes my jokes made people uncomfortable which still got me off, but that's just how my personality is. When I talked about what made me functional again and how Alicia brought me back outside to the world, no one really got it or understood where I was coming from. "Come on, Andrew, get in the fight!" One of the group members I was cool with said to me one time after a group session, while raising his fists up like a boxer. It's funny, a lot of people don't get or understand how someone can get dragged down into that deep dark hole, but it happens in stages.

First, you're put through a shitload of situations that reinforce the notion that "yup" you are indeed fucked and there's no way out of it, then it beats you down until you're a dead horse. Then, once you're completely lost without knowing your left from your right, that's where the games can and will without a doubt begin! Down at this level, it's all about survival and getting through the month, week, and the day, but most especially the night.

By this point, I was well within the system and institutionalized and just another person, male, and black individual stuck on medication like a zombie and hoping for a better tomorrow, but with no real expectations for much to change. With medication, I really felt like it was my only way out and like my savior and grace too thinking that it would "fix" everything. I even became obsessive with looking at different Mood and Anxiety pharmaceutical websites that claimed their NEW AND IMPROVED medication was the be all and end all as if I was waiting for a new toy to come out on the market. I mean, I sure as fuck couldn't help myself, so I obviously thought that the medications could, or so I thought, and this slowly became my life as I slipped back even further into a much worse state than before.

Feeling boxed in and with a repetitive schedule where I wasn't doing much slowly made me give up on my dreams and they truly ceased to exist. When I heard from or about friends going to school and doing what they wanted as they were achieving their goals, it didn't matter much by this point because I accepted that I was not THEM, nor would I ever be! Or like any other normal person. This is when I started to stay in my basement a lot more, and forgot about time and the world, and to be honest with you I liked it down there since it was cold and lifeless with barely any soul at all. Time didn't exist there, and if you really think about it, it's as if life and all the bullshit that comes with it is what stuffed me down there in the first place!

Basement

First, I was outside, then I started to avoid things, then I hid again, then avoided some more only for me to go out occasionally at certain times, but in the end the basement symbolized a safe place. It was like everything beat me and won, so down in a fuckin' basement was the only place where I could seek refuge. My mom doesn't know this, but there was even a time when I played it off like I went to school, but hid in the basement instead until everyone was gone and out of our house. I was twenty-one at the time and it was two-thousand-and-one. Later on that same day I did nothing but assure her that I went to school.

Early in the morning I walked in the darkness of our basement and then finally sat down once I felt one of our old coffee tables. I sat there for hours as I ate a ham and cheese sandwich, but once I was finally done I stayed still and pondered about life figuring the world got the best of me and that I lost. My dad always got up early for work and always went down to the basement to wash his face or brush his teeth since my mom usually had the washroom upstairs to herself, so I remember hearing the basement door open and that's when I sneaked off and over into a corner to hide myself, but I thought I was already caught! It was the oddest thing, though, because I thought he saw me but he never did or acted as if he didn't. He just continued to wash his face and sang by the sink as he always did, then went back upstairs like nothing, and I nearly busted out laughing too.

Later on that morning, the vibe seemed kind of different and once I heard my mom coming down the stairs and walking on the main floor of our house her footsteps even sounded different. It sounded like she went to check the locks on the front door, and although the door was locked the storm door was locked just the same which might have appeared to be strange to her. That's when I heard her make her way to the basement door, then she stopped and opened that door so I held my breath long enough until she closed the door. It's strange, but that all seemed like a prelude to what would eventually become my daily living, which was being stuck in the house and in my basement on a regular basis.

The Internet

My life, my daily schedule, and the way I simply lived day in and out was like a repetitive movie played over and over again. I was getting up at twelve p.m., then eleven p.m., and at times my sleep pattern was so dysfunctional I never really knew what dysfunctional really stood for anymore.

Humans are social creatures, though, and regardless of the situation we need some sort of human/social contact! Something, anything! And this was very true in my case, because despite how hard I felt I fell down the hole I still managed to find people, and you do find people because there are others similar to you.

Once I got up at whichever random time I usually got something to eat, then I would head straight for the basement and turn my computer on. In the beginning stages I surfed the net then looked at porn and listened to music, and even made some music until I fell asleep again. Some sites I ended up looking at helped, and others I just looked at them to look, but it wasn't like I was going anywhere anytime soon and I knew I had more than enough time to look. On an average day, I usually had anywhere between three-hundred to four-hundred plus sites opened, and the more I surfed the more I clicked like a nonstop cycle.

At times, I looked at the wallpaper on my computer's desktop, which showcased pictures of the city of Toronto, and I remember staring at these pictures for a good thirty minutes, then an hour or more thinking to myself if I would ever see those beautiful streets again. It seemed so close, but so far. Although my basement was in fact dark and had a soulless feel to it, something about it still drew me there, and I think I started to make it feel like a warm place. After a while it started to have this energizing feel to it, and that's maybe because I added a lamp down there.

I blasted music from my computer, listened to radio shows and just me being in front of a computer screen somehow connected me back with forms of human life since that was my only means of communication. That's how I found out about this site called Social Anxiety Support, and when I found this site I felt like I struck gold since it had a lot of information pertaining to my condition, plus there was a whole community of people already there who were just like me! I joined this site around two-thousand-and-three, but never started using it hardcore until two-thousand-and-six.

I avoided posting much until I randomly just kind of said whatever, but by this time I knew enough about the site to know which areas to stay clear of since some sections were kind of counterproductive. The sections I started posting in were motivation, inspiration, general, JUST FOR FUN and arts." The Arts section was right up my alley so I found myself becoming more comfortable and posting there since I got a big laugh out of the fuckery. One day while on this site and forum I posted in the Arts section and asked for people to listen to some music I made and asked if they liked it. I had my own personalized website that I made for my music too and went by the artist name "Slikkz." I got a few responses from people and them telling me what they thought of my music, and one of the first people to respond was this interesting guy with the user name "Funky President." My name on this site was "aka dru" so I don't know we just seemed to hit it off pretty well and quickly started messaging each other back and forth until we finally exchanged MSN Messenger names so we could speak more rapidly and naturally.

When we first started talking on Instant Messenger I was hyper, talking all crazy and he was pretty similar to me in that respect, and it just so happened that we had the same taste in music (hip hop, soul, drum and bass and alternative.) To me it was insane, and really made no sense how I could possibly find someone identical, but what made this even more of a mind fuck is the fact that this fuckin' kid ended up residing within the same city as me! What were the chances!?

Gradually, I met a couple of other neat and interesting people from the net and from that site specifically in and around this same time. Dani, a cool girlie tomboyish chick from Edmonton, Jessica a chill yet hyper and exciting girl from Philly where some of my relatives live, and Nikki from Baltimore, Maryland and I'm still close to them to this day!

Now with my new social circle full of people that could have been my long-lost friends what else can I say? I got up whenever I wanted, the days were random with no sense of order or control, and I conversed with my new social network every day. I had a dying need to laugh, talk, and "be" with other people, so these people right here? Made all the difference in the fuckin' world! Especially since we all supported one another!

Now with Mr. Funky and me, shit was just on a different level. And we both should have known early on that things would naturally escalate, because (surprise) that's exactly what ended up happening! It's jokes because after a while he told me that one of the only reasons for why he even contacted me in the first place is because he thought I was a girl! But I can't blame him since men and woman dealing with these types of things usually are pretty horny people.

By this point being so far down into my dysfunction and being housebound really did seem like a blessing. I mean, I got to work on my music and developed my own signature sound. I also got into the habit of looking up different underground music labels to submit my music to in the hopes that it would be released, along with uploading it to Myspace. Because of my situation and the bitter perfect timing of it all, I by default had a front-row seat when it came to witnessing what the internet currently represents today. I watched it morph and change right before my eyes. Finding celebrities on Myspace, finding long lost friends...it was craziness. Now, remember I am Mr. "tabs" and I could easily open three-hundred or so tabs like nothing. So, when it came to me and Myspace I was instantaneously addicted! Also, because it had that whole social element I lacked in actual real life how could I leave? Oh, and I almost forgot to mention that this is also around the same time that YouTube also hit!

On a daily basis, it seemed like more and more people were finding out new and creative ways for how to manipulate all these new forms of technology too, and things rapidly started to happen faster and faster. The INTERNET! It was like the new drug of choice, and slowly everyone was falling victim to it and getting hooked! Web chatrooms like Tinychat were becoming more popular and were popping up everywhere, and everyone wanted to be a part of the spectacle. The internet itself was a major coping tool for people, but no one really said, mentioned, or knew that at the time, but looking back at everything now? It was just another vice and addiction for those who had issues or those who were rejected by society.

With social interaction, though, people also have human and sexual needs, so by the time Funky, and I started feeling like that, we talked about joining a dating site, and that was something I NEVER thought I would ever do in my life! To go without sex or some form of natural interaction with the opposite sex for a long enough time can really fuck with you! When it came time for me to write something about myself on some of these dating sites I always found it to be hard, and I always drew a blank. I mean what was I to say? That I have severe Mood and Anxiety issues and that I've been locked up in my basement? And putting up a picture was always a teeth-grinding experience. This was around two-thousand-and-eight, and putting up too much information about oneself online was still very taboo and abnormal.

I eventually got around to writing up a profile intro for myself, but usually only after forty or so attempts, and I never quite knew what type of girl I wanted to talk to. Half of the girls on this one dating site

I started to use a lot seemed to be pretty bitchy, stuck up, and looked like girls who already had it all, so I felt very different from them and even a bit envious. At first I remember messaging girls and being very honest about who I was and my situation, saying things like "hey hello you look pretty nice blah-blah-blah." I put my heart and my soul into my messages that weren't too long, or too short, but sadly I hardly got any replies, which crushed my heart.

After attempting this same approach countless times for hours every other day, I finally said forget it and decided to call it quits, then out of nowhere I just…didn't give a fuck, like no fucks were given and I decided to have nothing but fun! From then on it was all about doing everything in the name of sex, and for sexual progress, and really? Why not? I was locked up in a jail-like environment and I wanted out! I had so much sexual tension built up inside, so all I wanted to do was release it and live out my wildest sexual fantasies while talking to whichever girl who happened to appeal to me…

I was wild and reckless and ditched my regular, nice sweet pictures and replaced them with random and fucked up pictures of me in my mom's church hat and another of me screwing my face while holding a long kitchen knife and smiling. And believe it or not, this is when I started to receive more messages. Messaging girls became a full-time job at this point, and was a game to me. I stopped writing semi-long messages expressing myself and just shot out one liners and got straight to the point! If a girl looked good, and I was digging her style and she turned me on? By the first or second message I would have her phone number and we would be on the verge of having phone sex. One of the first girls I had this sort of interaction with was this Native girl Jilly. We talked on the phone while I was downstairs in the basement and talking to my crew on MSN. I spazzed out typing to them while talking to Jilly at the same time, then that's when I started to stroke myself as we started to talk more sexual. I mean, I couldn't believe any of it. Wow, I was talking to a true to life girl again in a sexual way. And she gave both my heads a spin. We both talked and were beating around the bush for a while, but then I had enough and straight up told her to take off her shirt and for her to squeeze her nipples. Then all I heard was Jilly moan as she started to breathe in a shallow-like manner, then more heavily. At first I thought it was all an act, but nah, it was all pretty real.

"What else do you want me to do?" she asked. So that's when I got a wicked set of blue balls and my body started to tremble and shake since it was in shock from all the excitement. I stood up fast then I tried to find a chair in the dark basement for where I could lay back and continue our fun. Then I got so horny I didn't know what to really say, so I blanked out. That's when I took a deep breath, calmed down, and slowly directed her on what I wanted her to do...

I don't really care where you're from or who you are, when you're horny and have Anxiety or Shyness issues, self-doubt goes straight out the window! It's like you're in the world of sex and nothing else matters except for your sexual actions, and nothing can ruin that moment! My intentions that day and night, or that morning, was to have mind-blowing phone sex with Jilly and to make it last for as long as I possibly could. I got off on hearing her excited and in pleasure, so the hornier she was the more I liked it. I think we ended up talking on the phone past five a.m. that time...

Later on, during that same week I started bragging to Mr. Funky about how I talked to this girl from a dating site and how crazy our phone session was. Immediately he started to get excited and wanted in on all the "fun" I was having, so he made a profile on the exact dating site I was on and ended up talking to that same girl. When he went on to do that I was very confident in the fact that nothing could possibly happen between them because hey, she was talking to me. And I figured I was special since we connected so well and had a lot of fun. Or so I thought. That's when he jokingly told me that same exact girl I talked to did in fact message him back, but even then I still thought nothing of it. But then they ended up talking on the phone and all the "fun" I ended up having with her? She ended up having with him and dude had the nerve to tell me she was even freakier. And hearing all of that made me careless and made me not give a fuck even more. So now, my boy and me were both simultaneously doing this on the same site. I would message a girl, then he would message a girl, and sometimes we messaged the same girl who then in turn phone sexed both of us, just on different days. I can't lie, though, it still made me mad that my sweet messages didn't work, meanwhile the crazy other approach and method did.

It wasn't elaborate or anything of that nature either, we kept it simple and said things as basic as "I like how you look, now it's time to make you cum." Or, "it's late let's have phone sex sooner than later." There was even a time where I messaged this beautiful girl while being all chill and "regular" with little to no luck, so that's when I flipped the script and said, "oh, hey I know you don't remember me, but I know you do remember how many times I made you have an orgasm while we talked on the phone." And like nothing, she replied to me without striking up much conversation, and she just gave me her number so I called and we got straight down to business. Things beyond that point became so simple and erratic to the point that I started asking some of these girls how and why they liked talking to me and why they enjoyed everything so much?

This is what some of them said: The power, living out my fantasies, this is way more fun than being with my boyfriend, I love the control, I just had crazy sex, so I don't understand how it's possible for me to have such a powerful orgasm again! I love you and not my man, and I have to write an article on you and about all this! Even though I was having my fun, there were some girls that clued into or who became a little more curious about who I was and why I even liked doing what it was I was doing. I was obsessed with pleasing them and never cared to finish myself unless they did. But as a gentleman wouldn't you let a woman finish first? Ha! Yup, I was a bit too cocky and confident by this time, but I mean I wasn't getting out. I simply wanted to enjoy what others were experiencing out there in the world and I managed to achieve it.

Another encounter I had was with this other girl named Chantel which was pretty interesting...What made Chantel very interesting is when I first started talking to her I confidently told her in graphic detail what I planned to do with her and how intense and pleased she would be after and how hooked she would become. She eventually broke down and said "Really, huh? That's so hot, I love it already when can I call you?" We made up a time and decided to speak to one another at night around nine p.m.

As the day progressed falling into the night and the time now being ten minutes after nine p.m. the phone finally rang. That's when I ran for the phone to make sure no one in my house picked it up except me, then that's when I answered and did my cool guy thing as we slid into that "world." I don't know how she did it, but everything happened so fast! So, before I knew it she was telling me what to do and demanded I pull my dick out and stroke it until it threw up all over the damn place! She became pretty aggressive, and pretty fast saying to me, "I caught you off guard, huh? Didn't know I would run the show, did you!?" I replied saying "Na, but I love it..." I was kind of scared at first, but let her have her way with me regardless...

Her kink was getting men to do what she wanted them to, and I was okay with it until she took things a little too far to the point that I had to slow down the show. Then she bragged about how she had a boy toy she talks to that she ties up to the tree in the back of her house and beats him like a little bitch! That's when I knew she was into some SICK shit! So, after all her failed attempts at trying to get me to do some disturbing stuff all we ended up doing was dirty talk while rubbing ourselves. We did this a few times, and she always ended up falling asleep on the phone after then started snoring. That's when I stayed there thinking about my life for five to ten minutes, but also wondering what planet she was from?

There was also another girl who was pretty analytical like myself and always wanted to know why I got off on the certain things that I liked. She always wondered why I loved control as much as I did. So much so that she wrote an article about it in an independent magazine that she wrote for. I mean, she "loved" the phone, I mean fun just as much as I did, but always tried to pick my brain apart because she wanted to know what made me tick, which I thought was pretty cool because I was usually the one who took on that role. She even came up with a theory for why I liked control so much.

Her theory was that because I might have lacked control in my actual life that's one of the main reasons for why I needed control during my sexual encounters of any form. It was a pretty neat and eye-opening theory and all, but it's also one I rejected. She, along with all the other girls I talked to, never quite knew I was dealing with Anxiety issues, but for her to attempt to breakdown my actions was still a neat and crazy thing.

In the end I have always been, and shall remain, a very hypersexual person, and when it comes to things that have to do with sex I am willing to experiment, but within reason. And maybe there is a connection somewhere with what I like and how my personality tends to be, but I won't touch on that now. That whole experience taught me a hell of a lot about women, though, and really opened my eyes. I never truly knew how horny, kinky, and seductive a lot of them could be and how demanding they are.

Fifty percent, if not more, of the women on that specific dating site at the time probably engaged in phone sex with my boy and me. I later deleted my account and came back on three more times, but I saw the same faces, which made me wonder if they might be dealing with the same issues as myself?

It was fun while it lasted, but after a while more than enough of these girls wanted to actually meet in real life since they felt a connection, but since I made too many excuses and made it difficult to meet up, most of them stopped talking to me since they found it to be strange. Some of the other girls liked it, though, since it made me that much more mysterious and that got them off even more. That hurt me, though too, because I desperately wanted to meet up with some of them, but couldn't figure out how to make that happen at the time. Slowly, though, the same coping methods I was using just became reminders of why I was fucked in the first place, so little by little I wanted out more than ever! I mean, I wanted out before, but those feelings were at an all-time high now, which went on between two-thousand-and-six to two-thousand-and-nine.

CHAPTER 4

London

I was still using some of my old coping techniques to get through the day and lived the same lifestyle minus a few things while desperately still trying to get out.

Funky and myself were now chilling and skating after our group meetings and sessions held by Mental Health activist and advocate Earla Dunbar, and Paul Rennie, which was held on a weekly basis every Wednesday in the evenings. In and around March or April my dad asked me if I wanted to head to London, England to go and see my grandma, so without hesitation I said "yes." I didn't know and didn't really care how it was all gonna playout, but all I knew is I needed a change and needed to get away ASAP!

When it comes to my relatives and myself I have always felt excluded, and that's because... shit, I was! I was sheltered from them, and wished I knew more about that who side of my family. Growing up my grandmother always said to my parents to throw me on a plan and to have me come over to London but my mom was against it not wanting me to travel on my own. Anyhow, after agreeing to go everything was being set up and I really didn't think twice about how the trip would be, nor did I care much. And the trip itself was a month or so away so I never really had to think about it emotionally.

It was a planned trip, who the fuck cares! Just go, see FAM that you haven't seen in years or at all and comeback and that'll be that! Right!? Wrong! It was now May and the date of our flight was coming near, then finally it came down to just one week! As usual Funky and me skated after group, well, he was skating and I recorded since my weight alone could crush a board and I wasn't tryin' to do that, and we also had another one of our people with us that day too, since he drove us around.

It was a Wednesday, but we were having so much fun that we ended up staying out until two something in the morning. I was paranoid about the time, too, so I kept looking at my watch repeatedly thinking that the plane would leave me if I slept in for too long. Finally, we closed down shop and headed home. The day after I was so tired because I got little to no sleep since I was tossing and turning the whole night thinking about the damn trip! Who would be on the plane? How long would it take to get checked in, and would I be fully packed for my trip?

I don't even think I ate much that day. All I remember is saying to myself, what the FUCK did I just get myself into!? Did I not know how this would make me feel!? Something deep inside of me liked it though. I liked the unknown, and the challenge that came with not really knowing a damn thing, so I wasn't gonna stop or change my mind now! I couldn't anyhow, because I mean the tickets were already bought and this is what I signed up for.

Coming down to the last few hours of waiting before we would head to the airport was a lost and spaced out feeling, I just stayed there in my room packing my suitcase, but it wasn't like I was mentally there. In total I ended up packing two suitcases. One that was medium sized, and another that was a standard suitcase size and my dad was packed and prepped before I was, since he was more experienced. We somehow managed to make our way downstairs in one piece then I reminded my dad that I would call a cab for us since I knew a cabbie personally that was around whenever I needed him, or so I thought.

After waiting for fifteen or so minutes this cabbie friend Milo came turning right into the driveway, came out of his taxi, and helped us put our bags in the back of his taxi as soon as possible, and then we drove off. I was still feeling spaced out and felt like I was dreaming so the ride to the airport is something I don't even remember that well and it must have been on some next level shit, but really can you blame me? I had so much on my mind.

Once we arrived we got our bags then Milo sent us off. In the airport, I asked my pops if I could use his phone to text some of my friends since I kept this London trip mostly to myself since I thought by telling others I was leaving it would be like rubbing it in their faces. But I now know that most of my true friends would have been happy for me to get away. My homie and longtime friend and brother Hermano Griego (Greek brother) was one of the first people I sent a text to letting him know I would be leaving. Aside from my internet crew and a few people, like three or four on the outside, that's all who really knew I was gone! Oh, and my mom, sis and brother in-law of course.

After that I got checked in along with my dad, and then we waited around Toronto Pearson Airport until it was after eight p.m. then we headed to the departure area, which made half of my uneasiness go away. But once we were finally called to board onto our plane all I remember is my senses kicking in! Telling me not to be stupid! And to be smart! Like, my black common sense kept saying to me "Yo! Stay alive! Don't go on no plane!"

The first thought I started to get as we got closer to the walkway to board the plane was there's no way I'm going through, past, or on that tunnel! And on that big hunk of metal! Trusting it to get me across the Atlantic Ocean! It didn't seem logical to me... (Did I mention that this was my first time flying?) Reluctantly, I walked through this tunnel with my dad and onto the actual plane, then once inside we went to our seats and I calmed down for a bit as I kept reminding myself that going away was a good and positive thing for my health, and not a bad thing.

Once everyone was settled and seated the captain introduced himself to us and reassured everyone that everything was safe and that everything would be okay. All systems were a go, then the plane lined up on the runway and plowed down with engines that sounded powerful as fuck as we smelt the raw gasoline. "Yup, this is real." I said to myself.

When the plane finally lifted off, the force was like nothing I'll ever forget! It's like the plane raised up off the ground without ten fucks to give and then we shot straight up into the air. I purposely wanted a window seat too because this was my first time flying, and also because as the plane took off and spiraled away from the city all I wanted to do was is give the city of Toronto one big middle finger! The drama, the feeling trapped, the craziness, the not feeling I could ever get better... it was like I was leaving all that behind, with a huge weight lifted off my shoulders. "Later you twisted city," is what I said.

By the time we were up and on our path headed to London, most of my anxieties about flying or wondering if I could manage went straight out the window! At first what was hard to compute though is how calm most of the other passengers around me looked. I still didn't forget that I was in a hunk of metal, but for the most part everyone else around me seemed to be nonchalant about it. Maybe some were scared and they just did a good job at hiding it, but I visibly looked like that was the first time I was in the air. For me this was an experience of a lifetime and one thing that stayed on my mind while I looked out of the plane window was life and our existence as I looked on into this thin spectrum of light off into the distance. It looked like morning and we were in the evening which quickly phased into the night. I also wondered if my London relatives would be accepting of me, or not? Then before I knew it? *BAM!!!*

This plane dropped to the ground and made this huge noise that sounded like death calling your ass without your say so! "Shittt!" A guy sitting in front of me said as he turned around to me, so I freaked out too and said "fuckkkk" but as soon as that happened my dad grabbed my hand to calm me down, but his ass was freaked out too! He had way more air experience than me, but he later admitted that what we went through was the worst air turbulence he's ever gone through. I guess you could say that's when I lost my air virginity right then and there.

The captain came on the PA system shortly after stabilizing the plane and assured everyone that everything was okay and apologized for the turbulence. Everyone laughed after with a sigh of relief, so after we went back to being composed I took my windbreaker jacket right off and used it as a pillow and rested my head on the window. When I opened my eyes again that little spectrum of light I kept looking at wasn't so small anymore it was wider and we headed straight into it. I looked on for a good while, but nothing changed. It was like we were in limbo, but eventually we joined with it and then our plane lowered into this damp environment so I was like "huh?" Then that's when the captain simply said, "Welcome to London, we have arrived at our destination."

Our plane landed safely at Gatwick Airport so once we were connected to the skywalk we safely made our way off the plane and made sure we had all our belongings. While walking and familiarizing ourselves with our environment we finally made it to the check-in area. Then as we got closer this classy dressed-up couple looked at everyone who got off the plane and said, "they don't look like the liveliest bunch, they must be North American." And that was my first intro and welcoming into London!

Based off that indirect encounter I felt as though it was gonna be a long ass trip, so I braced myself for it. We waited in line for what seemed like forty minutes then finally got up to the front of the line and the passport guy asked me what I came for? So I said, "To see relatives, it's my first time in London." Then he smiled and said, "You need to have a pint on me, cheers!" This kind of brightened up my day a bit more!

From that point on we got our entire luggage then went to look outside for a family friend that came down to get us, and right off the bat I became confused since everything was inverted, but even more mad because I tried to warn myself that it would be like that anyhow. When we started to drive along we made small conversation and out of the blue he says "one thing people don't know about England is, that it has a lot of trees." He said it with a sense of pride, but being that we were from Canada? We didn't even bother to get into detail about "trees."

He was a proud Brit man though, so that's something I can't take away from him. Driving along trying to get into the city seemed like it was taking forever, but then the car finally made a sharp turn and then like nothing we were right there in the mix of it all! I was in awe and looked around like I was a child who was speechless taking in the sights. I viewed going away to London as an opportunity to get myself back into shape physically and mentally and this was all very important because I wanted to do this to be able to take on anything before heading back to Toronto. I also considered going to school in London so what better way to check out the scene?

We finally made it to where we'd be staying and that place was my granduncles house, well, one of them. He greeted us at the front door and helped us with our bags then we got settled in. I don't even think we stayed in the house long either. My dad, and I immediately hit the streets and he showed me around southwest London which is where we stayed at.

Seeing all the different types of people roaming around and hearing their accents was a major culture shock to me, but at the same time what really got me was is how similar London was to Toronto. We ventured towards this dense major intersection which seemed like a main hub for most people in and around that area, then out of nowhere we happened to bump into a family relative of ours who was our cousin. He greeted us then we went to a nearby bar to go and have some drinks. Now, I hardly did any of this shit back home so while we were there I was anxious but just put my mind on autopilot.

When we were done, we all headed back to my granduncles house then the drowsiness from the time difference hit me so my granduncle let me have whichever room I wanted then I passed out. Hours later I ended up waking up from the most intense and most beautiful rest I had in quite some time! I left my room and walked the hallway and then made my way down the stairs and into the main living room area to turn on some TV, then I jumped up going hyper being in disbelieve not understanding how I was literally across the ocean from where I was born and raised!

Those Brits sure do love their naked women and music! And so did I! There were half naked girls on nearly every other station I flipped through and it was almost like an early morning tease just to get everyone READY for the coming day. I became addicted to seeing them every morning too! Plus watching a lot of the UK music stations they had. At that time I had mixed emotions about the music thing though, because it made me wonder how and why Toronto and Canada didn't embrace Canadian urban music the way Brits prided theirs? Though, things have changed for the better...

Little by little I became sleepy again, so I went back to bed at four thirty in the morning. Later on that morning I was woken up by my dad and granduncles talking so I fixed myself up then headed down to see them then we eventually decided on going shopping for food. I brought my camera with me too since I wanted to document EVERYTHING so I took it with me before we left out. While shopping I noticed that my dad was almost as anxious as myself so, I tried to keep him together along with my own wellbeing.

When we finally finished up, my granduncle made a funny comment as we left... something about being a "scatter foot" or something? And I guess to say "oh, you don't like crowds either?" Being that this was my dad's side of our fam that we visited I wanted to see if I could get answers or if I would notice if anyone else was similar to me because I already knew for a fact this shit more than likely came from his side of the family. Witnessing my family was interesting because there was this whole culture and world I never knew about!? And I truly felt I was purposely hidden from it and them.

The Marshalls in London were really active! I loved it so much and it gave me a sense of pride I couldn't buy anywhere! They were go-getters, had ideas and implemented them! So, without a doubt seeing some of that resonated with me since I was always like that and now it made even more sense for why I had such high ambitions. Back in Toronto most people thought half of my ideas were crazy and it was almost a crime to be black and ambitious. Seeing their ambition made me buckle down and focus on what my goals were and made me want to push my issues to the side!

At night while in my room I would play on my dad's BlackBerry and since I installed MSN Messenger I got to chat with some of my friends back home. Funky of course updated me on all the crazy shit he was doing and since I left the country he went into hyper mode with the phone sex stuff.

It went from phone sex, to webcams, and then to him contemplating becoming a webcam model to make some extra coin. I also told this cute girl who I met from that dating site that I loved her... Being away gave my brain a chance to breathe and regroup because home was nothing more than a madhouse with me not getting exposed to much light or going out. There was something magical about my guest room in London though and I pondered a lot about what my game plan would be once I got back to Toronto. My sexual fantasies also became more intense and explosive in this magical room for whatever reason and they wouldn't stop...

After about a week and a half of being in London I was ready to head back home, and I was mentally prepared for it too! I thought we were only staying for two and a half weeks, but to my surprise my dad let me know it was for three and a half weeks, which I didn't feel mentally together enough to do. To be honest with you I freaked out, and everything started to feel like a nightmare! I mean, I was more than grateful for going, being accepted and being there but I was slowly becoming mentally tired from seeing so many of my relatives every day and having to put on a front like I was doing something with my life. Because I now knew that we had to do one more week and some change? I got up in the morning, napped in the afternoon, then was up at night until I passed out again and I carried on this pattern until the whole entire week blacked out. It worked too! And before I knew it? We were only down to a few days.

Believe it or not I started to miss home and all that I was familiar with but not necessarily my home, but stuff like my sister, my mom and missing Toronto. I mean, shoot, I loved London because it was so chill and laidback, but I didn't feel too comfortable eatin' up all my granduncles food and I felt guilty for not pulling my weight around, and people asking me every other day why I was single!

On one of the last nights I spent in London me along with a group of relatives went out to go eat to celebrate one of my other granduncles birthdays. I was scared shitless leading up to that night but once we were there it wasn't as bad as I figured it would have been. Two of my Cousins laughed at me while I made my way over to their table to socialize with them and I guess they saw my uncomfortableness from the jump! *Again with the questions*

One of my other Cousins I think might have seen how uncomfortable I was so they saved me by jumping into the conversation I was having with the others. We ended up talking about music, so, that was easy for me and it just so happened that she was into music as much as myself, and without her I don't know how I would have gotten through that night... *thank you*. Once again I was lying in bed and thinking about my goals, dreams and sexual fantasies. My window was open most of the time so I got plenty of fresh air and heard the pulse of the city.

I once heard a police helicopter searching for someone at four something in the morning, but I thought okay, regular cops don't carry guns in London so, who's running this operation? Maybe their special operations unit or something like that? Anyhow when the time came around for me to think about my goals, getting out of the house on a regular basis was one of them, I also wanted to start up a sex blog to let out all my sexual thoughts and feelings and I thought it would be cool to promote it too! You know what's funny though? Throughout my whole stay in London I only used my prescribed medication for sleep only three fuckin' times! Away from that I never really used it for sleep at all! I just went to sleep naturally so that made me know for sure that it might be my environment that was fucking me up so much.

The night before our flight back to Toronto I was worried. Well I of course wanted to desperately go back but thinking about the plane ride had me not as calm. I remembered how nerve-wracking it was going through the whole process of going to London in the first place so, going back? I felt like I'd experience it all over again, but I mean I had no choice. I had to. Feeling semi rested and tired I got up the day of our trip to head back home. As I was packing my bags my grandma came by to see my dad, and I off. She spoke with my dad for a while and cried since she didn't want him to go then she came to my room and hugged me. Right after that we made our way downstairs, ate something small then left the house, but before we left my granduncle said to me "Andrew rememba you is family."

We hugged and shook hands, then that same family friend who drove us into the city, was the same one to drive us out and back to Gatwick AirPort. It's like everything was going in reverse, but I felt good knowing I was going home! When we finally made it to the airport and got checked in my dad had to take a piss and this nearly costed us our trip back to Toronto. If I wasn't outside the washroom to hear our flight boarding, we would have been done for!

Rushing towards our gate, getting processed then boarded onto our plan was happy, sad, and a mixture of emotions. I didn't know if I wanted to leave or if I wanted to stay? My relatives from London made me feel proud to a Marshall and really? It was good to see them, but I felt like I was too antisocial towards them which they probably did/didn't understand. To my surprise, the plane ride back home was relaxing, and I remember looking out of the window again and just observed the land below wondering what everyone was doing? And if our plane would make it across the ocean. That's when I started to drift off to sleep calmly, but then got violently woken up out of my sleep since I had a nightmare of the devil with eyes that represented destruction and everything was in red like I went to hell. Then my dad tapped me on the shoulder and said, "We're nearly home."

This cute like white woman was seated next to us, so my dad had a cheerful chat with her and she calmed me down a bit too since her demeanor was happy and her voice was therapeutic. Within six hours the clouds cleared up and I saw our city all close-up and personal! That's when the captain said, "Ladies and gentlemen we have arrived in Toronto ahead of schedule." Now, London, I love you. But once I left that plane I wanted to kiss the pavement of Toronto like it was gold!

Heading back home was cool, and I felt like I was returning home after being in a rehab detox clinic for all the bullshit I needed to wash out of my system. When I finally got inside the house with my dad seeing my mom made me feel so good and EVERYTHING in Toronto seemed huge! One of the first things I did while getting settled in was is head to my computer in the basement to go and check my emails, then doing what I did best: use Instant Messenger. I talked to some friends to notify them that I was back home and in Toronto, then I started to surf the net again… but after thirty minutes or so I turned everything off since it didn't feel natural anymore.

It felt boring to me, and being exposed to so much while I was gone made me realize I could do so much more. I went upstairs to my room for a while, then slept until I finally got up around nine p.m. It didn't take me long to fix up my sleeping schedule either because within less than a week I was okay, but guess what? Within this timeframe, I also slipped back into my old habits.

CHAPTER 5

Down the Lanes

I came back on June the eighteenth and after a week and some change I fell right back into my old habits. I ended up looking at pictures and video I took of my dad and my granduncle walking the streets of London which made me a bit emotional.

It was a mind fuck to me, because it's like first you're there, and then all of the sudden you're not! All the plans, ideas and aspirations I thought about while in my bed in London were now on the verge of becoming a reality. Now remember one of my goals was is to make a sex blog, so that's exactly what I started to do and started to build a blog within a few weeks of being back home. It was all mapped out in my mind how I wanted the blog to be like too!

"Honestfreeak" was the name I chose to call my blog, and from there I developed different sections for it, like "about me, the main area, goodies and a contact section. Some girls I knew didn't mind me putting their pictures up either, just so long as it was in an anonymous way, they loved and supported me bigtime and I loved it! Day after day I found myself fine tuning this blog to perfection so that I could finally present it to people sooner than later. And I can't lie, knowing that I was exposing my feelings and sexual thoughts out there excited me as well as intrigued me.

When I was finally done, it was all about knowing how and when to promote my site, so I buried most of my fears of rejection, joined Twitter and posted up my first few blog postings! On my Twitter account, I had a negative inverted colour profile picture of myself, so once I posted my blog entries I slowly started talking to people and just "waited" for some positive responses. "Look at my blog! Look at this amazing freaky blog!"

While Tweeting I also managed to find a pocket, or, stream of people connected with Toronto and New York, so from there I started posting to them or maybe Twitter just knew my location. Within a day of online promotion, I gained over a-hundred followers and to me that was huge at the time, especially in two-thousand-and-ten. I gave my blog link out to girls, guys, REALLY sexy girls and it was trippy to me because I wasn't doing much talking, I just slapped my link to whoever I was having a conversation with and told them to go and see what I have! I also programed my blog to synch with Twitter, so whenever I posted it would show up on my timeline which meant less work for me.

With everything going so fast I gained three-hundred followers within a week. With all these events taking place I kept looking up different girls that were somewhat associated with other people I knew and there was this one girl I kept seeing more than once. My first impression upon seeing her profile picture was is to not talk to her because I figured she wouldn't want shit to do with me, but I kept seeing her profile pop up so I followed her and then she followed me right back! From that point on I said fuck it, why not? And sent her a message and link to my blog. I told her to tell me what she thinks of it once she's done looking at it, and really? I NEVER thought I would hear back from her again. Then, out of nowhere all I got was... "Your blog is hot, and it's really turning me on right now... I'm so fuckin' wet."

Her profile picture was a picture of her looking straight into the camera with this crazy excited look on her face and in her eyes with her tongue lunged out like she was this life of the party type of bitch! "Really?" Is what I said back to her. From there we started to chat back and forth talking about sex and psychology and revealed hidden truths about each other and there wasn't much that she had to pry out of me since some of my sexual thoughts were already out there on my blog which she read.

Even before meeting her that was basically the theme to what my blog was all about, sex, psychology and the psychology of sex. I eventually asked her if she wanted to talk on the phone. She knew I was from Toronto and I assumed she was from New York, so why not? She technically was and wasn't from NYC though since she lived in and around that whole Jersey and NYC metropolitan surrounding area. We hit it off good so I didn't really hesitate in asking for her number. I geared up to call her, and since I was still in phone sex mode I just got myself in that headspace. This cute brown ebony cat eyes looking girl from New Jersey not only looked oh so very cute, she SOUNDED cute! In my mind I was going crazy, but on the surface I played it chill and cool.

"Hey baby, it's... *the name I used on Twitter.*" She moaned and got turned on from my voice and how I was speaking then we both picked up right where our text left off. Just when we both started to get more excited that's when she said, "Hold on I gotta go to the bathroom so we can talk." So I said cool.

She was staying with her Sis and let out a sigh of disgust as she passed her. I said what's that all about? So she said, "Oh, she's drunk and basically doesn't know how to handle herself." I said "Ohhh" then, we got right back into what we were doing in the first place and I took it nice and slow with her, like how I love to do.

We talked all dirty and I teased her to the point she couldn't handle it any longer but it was what I loved. Something about this girl was different though, from me finally messaging her and then her getting back to me telling me how she loved my blog and then us talking on the phone, it was different! It was like we were one in the same! I asked her if she had a mirror around so that she could admire herself and so she could describe to me how beautiful she looked while looking at herself in the mirror. She went on to describe herself in a very detailed and seductive way to the point she was on the verge of cumming hard. Then I started stroking myself but only after I knew she was excited and ready... Then...*Orgasm* She came, I came and we were both out of it. Then she rushed off the phone since it was long distance, but we continued to talk through the net until we both fell asleep.

After that night this girl, who I shall call Heart, and myself were instantaneously connected and talked all the time, be it on Twitter or Instant Messenger. I was still doing crazy things here and there, phone sexing other girls that I knew before talking to Heart and going to my therapist sessions, all rolled up into one lifestyle. Although she was different and extremely compatible with me I didn't want to get too close since I was afraid of getting hurt and since I was an emotional wreck who had little to no trust in women at this point.

During the first stages of us starting to talk more I only signed on to my messaging app around eight thirty p.m., or nine p.m. for us to directly talk. Then one week she ended up telling me about this thesis she had to write up for the program she was in at school and how she got in contact with a porn director that I kind of knew of as well. She wanted his help in order for her to do the paper, so, right then and there? That's when my heart dropped! I didn't want her to have anything to do with him! I mean, I saw his videos, so I knew exactly what he was about! Ironically, I even emailed him the year before to ask him how to run a porn site even! Heart? Talkin' to him!? Never!

I felt pretty fucked up about it all, but never told her. I kept it all in and had this weird burn inside of me. I also felt helpless at the same time but didn't wanna lose my cool so I never told her how I was feeling. She talked about him a lot and ended up texting him too, so things just got to the point to where I knew I had to say something. It was difficult for me to express my emotions to a girl in that sort of way since before getting to know her I didn't really get that deep in terms of how I felt because I wanted to protect myself. The day right after I came out and told her how it is I felt she was in shock and I guess for many other girls they don't really know how it is you feel until you tell them. After that event and that point, my heart opened up for Heart.

From that day on? I was on Instant Messenger as soon as I got up and we started talking even more frequently. She even started to open up more than before and disclosed more things about herself that I never really would have known. She also expressed that she had feelings for me which is something she might have said weeks before but I was too afraid to acknowledge what she said then. In the end, we both had feelings for one another from day one though, but it's just that we never really said it to one another until now. She even let me know that she got very bothered and jealous when I would talk about other girls too!

"Well, yea... I mean I'm a girl! Of course that got to me! I obviously want to be the only one!" Heart said in her cute voice. When it came to her and that porn director dude I didn't care much until she said she was going to meet with him. So that's when I told her it needs to stop! From then on, she slowly stopped talking to him, or, talking about him, and a part of me always still felt like she might have still been doing it but not telling me, and really? I didn't wanna know!

From that day on our daily schedule was both of us getting up at slightly different times, I would then check Instant Messenger to see what sweet "good morning" message she left for me, then I'd head straight on to Twitter to promote my blog until she came home from work. Not much was known about my life and she never knew if I worked or not, where I stayed, or if I had a cell phone. She never asked, but I knew these were some of the things she wanted to know about me. Our conversations on our Twitter timelines were superficial, but once we talked direct, everything was about all things SEX! And since we were both heavily into psychology it was always a mixture of the two. It all seemed so perfect, so I wondered when it would end. But it never did and kept going.

"Babes, you need to write more poetry!"

"I know, I know... I'll get on that soon princess.

"Babes you really need to make a book!"

Huh? Me? Never! I don't even know how to get started.

She always encouraged me to the fullest and found out I did music so was my number-one supporter. This all took place in and around June two-thousand-and-ten into Christmas, then by February of two-thousand-and-eleven I fell hard for this girl to the point I was Aboboed! One of my closest friends from the outside world that I grew up with always checked in to see how I was doing and he knew the deal between Heart and I. "Guy, I don't live in her city! This is craziness and there's no way this can possibly work! I'll get hurt!" Is what I said to him.

Cool, calm, and collected he simply told me to go for it. See, with him he's been around the block and knew all too well how relationship dynamics were, but also believed in experiencing what life presents you with so that you can learn, that was Coolz. He let me know that I had nothing to lose and it would all be a learning experience so, I shrugged my shoulders, took a deep breath and stopped worrying about the future ahead as much.

During February, my sessions started to pick up again since the holidays were now over and I couldn't wait to tell Alicia about this new love interest of mine. We also had a break from each other for a while since I got sick of continuously going with little to no progress, and we stopped seeing eye to eye since I felt like we were both on different sides of the living spectrum.

"Alicia, I'm talking to this girl!!" "Really? Tell me more about her!?" Being all excited and eager to share more I told her that she was from NYC, is really cute but has a coke habit.

"Jesus Christ, Andrew. Are you an idiot!? Why would..." Then she stopped to compose herself. That's when I said, "Weren't you in a long-distance relationship?"

"Well, yea, but it didn't last, Andrew," she went on to say.

I asked her if I still had her blessings, so that's when she said, "Yes you do."

After seeing her I sometimes had the pleasure of seeing hot assistants that were working at the clinic who gave me tasks and homework to complete that revolved around my own personal goals. When one of these assistants asked me what my goals and plans were for the New Year without hesitation I told them that I wanted to fix myself up for my baby Heart so that I could be there for her mentally, physically and in a financially stable way. The more I started talking about my goals though is the more personalized and specific to me they started to sound. I just started to sound like someone who wanted better for himself and someone who wanted to break free. This was interesting and came as a surprise to me, but if I really think about it... I never confronted myself much at home, nor did I think about my dreams or aspirations because they never existed when I was inside.

See, being inside was tricky, and if I didn't say it before I'll say it now... my room was like my house, my house was like being outside, and being outside? Well that was like being in outer space. I visited this place once in a blue moon and had little to no understanding of it, with creatures that seemed strange and unusual to me. Or I could have said my life resembled this video game called *Silent Hill 4.*

When March came around, Heart and I were still doing our thing and we not only got attached to one another, but it was an addiction! Being that we were now officially in love that made me think about how things were before it got to that stage? I felt like our relationship started backwards and felt bad for the way I treated her in the beginning. Since her birthday was coming up in April, I wanted to get her something to let her know how thankful I was for having her in my life, but I kept it a secret from her and for me? That was hard to do.

In a million and one years, I never would have thought that me, Drew, would be shopping online for a girl I like and at a jewelry store at that! It just went against my character at the time. "What happens if I buy this and then she turns around and plays me? Whatever." I just went with the flow.

After a couple days of searching, I narrowed it down to this one piece that I felt spoke for our relationship... "Yes, the shared HEART! I'll get that!" The Shared Heart was this neckless and pendent with a heart on the front saying "The Shared Heart" and on the back it was a heart made out of diamonds. I hesitated for a moment, then...*Click* "Order being processed."

I tracked the order and waited for it to arrive at my place, but if I had it my way I would have sent it directly down to her Jersey/New York area. "What is it? What is it!?" I dropped a few hints to her here and there, but kept quiet about what I was gonna send down...

The order finally made its way to my place so I grabbed it and ripped it open to see how it looked. The neckless and pendent were beautiful looking exactly how they appeared to look like online. Soon after I wasted little to no time and headed straight to the nearest post office, and demanded that they send out my package to the States for my "girlfriend" before it was her birthday!

The customer service associate was a girl and went "aww" as I explained everything to her so she was more than willing to help me to get my package down to Heart ASAP. I was close and running out of time too, because they were just on the verge of closing their shop for the night! We did overnight shipping, and from there I crossed my fingers and hoped for the best! Hoping that it would get past the border and to her place on time. Needless to say, I hardly got any sleep that night since my only concern was is getting my gift down to my baby.

The following morning, I got up and the first thing I did was is track my order to see if it reached down, and it did! But nobody had opened it yet! After a long ass day of working she finally got home, so we went on cam to talk as we usually did during the evening. She had no issues with webcams but I did and later told her that I had issues with that. "Did you get my neckless, baby!?" I asked her while being all excited and she said "Yes!" And damn right then and there she was wearing the neckless for me to see, and I couldn't believe it!

She looked like my fuckin' wife man, my fuckin' wifey! I remember asking her what her mom said and thought about it all? And she said that her mom said who loves you that much to give that to you? Then we both laughed. But I didn't care about all that because all I noticed was is the girl of my dreams that I was now madly in love with was finally wearing my chain.

Days later when we talked on cam I noticed she didn't have the chain on though so I said, "Where's the chain?" So she said, "Oh I was painting, you don't want me to wreck it, do you?" She walked out of her room and came back in with the chain and kissed it. I was relieved and assured that she still had it. We both ended up saying we loved each other minutes right after me questioning her and the raw emotions that we felt for one another was like nothing else. It was overwhelming at times, like whenever we didn't talk I needed to talk to her and felt off whenever she wasn't around.

Right after that I started to ask myself rational questions like what I could possibly offer her? Was I any good? What do I have going for myself? And, if we had a kid that meant I would have to be on point with my shit being together! We increasingly talked about meeting each other and we always joked about it but it wasn't just a simple joke anymore. We both talked about what the other would do as soon as we laid eyes on one another, and she always said to me one of the first things she would do upon seeing me is touch me to make sure I was fuckin' real!

She felt like she wasn't worthy of having someone love her the way that I did or having someone in her life that was as caring because of her past dysfunctional relationships she always found herself in. I even asked her how I measured up to the other guys she was in past relationships with? And she told me not to worry about it since the other guys were assholes who did her wrong and who tried to take advantage of her.

To be in more frequent contact with her I got myself a laptop and that helped me to get out of the basement which was killing me slowly. Talking in my room was becoming the "new" thing and the vibe was different from the basement so I felt like I was turning my life around. The situation I had with Heart represented everything that was good. It was change and a new beginning which developed out of this thing called love that I haven't experienced ever to such a high level. On days we didn't talk I felt terrible! I felt like I wasn't living anymore, and likewise for her too. Anytime away from my computer was time spent thinking about her so if I was out I rushed back home as fast as I could and usually saw my screen filled with messages from her wondering where I was? We purposely left our devices on for each other too.

I have to admit, though, that the more I witnessed how active and up and about Heart was I envied it, and the more I kind of envied her. She was going out and met with a lot of her friends and went out with her mom to a lot of lively places. In terms of working, it seemed as though she was already living the dream too! I mean she loved theatre and dancing and was working as a stage manager in Jersey and NYC. I always felt I should have been doing as much as her if not more! When it came to work, all I mostly said was that I'm working with my dad. I admired her ambition too and because of the fact that she was so active that was one of the many reasons for why she had a five-page resume.

So, what was Drew doing? I felt like none of what I wanted to do was going in my favour at all except for me making music and trying to get it out to labels that really didn't give two shits about someone they didn't know. I really felt I needed to be equal to this girl as well as being someone she could depend on, and maybe I already was in her eyes but I didn't feel like that at all. Anyhow, that's when I stopped and evaluated my situation in a whole.

Okay, Drew, what needs to happen? You need to head to school for social work so you can work within that field, get your ass paid then you can be there for her. Then relocate down to NYC to move in with her to get everything rolling, but before that we gotta meet to see how everything goes.

It was nearing the summer so I wanted to be down there before it hit, and if I wasn't I didn't see why she should just stay there and not have any type of "fun." So, out of the blue I said, "Baby? It's gonna be the summer and all so... I mean don't you wanna fuck?" See, I knew and understood that we were in a long-distance relationship so although I was in love I also didn't try to fool myself. She had needs just like I did, so I wanted things to be open between us.

"Na, I'm good, but I'll let you know though," she said.

I don't think she thought I'd ever come down, but I threw my hands up one day and finally said enough is enough! Then bought Amtrak tickets to New York City to see my lady. My departure date was set for July twenty-eighth, ten twenty-seven a.m. and my coming back date was August second. I thought nothing of me going until it came down to the last few days, similar to London. So I freaked out... What? Me? Mr. Anxiety and housebound going down to New York City!? The fuck!? Then I caught myself and my thoughts and reminded myself that I was doing this for Heart! And nothing was going to stop me because it was the next logical step!

The morning of the trip I remember waking up feeling intensely spaced out of my mind, so it was a good thing that my bags were already prepacked. I felt like I was watching myself from the outside since everything felt so surreal. Remember Coolz? Well, I told him that I bought tickets to head down to NY, so he offered to drive me to Union Station in downtown Toronto so that I could catch my train. On our way down, we talked about life and how the craziest things happen when you take chances. When we arrived at Union Station, he asked if I was alright, threw me a bottle of water, and made sure that I had all my luggage with me, then drove off. While walking across the street headed towards the station that's when everything hit me harder but I proceeded to keep it cool even though I knew I was a-hundred percent on my own.

I physically started to shake in my knees, but the objective still remained the same. As I stood in front of the station one of my first thoughts was is a hostage suicide situation that took place a few years ago, but I snapped out of it and tunnel versioned straight to the station. I still felt unsure of my whereabouts so that's when I quickly stopped the first person I saw for directions.

"Excuse me, sir? How do I get into Union Station?"

"Over there," the sharply dressed forty-something-year old

businessman said to me without a care while he leaned back on the wall smoking in his grey suit.

I walked into the direction he motioned me to go towards. It was a steep concrete ramp where it seemed like everyone else was headed to, so, I went too! The movement of people was crazy! With people coming and going through these few set of doors. So, like everyone else I went straight in and then found myself right in the Centre of one of Toronto's biggest transit hubs. All I saw around me was ticket booths, so I took a moment to look around until I found the Via Rail and Amtrak booth. That's when I approached this cute Asian girl working there and told her where I was going. She was friendly as she directed me to the gate I needed to be at, then I split fast. Amongst all the confusion, I managed to find the gates to where I needed to be, so I waited along with everyone else.

A week before going I assured my mom that I would be alright but my mom along with my dad thought I was crazy. Can you believe all I took down with me was one medium sized suitcase and a little strap bag holding my laptop? No phone, hardly any food just my wallet and some snacks to munch on like Jell-O Pudding. When I got relaxed and seated, I took the window seat (of course) and I laidback and allowed myself to take it easy, even if just for a few minutes. As I waited, I witnessed so many other different people getting on too! Like this one white kid that sat right across from me that I ended up talking to. I asked him where he was going and he told me "Oh, I'm headed to Boston!" He then told me that his dad lived out there while he lived with his mom in Toronto, and that he's been doing this since the age of twelve.

"F'real?" I said to him, then he told me he had a dual citizenship which is why it's so easy for him, so I told him he was lucky to have one. Then I went on to tell him that I was seeing a girl and that I was excited, so he shared in my excitement and said, "I'm stoked for you man! Cool!" He also lent me a pen so that I could fill out the passport forms we had, and he never wanted it back, so I'll always remember him to this day for that.

With everything mostly being finalized with everyone on the train that's when we started to move out of the train yard heading westbound out of the city. I never ate anything that morning because of my nerves and the more our train started to pick up with momentum my stomach started to turn, but luckily I had nothing in my system so there was nothing to throw up. Oh my god, I was headed to Penn Station in NYC to see Heart!

I tried to do some deep breathing exercises I learned from my doctor like breathe in, breathe out, breathe in, then HOLD for four seconds and out, then do it again! After doing that I ignored my physical worries and thought to myself that I couldn't just show up like that. I reached into my bag for my laptop and plugged it into a nearby outlet on the train, then I laid it on the food trey then opened my iTunes player to listen to some music. While listening with my headphones on I went through my Hip Hop, Reggae and Dance Hall, R & B, and Other, going through tracks while trying to meditate. Then out of nowhere *"Inside my love"* by *Minnie Riperton* started to play.

This was all ironic and crazy to me for a few reasons.

#1. I used to play this track in *GTA 4 Liberty City* which was based off New York City.
#2. I never even knew I had this song in my iTunes playlist to begin with!

So, as I sat there in shock while listening to this song that's when the idea hit me! "I got it!" I said! Right then and there it just made sense to me to write a poem to Heart to express how it is I truly felt towards her, and how much she meant to me. While heading down to the states there were still a few seats on the train that were empty, and I mean I wasn't complaining because I liked it like that.

The route that was taken was called The Maple Leaf Line which connected Toronto with NYC. The line headed west then turned going southeast towards Niagara Falls and the Canadian/American border, then into Buffalo going east then shooting down south to New York City. With the train moving and with me being exposed to different sceneries along the way, and with my music playing it didn't take long for me to write up a poem that articulated how I felt and that conveyed the right message.

At that point, it was just a thinking game of wondering how I'd present it to her, but my nervousness turned into excitement at that point since I now felt more at ease. When we finally got around to the Niagara Falls border that's when our train slowly stopped to let the American Border Patrol guys get on to feel us out. This freaked me out because I knew it wouldn't take much for them to interrogate me if something seemed off. I tried to remain cool while telling myself to simply show them my paystub ticket, and don't stutter!

With loud-sounding footsteps, my heart started to beat faster as I heard them getting closer and closer to our cart. There were two Asian kids seated behind me that got questioned first with one of the patrol guys asking them where they were headed? They said Texas, so that's when the patrol guys said to them "if you're headed to Texas why are you on a train headed to New York?" That's when the kids said, "Ah, it's cheaper, and we're meeting a cousin at their university."

"Come with us!" The Boarder Patrol Officer said after hearing their story. When I heard that, I knew not to say anything stupid along those lines and I was Black so I knew my story had to be good and make sense!

Guard walks up

"Where are you going?"

"Um, I am going to New York to see a friend." Then I made a joke about not seeing them for some time. He didn't crack a smile or laugh, he just eyed me down with a stone-cold look and asked me what my relationship was to this friend, how I met her, and what I planned to do with her while down in the city?

"Ah, she's my girlfriend and I plan to have fun..." I thought he would have at least cracked a smile over that, but he gave me back my questionnaire form and said, "Have a nice trip" before walking off.

The white kid seated across from me had the same guard but he seemed to know the drill all too well, so he winged it smooth like an ace. This girl on our train who was also from Toronto had like five bad ass kids with her that were loud and annoying, but similar to myself it seemed as though she was seeing a significant other.

Once we got to the border she wasted little to no time in getting off the train after she was questioned, and when I looked out the window I saw a dude with dreads who looked like he might have been her man since he was smiling and waving and she waved back. She ran out of that train so fast with her kids and over the tracks and into his arms and hugged him, so I was right. Twenty to forty minutes later the train started up and began to take its course after everyone was checked out, and like that I was in America.

CHAPTER 6

NYC

*P*assing through Buffalo was a trip since the places where we past looked all abandoned like a ghost town. From that point, it was just a straight line that continued for hours that picked people up at different stops ever so often.

The train stops became more frequent once it finally made a right and headed south for NYC, and it all tripped me out because I never knew the train would have gotten filled but it did. I don't remember who sat beside me but my frame of mind was probably somewhere else and for good reason. I thought the train operators were American from jump but later realized they were Canadian, but switched once we got to Niagara. "Ladies and Gentlemen, we will be at our destination shortly."

Although the train ride seemed like forever I knew damn well when we arrived closer into the city because the surroundings and vibes were noticeably different. Houses, buildings, then bigger buildings and then even bigger buildings until it seemed like we were gonna plow right into the city then before I knew it the train magically headed underground to Penn Station. As we made our way through this tunnel our train finally stopped as everyone started to gather their belongings to get off the train.

Penn Station was their equivalent to our Union station and really their Grand Central Station since it had so many metro lines and transit hubs all around. Along with mostly everyone else I headed up this escalator and that's when my nervousness got triggered again since I didn't know what to expect! So there I went again with the deep breathing as I tried to brace myself.

Busyness

It was Union Station all over again, except this time it was at night and in another city and country. I tried to prep myself before heading down the best that I could and learned about the taxi line-up that most people go to, but while in the moment of craziness you lose your mind. All I know is I wanted a fast way out and away from it all.

I crossed paths with this black dude who was around my age and on my train trying to flirt with the girl seated next to him. So I called out to him. "This is my first time in the city. Where are you going?" He said, "Ah cool! I'm goin' to Brooklyn." I asked how the fuck to get out of the station, then said, "I hope all is cool and that I don't get jacked." I laughed and kept walking but his cheerful smile and demeanor slowly changed...

With a look of confusion on his face mixed with a facial expression as if to say nigga, don't be sayin' that type of shit to random people down here. Then he walked off going to the taxi waiting line. From that moment on it was just another clear reminder that I was pretty much on my own if I didn't already notice that by then. I stopped everything I was doing and scanned my environment then off into the distance I saw another escalator, then I saw this tall dude who seemed chill so I said "yo, how do I get out of this place?" He was the splitting image of Eddy Murphy's brother, Charlie Murphy. He gave me this big smile and said, "Heh, yea I can help you, follow me." So, like a simpleton I followed him as we bobbed and weaved our way out of the insanity and up the escalator I saw in the distance before seeing him.

Bitch slap

The city that I always read and heard about was right in front of my face and instantaneously gave me a wave of energy I have never felt before! Cars were going in every direction then this Charlie Murphy look alike said, "You need a cab!?" I said yea so he nonchalantly walked in the middle of the street as if immortality was his best friend and forced a cab to stop for him.

This white woman who was also waiting started to get into the cab that he stopped, so she screamed and said "HEY!!! This is mine!" He shrugged it off and stopped another cab for me then said to me, "Aight cool, ten bucks." I gave him an American twenty-dollar bill, then he quickly got me my change at a nearby stand. He helped me to shove all my luggage into the back of the taxi then gave me my change back once I got in. I let my driver know that I needed to head to the Times Square Hilton located at 42nd and 8th street so he wasted little to no time in getting there.

Passing through the New York streets was a mind-fuck because there was so much action and movement going on that got more intense. The insides of the cab were bordered off with glass, a payment machine and TV screen in the back which was crazy to me because it made me feel like an animal, and almost as if they were expecting you to do something crazy.

Man stabbed in Brooklyn

The TV screen was turned to a news station, and all they talked about was is robberies and stabbings that were going on. "Here you go mannn!" the cabbie said to me as we arrived at the Hilton. I gave him three or four bucks before I got out taking my bags then he pulled off. I just stood there for a moment to take in all the craziness and flashing lights that surrounded me, and couldn't believe that I made it to my destination. While staring in amazement at everything I gave myself a random security pat down as I usually do to myself to make sure I didn't lose anything, but something felt off though…

"Fuck!!! Where's my wallet!?" Within minutes from getting out of the cab my mood went from experiencing extreme happiness to switching to doubt and worry, then disappointment. "Where is my wallet!?" I backtracked and recounted all that I did up to that point and knew for damn sure my wallet was with me while I was in the cab.

"Ah, shit! I left my wallet in the back of the taxi!" Thinking back at what I did, I knew I left it in the back of the taxi while taking out my luggage. It was a madhouse of fun all around me, I was in another country, but my wallet was gone so…I just stood there as the city carried on moving in one crazy direction without me, then my luggage dropped.

When I went to go pick up my luggage I noticed a cute young couple getting a portrait of themselves done to my left. They, looked so happy too, but little did they know that to their right I was going through a world of shit, the contrast was crazy! What else can I really do? Is what I said to myself and knew I had to un-fuck myself out of and from this crazy situation. I started to become scared but shook that out of my system and told myself I couldn't be a little bitch! I have to solve this situation out! Plus, I was in the city for Heart and she was depending on me but she knew nothing of what was going on nor did anyone else because I had no phone! I took all the courage I had and turned around to head straight into the Hilton to check myself in but explained to them that I lost my wallet. Somehow some way I managed to convince them that I was who I said I was so everything was cool with the room I booked.

Feeling overwhelmed and extremely tired I dropped my luggage again before getting my hotel documents and access card to my room. The room they ended up giving me was room 2727 which was so weird. And just by chance it just so happened that the room had two queen beds in it!

Making my way up the elevator to the twenty-seventh floor and to my room, I instantaneously turned into this different person, it was all about sorting things out, getting things done and not standing for any type of bullshit!

Until that point most of my troubled life was being lived indoors, so it almost seemed as though being outside for that long really made my mind decompress which made my thinking become clearer along with my actions.

I took a relaxing, but quick, shower before drying myself off so that I could head back down to the main lobby, that's when I asked one of the girls working at the front desk if I could use their main phone since I didn't have one. Feeling not too concerned about much except for my current situation I called up my credit card company and filled them in on all that took place and that I lost my identification, so I needed money wired to me quick!

"Okay, Mr. Marshall, we will assist you, lookout for our call in the morning."

Automatically I just started to deal with situations as they came, and there wasn't much worry or doubt what so ever because I just simply did what I felt needed to be done! It was either I fold or I would survive. I hung out in the lounge area of the hotel for about twenty-five minutes looking around at happy people again, and then thought to myself how close I became to being like them. Then I headed back up to my room took my clothes off and jumped in my big ass comfy bed and passed out...

Ring-Ring-Ring

Alarmed and in a daze, I woke up early the next morning out of my deep sleep. "Mr. Marshall?" "Yes?"

"Your credit company called. You need to come downstairs so you can call them back," is what the front desk girl notified me about, since I told them the night before to wake me up when my card company calls back.

Still tired and in a daze, I rushed downstairs to the lobby and to the front desk where they gave me more details and a piece of paper showing me a number to call back.

"Is this Mr. Marshall?" I said yea then it got all secretive "Okay,

Mr. Marshall, here is a code number we are going to provide you with. You need to head over to Western Union with this code then you will be granted some money."

"Is that it?"

"Yes." So, with that information I wasted no time hung up and left the lobby to head down to the main ground level. When I got to the street level one of the bellboys asked if I needed a cab? I said "yup!" He helped me out by standing in the road like how Mr. Charlie Murphy did, then I jumped in.

"Where do you need to go?" I said I needed to head to 41st and Broadway. I studied the maps so crazy the night before to the point I knew exactly where I was going. All I had on me was is my credit card, my passport, my keys and pass to get back into my room. The cabbie ended up pulling right over at the intersection and on the opposite side was where Western Union was. I knew I had no money on me so I planned to pay the driver once I got some.

"Do you trust me?" He hesitated and didn't know what to make of what I said, so in one motion I jumped out of the cab and screamed at him saying, "Wait for me! Imma get paid! And you'll be paid! Just wait!"

And just like that there I was this guy who thought he had so many limitations and issues who figured he couldn't amount to shit running out on the streets of New York City of all places in the rain around five a.m. without a fuck to give feeling free and on a mission...

I busted my way through the doors at that specific Western Union location and only saw five people in the lineup. Two of them were Somali and the other three were regular looking white guys. I kept looking outside repeatedly like I stole something, but I was just looking out for my cabbie and I even waved to him so he knew that I wasn't trying to ditch him.

One of the Somalian dudes within this lineup sensed how impatient and in a rush I was so he motioned for me to go ahead of him so I nodded and smiled to thank him. When I got to one of the booths I gave one of the agents the secret number I was provided with, "Sir, this number does not work," the agent said, who was an unkempt looking white dude who could care less about his job. I looked over the information I was given and gave him a different number. That's when everything started to work! It couldn't have happened at a better time too since my cabbie came in yelling at me!

"I'm done, I'm done!" I said then ran out and jumped back into the cab. When we made it back to the hotel I paid him then jokingly said,

"See? I might have run off, but I came back, you're good man!" The fare was way cheaper down there compared to Toronto taxi rides too!

By this time, it was probably around six-thirty a.m., and it is true what they say about New York City, it really does not sleep! There were still people everywhere. When I got back to the lobby and front desk I paid for a couple more nights and for the phone in my room. This is all of what I had to go through and deal with before ever even thinking about meeting Heart for the first time, but I managed to do it. Now all I had to worry about was if Heart was going to see me, or if she was gonna ditch me and not even come.

With a big boost of confidence from all that I did, I headed back to my room with a mean strut and felt more mentally clear. That's when I flung all my clothes off, got settled in and connected my laptop to the hotels Wi-Fi services so that I could communicate with Heart.

Heart: "Babes, you're actually here!? My god, okay I'm coming to see you before work!"

Me: "Yes, baby, I'm here for you, and we finally did it! I'm waiting for you!"

Heart was a vegetarian, but she always let me know that if she really liked a guy she would make it painfully obvious by cooking good for him, and that he would know. She often fantasized about giving a nice juicy meal to a guy serving him while walking around all sexy in a cute thong knowing that it was her who fed and pleased him. I always thought that was pretty hot and seductive too, and sure as hell didn't object to that idea.

After telling her I was finally in the city and making her aware of my whereabouts I tried to catch an hour-long nap to refresh myself since I wanted to be ready for our first encounter. When I finally got up it was probably around nine-thirty a.m., so we must have coordinated how we were going to work out this first meeting by then. The details with that are blurry, but I do remember that once I mentioned to her that I was staying at the Times Square Hilton she was in shock!

"You're staying where!? I work right across the street from where you're staying!" Which made me go into shock. "Are you fuckin' serious!? How does that even make sense!?"

"Yea, now I can see you on my lunchbreak too!"

While she was on her way I gave the room a little clean since I messed it up a bit along with its two queen sized beds with one of them having my opened suitcase with clothes all around on it. Now remember that poem to Heart I randomly came up with while on the train? Well it wasn't until now that I knew how to fully present it.

There was a writing desk with a nice sleek chair near the window in the back of my room, so what I decided to do is take that desk and put it in the corner and position the chair so it faced the window instead of facing towards the front door, then placed my laptop right in the middle of this desk.

After that was fixed, I took a nice shower then creamed my skin with nice smelling coco butter then finished it all off with some not so harsh smelling Axe Spray scented as chocolate. Now, before even heading down I warned Heart that I was in a rough spot in my life and that I was fucked up. Dress wise, there was nothing special about me and even my Payless shoes were fucked up. At this point since I was done with preparing myself room wise and body wise, all I did from that point on was is sit patiently on my bed in dead silence until I got more nervous.

Fifteen-minutes passed…

Knock-Knock-Knock

My heart dropped instantaneously! What was my plan? Simple: to hide in the closet have her come in and read my poem *shrugs shoulders* what? I'm no magician so I just wanted the simplest plan since less is more… As she knocked, and once the flash sequence ceased right before my eyes, my first impulse was to run right up to the door. Then I just said hold up. I looked into the peephole to make sure it was her. I know it might sound dumb, but I thought if there were ever a good time to pull a stickup or any type of sick joke on me it would be now!

All my doubt and semi-irrational thinking went out of the window at that point though because there she was, my beautiful Heart standing all clueless at the door looking exactly like how she looked like on cam while we would talk except ten times better! I opened the door halfway and I said, "I need you to do something for me"

"Okay…" Heart said in an unsure voice. I said to her I was gonna hide in the closet and instructed her to walk into the room and sit down right where my laptop was and for her to read what was on the screen, then to call me once she was done.

"This is weird…" Heart said, but I was still confident in my plan.

Before she even made her way up to my room I made sure to have my poem opened on my laptop and cued up that Minnie Riperton "Inside My Love" song that I randomly discovered on the train.

"Come out…" she said, so slowly I left the closet and walked over to her while her eyes were closed… then slowly put my hands on her shoulders as she began to slowly get up and move towards the window.

"I've been waiting for this for so long, princess."

"I know, daddy..." she replied, then, we made out and kissed overlooking the city of New York. We held each other as we looked at the view, then Heart being the typical Jersey/New Yorker she is said, "The view is actually better on the other side, baby." I didn't care, though, I was there with my other half and by the looks of everything phase 1 of my plan worked. She was happy along with myself being happy.

NYC Hotel View

There was a comfy lazy boy chair behind us so I took her by the hand to lead her as I sat down. Then she followed me and sat right on my lap, which is exactly how we both envisioned everything to slowly progress. All nervousness went away as we both talked all sexy to one another and made out again for a second or third time. Heart was more than what I expected. She was five-eight, with nice chocolate skin. Her style was artsy, but edgy and calm. Her background was African and Puerto Rican and she knew how to seduce with her Spanish speaking if need be.

When we were making out, Heart's head turned and looked all embarrassed and I never knew why. Then I realized that a maid was watching us for a while, but I didn't care. I was with Heart and being watched kind of turned me on. Stunned, but intrigued, the maid finally closed our door, so we went back to what we were doing. Without hesitation, Heart got up, took me by the hand, and led me right to one of the beds then we started kissing some more as she gradually started taking off some of her clothes along with my help. Did I mention I was hard as fuck while she was sitting on me?

There she was all mine, bare and exposed, looking picture perfect with just a cute tiny black thong on.

"See? I wore a black thong for you." She looked like a goddess and left me speechless. She never had a guy go down on her in a mad while so that's what I did while making her clit throb as she became hornier. Being that I was her dude, I wanted to take care of her like how a man should, so I did and never left any part of her body unattended to.

When it comes to dick size, I'm not afraid to admit that I don't have a big one, and it doesn't really matter because straight up I'm way too freaky to let something like that stop me! I have no shortcomings!

Although we were having a lot of fun exploring each other, we had to stop since she had to head back to work, but promised she would be back. But once she started getting dressed I made circles around her bellybutton. She slapped my hands at first and said for me to behave, but eventually gave up letting out a relaxing moan of pleasure with a blissful smile on her face. I held her down and teased her for a while until she got close again and finally said, "Seriously, I got to get back to work!" So we stopped as she got dressed then she gave me a kiss before leaving.

What Heart made

After she left I tried to occupy myself in my room until she came back, and true to her words in regards to guys she really liked, she made a hell of a lot of bacon for me to eat which tasted damn nice! After hours of waiting, she finally came back and one of the first things I ended up telling her was is how I lost my wallet so I couldn't stay as long as I would have liked to have in the city.

"Oh, baby, that's crazy," she said while giving me a slice of her vegetarian pizza she got for lunch. The bacon she prepared for me was wrapped in tinfoil, which I never threw away, so while we talked she started playing with it and subconsciously made a heart out of it, which I ended up taking a picture of.

Once we finished eating and talking, we started up with a second round of fun! Some nervousness came back in because I might have worried about sexual performance but it was all good. By the time we were done with our fun, Heart laid her head on my chest then we both ended up resting. Out of nowhere, it started to rain with lightning and thunder which seemed sexy because of the perfect timing as though we were in a movie.

"Oh my god, what time is it!?" We slept for so long that by the time we got up Heart freaked and I didn't know why. But it was because of her bus transportation back home which she needed to catch. She quickly got dressed, we kissed, then she ran and rushed out of the place, but said "call me" as she left.

After twenty minutes I did call her, but she seemed too shy to talk on the bus and said she would call me back. With an action-packed day filled with so many highs then higher highs, I really had to sit back to process it all and thought about myself in a whole as a person. Was I dreaming? I was actually doing and living out all this crazy shit. I was in the Hilton in NYC and just had sex with my love. The room still had Heart's signature scent in it too as a reminder.

"Drew, what holds you back in Toronto?" I started to say out loud to myself while trying to analyze my dysfunction. Then I asked myself why I was so successful in NYC but not Toronto. But the answer was clear... my living situation along with my environment was fucked up. New York forced me to become independent and was a damn challenge, and because of this new-found freedom my brain started to process things more clearly for what they were.

"Wow, I was really messed up," is what I said. I couldn't really relate to the sickly guy from Toronto anymore as much, and didn't want to reconnect with him either. Nightfall slowly made its way into the city and I didn't take notice since I was watching TV. I mean I was a "new" person, but I still had some issues about myself and didn't leave my room really. I turned on the night lamps once it got dark and started acting out all crazy because I was on a high from everything that went on.

In a sick and twisted way, I felt I wasn't deserving of everything positive that started happening, but snapped out of that thinking and told myself that if I died the next day I at least had this moment before I died! Feeling hyper and excited I went to the hotel curtains, opened them up wide as fuck, and stripped myself naked so everyone could see me, so what did I do? I mooned them and loved it! Followed by a free dance show that went on for a while, and really, why not?

During and after some of that, I opened my laptop and connected to Skype so that I could talk to my boy Funky. He knew I was going to NYC but didn't believe it until he saw it with his own eyes.

"You crazy fuck!" he said while laughing at me as I danced and fell into my bed mumbling help, help, help.

Some of what happened that night is a blur because I went from moaning for help to Mr. Funky to completely passing out then waking up the next morning with my laptop closed which I don't remember doing at all. I also found out that I overused my hotel phone hours and racked up a big bill so they cut me off. They later ended up telling me that since I was making calls to Jersey, it was basically like me calling long distance which was stupid to me.

Again, the Jersey and NYC metropolitan area should all be one system because that's what I assumed it is along with many other people including residence who actually live there! And really it is! I managed to clear it all up though, so, once I got my phone up and running again I called my parents to let them know I was alright since they never heard from me since the day I left. After that I had to call Amtrak to see if I could get an earlier return date back to Toronto since I lost my wallet.

This was now day three and most of the snacks I had in my suitcase were draining out. I didn't know what to do so I started freaking out and contemplated whether to starve myself, or to leave my room to head out on the street and face it to find food. Walking back and forth in my room was my way of trying to kill my hunger pains with sips of water here and there from the bathroom sink. All I had to my name were three Jell-O Pudding snacks and I went one full day and a half without eating any solids. I tried to remind myself though that REAL hunger would feel way worse than what I was going through.

I had a pair of sneakers that were damaged from the rain that I wore while coming down and I kept looking at them since they were off to the corner of my room as I continued pacing. The more I looked at them the more they symbolized mobility and my emotions for freedom kept growing stronger. That's when I finally snapped and stopped pacing my room and screamed out "man up!" Then gathered all the energy and will I had along with a big deep breath and put my fuckin' shoes on. I made sure I had some money on me and then stormed out of my room, to head onto the street!

Where could I go? I thought. Oh! Duane Reade! That's what came to mind since Heart mentioned it to me earlier and even someone from the front desk at the lobby too. Now the only problem was I had to find it along the busy streets of New York City, which I have only been acquainted with for a few days. For a moment, I reminded myself of all I had already done and accomplished while being in New York, so that encouraged me.

I headed east on 41st Street then headed back once my senses told me I might wanna turn around. I walked until I hit an intersection then headed south on 8th Avenue and loan behold Duane Reade was there! I felt like I was in a candy store! Food, big ass bags of chips, water and vitamin drinks! And any and everything else I might have taken for granted was there! I bought two big ass bags of chips and two or three vitamin drinks. I always saw them at Shoppers Drug Mart (our equivalent to Duane Reade) in Toronto, but it wasn't until now that I bought it.

There were some fine girls there doing their shopping just like me, and one of them in a group even check me out. They didn't seem like they were from NY either. Waiting in line to pay was nerve-wracking too. But I thankfully made it out in one piece. After that, my intentions were to head back to my room and just sit there, but I told myself no, go and walk around for a bit. So, that's exactly what I did. Nice and slowly I strolled the streets and took in all the sights and analyzed them and all the people passing by me. Then hit 7th Avenue and crossed the street until I was on the same side as the Hilton.

Once I got back upstairs to my room I felt so damn good so one of the first things I did was is slam the chips I bought right into my face nice and fast as I tried to calm my hunger! Then downed one of my drinks! Where is she, I wondered? Heart and I talked in the morning and planned to spend the whole day with each other, but since she was nowhere to be found I just maintained myself the best I could. I can't lie though, because I did become increasingly more pissed throughout the day since she was nowhere in sight!

When the evening hit, I was already on Skype updating Funky on the latest that was happening with me. Then around this time I heard someone racing to my room and it was Heart! When I let her inside, I introduced her to Funky since Skype was running, but they sort of already knew each other since I briefly introduced them to one another online.

"Okay, we gotta go," is what I said out loud after everyone greeted one another. I then closed the conversation window and then we started to make out as if it was the first time we met.

Bam

We fell right on the bed while we started kissing, then feeling each other as we held one another. Now, although I was staying in midtown New York, I found myself going downtown with her pretty fast if you get what I'm sayin.' We started to play fight a bit, so I got some of the Jell-O Pudding I had and put it all over her chest and licked it off, then we rolled around on the bed until we faced each other and gazed in each other's eyes talking all sweet. Then just as everything was going sweet she had to leave again, so I pinned her to the door while making out with her as I said I didn't want her to leave but she was trying to catch her bus.

"Let me walk you downstairs."

"Babes, your shirt is covered in pudding," she said.

"Who cares!" is what I said back so we left my room and headed down to the lobby as she grabbed my hand holding onto it nice and tight and not letting go, which felt damn good. When we got to the ground level I walked her right to the doors then she freaked out worrying about her bus and the time. We made out again, then I kissed her on her forehead and told her to message me.

With all the crazy New York lights and commotion, I watched Heart run all cute heading west on 41st street until she disappeared and vanished into the sea of people no longer to be seen. It broke my heart, so I stood there already missing her. While turning around to head back into the hotel I saw a pretty hot girl with this tall dude along with his boy, it seemed like their romantic escapade was just about to begin one minute after mine ended.

"You need an elevator?" I asked to all three of them. "I can't make luv to her while you're there," the guy with the girl said, so I was like "cool" and headed back to my room to pack my bags for the next day since I would be leaving.

Buzz-Buzz-Buzz

Slowly waking up on my fourth day, my alarm clock was set to go off at five-thirty in the morning since I knew that I had to be at Penn Station for six-thirty to catch my train. I packed and made sure I was set the night before. I double checked the room and my bags then gave the room one last look as I thought about what took place in the span of four days.

There was a stuffed teddy bear I surprised Heart with on our last day together and that was something I kept thinking about as I scanned my room while getting emotional. Damn, fear, love, sex, romance and victory all rolled up into four days. Bye room 2727...

Leaving my room then checking out at the front desk lobby was bittersweet, while I was in the elevator with this other couple they asked me where I was from. So I said Toronto. "Ah, I knew it!" the girlfriend said, and then as the doors opened they wished me good luck then the boyfriend said "give my best to Yonge Street." I gave him a fist bump once we all got out. As I reached the street level the bellboy caught me another cab then I took off. The driver was Asian and that was unique to me so the joke I made to him was get me there alive, man. "What you do after you drop me off is your business." We both laughed.

On arrival at Penn Station I hopped out the cab then headed to the escalator but saw this black dude selling perfumes and incense that I decided to buy at the last minute. It was all for a dollar so I figured to just take a chance. Looking around as I headed down to the lower level made me think of the first day I came, it looked so different, but also I arrived at night when things were busier and more crowded. I rushed to get processed quickly so I could board the train with everyone else. Shit, it was literally like doing everything but in reverse heading back to Toronto.

This cool Jewish guy ended up sitting beside me and was headed to Toronto for the first time and started asking ME everything there is to know about the city since he knew little to nothing. I was more than happy to inform him.

"Oh, Andrew, New York is a beautiful place, Giuliani really cleaned it up! I'm glad you got to see it. By the way my name is David."

David looked young, but he insisted that he was retired. He was also I true to life loud and proud Jewish New Yorker from Queens, with the full accent and all. "You know, Andrew, although I've never been to Toronto I've been to Montreal and loved it! I also hate flying so traveling by ground is all I do. So, tell me more about Toronto how's it like? And tell me more about this girl you saw where is she from?"

I told David that my lovely was from New Jersey but loved spending most her time in the city referring to Jersey as being New York's ugly cousin that's hidden in the basement that never gets acknowledged.

HA-HA-HA

David laughed all hard and said, "Wow, that is rich, that's really cheeky! I gotta tell my sister out in Jersey about that one."

"You know, Andrew? Jersey isn't that bad of a place. I actually used to live out there before and loved it!"

I always used to encourage and tell Heart to be proud of where she comes from, and I always jokingly called her my "Jersey Princess." I mean, I'm from Scarborough which could be our equivalent to what Jersey is to New York and I'm proud regardless what others have to say!

David and I struck up such good conversation that I barely even noticed that we left Penn Station, and by the time I noticed we were WAY out of the city by then. I also felt liberated heading back home too because of all that I did... and the trip back seemed faster than going down, but we had to get out of the train to get checked at the Canadian border.

When we were being processed, I slipped up with something I said and the police were all over me. I was forced into a room and they looked at my laptop from top to bottom since they thought it was a bomb! The Canadian border patrol really took their jobs seriously whereas the American side didn't give two shits even though they were strict as well. When everything was all said and done, we boarded back onto the train but now I was separated from my boy David and other noticeable faces.

I sat in a seat by myself and thought about life as I watched the buildings pass by. The train past this condo as we cut through St. Catharines which made me say, "Damn, I need to be on my own, I can't go back home living like how I used to. I lived man. I lived!" We went all the way right and around until we got to Toronto then we all finally boarded off, I remember randomly reconnecting with David and he seemed lost and freaked out. "Oh my god, Andrew, us bumping into each other again must be fate! How do I get out of here where are the cabs!?"

Interesting, the helpless has now become the helper, and I was more than happy to do so. I showed him where the cabstand was before we parted ways but before I walked off he said, "Andrew, if you're ever in New York again please look me up and we can catch some shows." Then he waved to me as I said, "No problem!"

"Hey, David if you're reading this and you remember Andrew, get at me!!!"

There I was back in Toronto at Union Station looking around. After ten minutes, I managed to get some change and called my dear sister to see if she could pick me up and luckily for me she did. As soon as I saw her I gave her a huge hug! Then told her how my trip was but left out all the freaky shit of course.

Leaving Union Station and getting out of the downtown core was nuts but once we did we headed straight for the highway and headed east back to Scarborough. The closer we got to home the more terrible I felt inside, my stomach literally became sick and I felt all the toxic energy from the environment making its way back into my body. It felt like willingly heading back into a deathtrap.

Psychologically, I felt like I shit myself, then suicidal thoughts started to run through my head. If I feel like this and I haven't even gone inside of my house yet, how would I feel once I get in? My sister stopped at a nearby gas station to fill up the car so this in a way kind of gave me some time to brace myself for my unwanted reality. "We're home!" My sister screamed as we arrived entering the house, my parents welcomed me back and I generally told them how my trip was. My mom never wanted me to go, but my dad knew the deal, so, we spoke the unspoken truths that men sometimes do at times without saying one word to one another.

CHAPTER 7

On My Own

Back in Toronto from NYC, with stuff from the hotel

After being home for about a month or so and with fall coming around the corner communication between Heart and I progressively slowed down. No Instant Messenger apps, no easy way to get in contact with her, if I had to speak to her I had to go out of my way to do it.

When it first started happening, I played it cool, but after waiting for so long to talk with her I lost it and went back to the same place we connected at. Twitter! She messaged me back here and there, but our communication was fickle with us hardly having any regular type of conversation, so I figured she didn't dig me much anymore. When I did finally hear from Heart it was as if I won a jackpot of gold! Anytime we talked it was unpredictable so I let her know that by putting all my concerns and issues on the table.

"Baby? You KNOW I love you! And I'm keeping you out of this for your OWN GOOD!" Heart said. That was one of the last messages I ever got from her with other undisclosed pieces of information because it goes too deep, but yeah...Being left in that sort of headspace made me not sleep at night since I felt high strung, and getting up the next morning feeling even worse! Then I read a posting of hers that kind of sealed the deal for me making me realize that nothing more was ever going to be happening with us, so I said fuck it! Back down the drain I go...

Girls I once pushed away were now girls I started talking to again and I started getting crazier and erratic on the net without giving a shit. Emotionally and psychologically I was really messed up, thinking about her and not talking to her triggered me to space out from all the anxiety I felt, and looking at her social media profiles was the same. A girl I used to be distant towards slowly became someone I started talking to, she always wanted to meet up, but we never took things beyond our conversations since we rarely talked on the phone.

Since I was in a fucked-up spot, I said fuck it, why not? So we set something up so we could meet but I kind of felt hesitant about it all. "Here's some motivation," the text message read. Getting up the next day I got up reading that as my first message on my phone with a shot of her ass followed by a wink. The whole reason behind why I even owned a phone now in the first place was so that I could keep in contact with my baby, but as I got the phone things fell apart.

I am a true believer in energy and vibrations though, so before going to bed every night I would text Heart, but after we weren't really talking anymore I just hoped that she felt me thinking of her and hoped she was thinking of me too. Peaches is the girl I ended up going out with on a little date at a local movie theatre, I really had no idea what I was doing there and I kept thinking of who I was in love with. When Peaches finally came, all of what we mostly talked about was is Heart and she sat there and listened to me.

"Let's go in this room," Peaches said so I went with her since she knew the layout of the place better than myself. Peaches was VERY attractive but my mind was elsewhere even though we did get frisky as I put my hand up her skirt. "I love Heart so much," is what I said as I leaned in to kiss Peaches and it all was confusing. We quickly stopped then like ninjas we made our way to another movie room that had little to no people inside of it, so we could get down to, um, business!

"Um, Drew?"

"Yea?"

"Maybe we shouldn't be here. There's security coming up." Man, I was so lucky she told me that too because my ass was literally all the way out!

After that we just left and called it a night, then I waited with her until the right bus came. She wanted me to come on with her but I made up an excuse since I didn't like buses that much. "Oh, yea… your issues." She went on to say since she caught on to the fact I didn't want to be around crowds.

Once she left I sent Heart a text message and video of me walking around in the hopes that she would return my message, but she never did. My life fell apart and so many of my dreams were tied to Heart, I might have been in Toronto physically but mentally I was down there in NYC with her.

My mind was warped with me having a one-track mind which didn't include me living in Toronto at all. I was living off hope and the notion that I eventually would be in New York, so when that option was crushed I was forced to face the ugliness of my life. No fantasies, no more looking into the clouds and no more wishing upon a star for fuckin' hope! I was smacked right back into reality and hard! Heart represented change and that change didn't really happen, so once I turned around looking at the big bad city of Toronto I had no choice but to take on the things I was avoiding. For as abrupt as things ended with Heart and myself, I always felt like we would eventually speak again but all in time. Until then I just had to confront my demons.

It was now the beginning of two-thousand-and-twelve, and although I was still connected to Heart on social media sites we weren't even communicating, so I waited for her to inevitably unfriend me since I couldn't do it myself. Believe it or not, though, there was a grey period where we somewhat started to talk but our conversations weren't very consistent. She said she needed "space" and even then I didn't want to let her go. From January to March of two-thousand-and-twelve we hardly talked and most of what I said was is wanting to get myself cleaned up in a rehab program so I could still see if there was a bit of hope! She was on the verge of living in Brooklyn, so, I felt like time was ticking.

She eventually blocked me on all sites though and I saw her hugged up with another guy I knew NOTHING about which was another major blow to my ego but I saw it coming. I was still seeing my therapist during this time and felt as though the world was really taking a serious shit on me. My credit card was burning out from excessive taxi use, I became unwell, and I felt like I couldn't do any better.

"How come everyone is winning?" I said to myself on one of the days of my therapy sessions. I walked out of the office depleted of energy and saw a new high profile luxury car in front of me, I paused then walked off.

A month and a half later Alicia dropped half of her patients, me being one of them, so the head director of the clinic told me he would set me up with someone new and her name was Dr. Pierotti, which I was pessimistic about but still willing to try. It was going to be a month-long wait before I got to see this new doctor, so until then I saw the head director of the clinic which was part of what I would do anyhow.

I expressed to him that I wanted to go into rehab at one of Toronto's most well-known mental health/psych hospitals. He didn't want to see me go so I got my family doctor to process me in and to fax the forms to the hospital. The standard wait time for the program was a wait time of six months or so and the name of the program was called The "AIM" Program. Feeling very desperate, I even called a help line and a mobile crisis team to see if I could get hospitalized, but the helpline I called put me on hold then disconnected, and the mobile crisis team never bothered to come out to see me.

"Well, we thought about it and it's not like we could drag you out and help you." I pleaded with them, but all the dispatcher said to me is, "Ha-ha, good luck" in an uncomfortable way then he hung up on me. If I ever felt like the world didn't give a fuck about me, it would have been then!

From that point on I accepted that I was on my own and for the most part I felt like most people just cared about their own skin! And I felt betrayed by a system that refused to help me. "Okay, things have to get straight back down to the basics," is what I said to myself from that moment on. I was on the verge of psychosis and it just seemed logical to hurt and/or kill myself, plus I was having dreams of my mom coming home from church dressed all nice but screaming at me to kill myself!

"KILL YOURSELF, KILL YOURSELF!" she would say in a black dress with white trimmings around it and a black church hat on with mesh covering her face a bit. I went back to my doctor to redo a submission form for the rehab program I wanted to get into then headed home paranoid screaming "This is my fuckin' life!?" As I walked up my driveway. Then I ended up having another dream where I was encouraged to X myself out. By the next morning, I headed to the emergency room of that same hospital I was trying to get into. They knew me well at that hospital since I have been there before, so getting processed in didn't take long at all. All I had to do now was is endure sitting in the waiting room.

Intense psychosis, people off their medications, the classic white girl with an eating disorder off to the corner, someone getting pinned to the ground in a private room then forcefully sedated. This was all there and is what I witnessed.

After waiting through the usual chaos and Lusions, I finally got to see a social worker and then a doctor. I let them know I wanted to get into their rehab program because I felt all my other options left me out to dry. They wrote up a referral form then submitted it, but asked me if I was suicidal? "Off and on yes," is what I said. They followed up by asking "Yes, but are you suicidal now?" That was their classic line they would use to not keep you there then would give you ten minutes to collect yourself before telling you to leave.

Weeks later I ended up seeing the head director at the clinic I always went to and since medical records and whereabouts are traceable he knew fully well where I had been in the past couple of weeks, but I didn't care because at that point all I wanted was is to go into rehab. By the weekend, one of my friends invited me to hang out with her and another friend of hers so being out of character I agreed, but then we ended up walking around aimlessly in the winter cold until we decided to head into a nearby mall.

We were at the Eaton Centre and I felt good being out with her and her friend, but being out in the cold for too long depressed me a bit, so by the time it hit five p.m. I parted ways with them and headed on the train to head back home. Since Dundas Station was inside of the Eaton Centre I hopped on at that station and made my way north to Yonge and Bloor station, then headed east on the Bloor line. Because it was a Sunday, the train system wasn't as busy, plus it was almost past six p.m. By the time I got onto a train, I noticed this girl sitting right across from me; she looked cute. She was a black girl with a curvy body, and had wild and puffy hair that went in every direction, and I dug it! The more I glanced over at her, the more she seemed like someone I had met before, but I just couldn't put my finger on where.

Oh, shit! I saw her a week and a half ago! I realized and remembered I saw her on a day when the train was packed but she vanished within the busy crowd, and I was too socially anxious to do anything about it anyhow. The way I viewed the situation at that moment in time is I felt like I truly needed to speak to her since things like that rarely happened twice.

Arriving at Kennedy, Kennedy Station

The train announcement sounded as we headed deep into the tunnel towards our final stop, so as this happened I said to myself, "Drew? You better time this shit good!" The train started to slow down, and I didn't want to be the first one to get up so I waited for her to get up and feel safe, I then got up and walked beside her and tapped her on the shoulder while my heart was beating miles a minute. She did this elegant turn and spin all in one motion like a model while taking off her music earphones then looked at me as I looked at her. I paused for about a few seconds then said, "I've seen you around and I just wanted to tell you that you're beautiful!"

She cracked a smile, then broke into hard laughter as she slowly raised her head up to the ceiling and said, "Oh my god, thank you." So I said, "Hey, we only have one life to live so, why not? What's your name?"

"My name is..." Let's just call her Sky for now. I followed up by telling her what my name is, then we stood there and talked as we looked at each other, and leaned into one another then we randomly hugged since our energy felt loving. Right after that we exchanged contact information.

"That felt nice," I must have said right after and then we headed upstairs to where the buses were at Kennedy Station. "So, what do you do?" I asked, then she told me she was going to college studying business finance, so I told her I thought of going to her school since I was interested in their Social Service Worker program. We kept talking as we went up the escalator. When we finally got up to the top I asked her what direction she was going into then I headed in my direction to the cabstand, but not before giving her one more big hug once again then we both promised that we would text one another.

I can't lie, I felt like a king knowing I took the opportunity to speak to her instead of letting that place in time slip by. I was so hype about it all to the point I even told the cabbie I ended up driving home with, saying I met a pretty chill girl! And true to her word once she got home? She sent me a text message. Our conversation was flowing and everything was on a good vibe tip, so because of that I decided to close off the convo for the night with both of our spirits in a good place.

That night just felt right, and if I didn't choose to leave my friend and her other friend none of this would have happened. Sky and I ended up talking the day after but our warm, cute and fuzzy conversation slowly turned into her questioning me, my age, background and what my intentions were with her. It all came as a shock to me because she hit me with all of this during the night and it was like a cross examination!

"Oh, I'm thirty-two, background Jamaican and you're a cool girl and I would like to get to know you," is what I said back to her. Slowly in time, though, I gradually got to know more about Sky and later found out that she had one too many run-ins with guys who never really treated her right, which is why she was so guarded when it came to me. From that point on, we kept in contact with each another off and on. Call me crazy, but I felt a connection...

Ring-Ring-Ring

The rehab Centre I was so eager to get into finally called me back and it was now the end of April. Before than I kept bitching about no one getting back to me, but as fast as they called wanting me in their program I stalled and told them I would call them back. I held out from calling them for a couple of weeks, but eventually ended up calling back, but all they said was is we're fully booked, and you didn't reserve your spot like we told you to do. There was really nothing else I could do at that point, so I put myself back on their waiting list and promised myself I was going to take them up on their offer next time.

Once again I was waiting, but in and around this time I finally got set up to see my new talk therapist, Dr. Pierotti. I noticed she was nice from the first visit I had with her, so I let her know. "You don't have to say all of that," she said to me, and her style of doing things was way different than Alicia. Dr. Pierotti let me talk then added her two cents on what my situation was, whereas Alicia's style was more okay, this is what the fuck we're gonna do! Pull up your boxers and I'll grab you by the hand if I have to! Although Alicia somewhat helped me out a bit, I never got to express myself as much when it came to my own treatment since she seemed to like to do what she wanted.

Dr. Pierotti was different in that respect and gave me room to speak and because of that I never really knew where or how to express myself since I was finally given so much freedom with my own voice! My mind was scrambled all over.

Around this time I made another blog for myself to get out all my thoughts and the gunk in my head. I couldn't keep anything in anymore and had to place my thoughts somewhere since there was no one else to rely on. After blogging and seeing my thoughts written down I got a good look at how fucked up and distorted my own thoughts were, it also revealed how hurt I really was. Most of my postings were done while I was in a state of psychosis and on the verge of a breakdown. The more I expressed myself on this blog, the more I started to understand myself, thought patterns, and even my behavior, which ended up helping me tremendously when talking with Dr. Pierotti. I talked about Heart and rehab a lot during this time, and I never knew what I was living for anymore... rehab? A second shot with Heart or a life?

My erratic behavior on the net persisted too since I felt like I had nothing else going on and I started talking with old and new social media friends then Funky and me started to microblog. It was all about who did what better, and about how many followers one could get! Being all up in the mix like in the past, seeing my doctor and doing my own personal blog made me start to question everything that was around me as I looked at these social media sites. "Mental Illness!"

If people weren't talking about extreme sexual acts, then they were talking about extreme cutting, suicide or how they didn't like themselves and the world around them. It was almost like being right in the middle of the twelfth sublevel of hell! By this point I knew all the hallmark signs and knew everything there is to know when it came to sensing whether someone was dealing with shit, so it didn't take me long before I full out deleted most of my accounts again.

Before completely deleting my account though I gave this regular girl my number since our interactions were always laidback and normal. "Hey, it's me" the girl said as she wasted little to no time with sending me a text message, so I asked what her name is? Shay is what she said.

I hardy talked to her even though she seemed regular, but I was guarded by that point plus I didn't want to associate myself with the internet world, so I brushed her off at times and never responded to her messages. Shay was persistent though, she always seemed to catch me off guard and when I least expected it.

Ring-Ring-Ring

"Hello?"

"It's Shay..."

When she caught me on the phone I had little to say to her since our text conversations didn't flow as much, so, I always tried to rush her off the phone but after a while she grew on me.

I never knew where to place Shay in my life since I considered myself someone who was going through a transition, but I had no direction.

What could she possibly want from me? I was too confused. Shay and I kept talking, I continued to see Dr. Pierotti, and summer crept in. Then, before I knew it, it was only two weeks away from August!

The rehab Centre finally called me back, but I missed their call since I was deep in sleep... "Um, I believe this is Andrew Marshall's phone? So... if you would like to get into the Aim Program please give us a call back. Thank you." *Click*

I was scared and nervous, but I knew it was something I had to do. So I called them back and spoke with the secretary. I told her my name and to mark me down as coming.

She told me a few people couldn't make it into the program. So, it just so happened that since I was on their waiting list, I was one of the lucky ones to get a call for a spot!

"Yes... I'll take that spot..."

"Are you sure?" The secretary said.

I just said "Yeah."

The next intake date for new patients was at the end of August, so I waited it out for a couple of weeks before I got myself packing on my actual intake day.

Feeling reluctant and filled with fear, not wanting to really go, I got my sister to agree to take me to the Centre. My mom also came as moral support but she couldn't express it to me.

They both kept asking if I was fully packed and if I had everything I needed. I let them know I was okay but felt a bit restless in my legs because of the new meds I had started to take.

It was something to ten in the morning and we had to make it to the Centre by twelve. While driving, my sis had Usher's album playing and the song *Climax* came on, so as I listened, all I could think about was Heart. I felt mixed emotions about my life as a whole since nothing made sense.

Climax represented everything in my life that wasn't going right – a scary blank road that had little to no directions.

Despite the traffic on the road, we managed to make it to the Centre on time. I got checked in, then I just stood there in front of the program coordinator. Then she gave me a tour of the place.

"Well, Andrew, AIM is a rehabilitation program for people with Mood and Anxiety Disorders who are trying to cope with and/or transition themselves back into society..."

Actually, I had heard about how good the newly developed AIM program was through a friend. I loved how the building looked. It was a new building with five or six floors that allowed up to six people to live on one floor and twenty four in total in the whole building.

The AIM program might not exist anymore or might be called something else though since this program and department merged with a few others.

After giving me this little introduction of the place, the coordinator took me into the elevator along with my mom and sister. I was placed on the third floor. I gave my mom and sister hugs as I was greeted by the nurses, and then my mom and sis quietly left.

It was a naked feeling once my FAM left, but I hardly had anytime to keep feeling like that. Right away, I was asked to talk to one of the head nurses in order to get me started.

She asked me what medications was I on? And how I was feeling? She went over my information and assured me everything would be okay, and I can't even lie, she was hot. She always smiled, which made me more comfortable along with the room being cozy.

I was asked to hand over my medications, and I did so not knowing if I'd ever get them back.

After our "meeting", I was escorted back to the room I would be staying in for a month. I passed this lounge area with seats and a TV but no one was there at the time. When I was finally brought to my room, the nurse told me to make myself comfortable and to mingle with people if I felt like it.

With my luggage to the side and with this room all to myself, I just looked in amazement. "Damn," I said under my breath while scanning the room and noticing how big and bright it was. There were huge windows for every room too! And even a cute little chair right near the window, so I could look outside.

Chatter and noise

It was past noon and I started to hear noise that became more pronounced the closer it got. It sounded like people talking, so I figured it was the others who were assigned to my floor.

They were more social with one another so I assumed it was because they started a few weeks into the program before I got there.

It felt nerve-wracking but I knew I had to leave my room sooner or later in order to introduce myself to them. So that's exactly what I did, saying "here goes nothing" before I stepped out of my room.

I walked up to this chill-looking punk rocker/skater kid sitting in one of the seats watching TV. "Hey, what's up?" I said.

Beside him was this wholesome, plain Jane looking girl, and then this five-eleven, slim, raver-looking dude.

They all seemed cool and said "what's up" to me right after I said it to them. Then I went right back into my room.

Fifteen-minutes later, we were all called to the main eating area for lunch. Eating together was something the staff promoted, but it wasn't mandatory.

I might have stalled until the last minute before I pulled myself out from my room again to go and eat with everyone. The person who was in charge of giving out food let me know that since I was a newcomer, I couldn't pick and choose until I stayed for a while.

"Ah! This sucks!!!" This girl with a buzz cut said out loud.

I asked her how long she'd been in the program for. She said to me it was her second time around.

I felt thankful for the simple fact that I was getting free food! Plus, I loved how my soup tasted, and really? Beggars can't be choosers was how I looked at it.

When everyone was finished, we all gradually dispersed, with some of us heading back to our rooms while some others went back to the lounging area to chill out and watch some TV.

As for myself? Well, you know I went back to my room.

Buzz!!! Buzz!!!

My phone vibrated as I walked over to the laidback chair in my room by the window. I looked to see who it was.

"Hey, how are you?" It was Shay.

"Um, I'm just chillin'. I'm getting back inside the house after being out for so long." Shay was under the impression that I worked during the day.

I carried on a normal conversation with her as if I wasn't even in a rehab Centre, away from my family and friends. When it came to my friends, only three of them even knew I was going. My girl Soul, who I recently reconnected with again since I got a phone, Rebel, who is actually the girl I was at the Eaton Centre with, and Heart.

Rebel and Soul were the main people to help me out when I was in a terrible wreck during all the Heart stuff. I even cried on the phone with Rebel like a little bitch while my mind kept rushing...

"Fuck!" My phone battery was dying and I realized I had left my charger at home. Our program allowed for us to go home on the weekends if we wanted to, so I figured I'd get it then. We had to be back by Sunday night or else.

Even though my phone was dying, I told myself it wasn't really a life or death situation. I mean, shit, I was in a place I'd been trying to get into for months, and I already planned to get my charger back on the weekend.

Shay started getting real personal and started asking me more about my life and what I do. The more she asked, the more comical I found it because she really had NO idea what was really happening.

As we messaged each other back and forth, I was also talking to Soul. Then I noticed a few of the rehab crew headed outside to the courtyard to play ball. I remember looking at them as they played and feeling left out when more of them came out to play.

There was one guy I noticed off to the corner with his hands in his pockets. He seemed like he might have been new like me since he wasn't as social with everyone else – similar to myself. He seemed guarded, but not to the extent that I was.

I watched them play until it got dark, and then everyone went back inside for dinner time.

Andrew Marshall, come to the fourth floor

The p.a. system sounded for me to head up to the fourth floor since it was winding down to bed time and they were making sure everyone got their prescribed dose of medication. I had avoided a hell of a lot of people on my first day alone, but I had to face everyone now.

Making my way up, I remember seeing this really cute tomboyish looking girl in suspenders with purple hair that giggled as I passed by, trying to make my way to the nurses.

I finally noticed the nurse's station off into the distance and to my left, so I headed over, not really knowing what to expect.

The same medications they took from me were right there at the station, so I assumed I would get them back, but NOPE! The nurse handed me a clear plastic cup of meds in order for me to down it all with some water as they witnessed me.

Right after that, I passed that same tomboy-looking girl, but she was now having an intense conversation with that other newcomer guy I saw earlier. I overheard them talking about Panic Attacks as I headed to the elevator to head back down to the third floor and into my room.

It was now past nine-thirty, and ten p.m. was lights out, so the nurse for our floor made sure everyone was in their rooms and all main building doors were closed to the Centre. The effect from my meds started to kick in and I passed out.

Knock-Knock-Knock

"Get up, get up," the sexy voice said.

It was seven-thirty in the morning so the nurse for our floor made her rounds, walking down the hall to wake everyone up! It was mandatory to be up and out of bed around that time so that we could eat and attend wellness groups or to speak with a psychiatrist.

"I'm up, I'm up," I said with a semi-sleepy voice as I sat up slowly... realizing that I hadn't noticed my legs getting restless before bed the night before.

I used some of my clothes for a pillow since I never had one and sat there for twenty minutes not doing much. Then the nurse came into my room asking, was I okay? I had phlegm in my mouth and wanted to spit it out so bad but swallowed it since she wanted me to speak.

She asked me if I felt comfortable, so I let her know that everything was cool with me so far. She smiled and told me that if I ever needed any sort of assistance to just to let her know. Then she left.

After that, I walked over to the washroom, which was conveniently designed inside of the room with the toilet, sink, shower, and mirror all designed in one space with the drain in the middle.

I brushed my teeth, took a shower, then readied myself to head out of my room so that I could join my other roommates for breakfast around the table.

Some of them were long gone since they ate fast and were already on their routine, which consisted of group therapy to help with stress management and seeing the therapist. We all got a chance to see the resident therapist three to four times during the week.

Throat choking noises

"You okay?" I looked to the left. That cool raver dude was in the kitchen area making all these fucked up sounds from his throat.

"Yeah, I'm okay, I'm just doing an experiment to check something."

"Okay," I said, then sat down and looked around at my surroundings. Then I slowly got up and said "I'm going to my room for a bit, okay?"

"Cool," the raver guy said, still choking himself as I walked back to my room.

I had felt happy and hopeful, but right then and there, something started to consume me. I thought about that kid choking himself and how many more weeks I would have to be at the Centre with everyone. Then I started counting down the days to when I would be finished the program.

Once my mind went in that direction? It was a domino effect from that point on. I clicked and said "fuck it" and wanted out!

I think there was a phone in my room that I used to call down one of the nurses to let her know I wanted out. The nurses and the residential psychiatrist tried to talk me out of it, but I kept saying the same thing. "I wanna leave."

"Andrew, why do you want to leave? You're not giving this a fair shot. Stay, we can talk this out," the psychiatrist said.

"Nah, I can't deal with this, it's not for me, it's just... not."

Frustrated and running out of ideas, the resident psychiatrist stopped everything he was doing and kept looking at me, and I guess maybe he was thinking of ways to keep me at the Centre so he tried to get me to say something reckless or crazy.

See, since I willingly admitted myself, I was technically free to leave at any damn time I wanted, but had I been there by way of a court order, they would have had all the authority in the world to keep me.

"Okay, fine you can leave. Oh, wait, you actually can't. You can only leave once you're done this program!"

"Um, no... I can leave whenever I want. I'm the one who actually admitted myself."

When he heard me say that? He paused again, then said "Okay, fine. You can leave. Oh, but before you go... tell me something, are you suicidal?"

Because I somewhat knew my way around the system by this point because of all the hospital experience I already had, I knew to say "no". If I had said "yes", he would have kept me there despite my own will.

Now, was I suicidal? I really don't know. All I knew was I didn't want to live and I didn't wanna die...

"Well, if you leave? Remember you can't just come back through those doors a week from now. Someone else will have taken your spot," he said. But I didn't care, I just wanted out!

I signed my papers, packed my bags, then headed out of the Centre, walking down the street and past the hospital until I got to the nearest bus stop.

I... felt free...

I always used to watch shows like Intervention, laughing at people that go to rehab and then snap, wanting to leave. I never understood it and thought they were stupid for blowing such an amazing chance at becoming better. Until it actually happened to me and I was the one in that actual situation. The reality of change can be a very scary thing.

I took the bus to the subway station and then I took the train to my clinic. I walked in with my entire luggage and asked if I could speak with Dr. Pierotti.

She happened to be there, so I went upstairs to talk to her about all that happened. Then realized I had left my meds at the Centre, I asked if she could write me up a new prescription – or if she thought I should go back?

She wanted me to go back. Her office called me a cab so that I could head back to the Centre to get my medication. When I got back there, I dipped out as fast as I could before anyone had the chance to talk me into staying.

I told the cabbie that I needed to head over to my friend's house, so once I gave him the directions, we were on our way.

We made it to the edge of East York/Scarborough. I got out, thanked my driver, and walked off dragging all my shit to her place.

This friend was Rebel. She recently got her own apartment. She was the first and only person I really wanted to make contact with after leaving. I don't even have much recollection of what happened except that I saw her, stayed for a while, then probably caught myself a taxi after leaving around eleven p.m. to head back home.

I got my luggage, then my driver pulled out and I walked right up to my door. I knocked repeatedly until someone finally came to open it…

The door had a long glass windowpane in the middle so I could at least make out a figure was coming to answer. The door opened up slowly as I heard the person on the other side unlocking the top and bottom locks.

"Andrew?" It was my mom. She was in shock that I was home. She had this puzzled yet familiar look on her face, the one parents give their kids when they expect them to do something. "I knew it! I knew you weren't gonna stay there for long. Why are you back?"

I told her the program didn't seem like it was for me and that I didn't have my phone charger, but looking back, that was obviously an excuse.

After being home for a couple of hours, my mood sank and I felt like a failure. I realized I had blown my chance and this had been a really big opportunity for me, but my fear? Yeah, my fear drove me away from it.

After being back for a day or two, I got dressed and headed over to Rebel's house to hang out and have a miniature housewarming. We talked while I sat on her sofa as she sat on this summer beach chair she had. I slept over for the night and had a little fan blowing on my head as I slept on the floor.

Waking up the next morning, I remember feeling the hard floor beneath me with the fan still going and her looking at me while I looked up.

"I was going to wake you, but you were enjoying your sleep so I didn't want to disturb you." Rebel was always nice and kind like that, along with being very accommodating to those she loved.

We planned to go out for the day, so we both took showers one after the other... she went first, and seeing her after her shower was sexy... hair wrapped in a towel, she looked like a model and she didn't even know it...

CHAPTER 8

Grey/Transition

*S*ummer came, summer went, and the fall arrived. Rebel and I were going out here and there and I loved it. Having her in my life really helped and encouraged me to go out more. I was also hanging out with Soul, who got out of a crazy relationship, and of course my homie Coolz.

One person who I should have mentioned earlier was this mystical figure named Sigz. He was one of the other main people I talked to about heading down to NYC, and we met for the first time in two-thousand-and-eleven after he sent me a friend request on Facebook.

Sigz and I had a lot of friends in common. We were both doing our music, him more so than me, and a lot of the people we had in common were from the hip hop and electronic music scene in Toronto so, I mean... it was bound to happen.

"Hey Drew, let's meet up somewhere, you down?"

"Ah, sure."

He always had this way about him always popping up out of nowhere on cue, it was "strange" because his timing was mostly always on point. We slowly started chillin' a bit right after I left that rehab Centre. I had told him about it before and he had been supportive of me going.

With all the commotion that went on and all of it winding down, I couldn't get myself to tell Coolz I was going to rehab. I guess maybe I didn't want to let him down and never really let on how fucked I actually was, but I think he knew and wanted the best for me.

I tried rehab and left, I went back to going to the clinic and saw Dr. Pierotti, and now I was kind of back to square one.

"Baby? I gotta go to bed, man, I'm stayin' up too late."

"Hmm ... let's sleep on the phone."

It was the middle of October and getting chilly, reminding me that winter was around the corner. By this time, Shay and I were talking on a very regular basis, and our twice a week conversations turned into everyday conversations.

If it wasn't talking on the phone, it was texting, and I do admit that some fun things happened around that time. The feeling was nostalgic and reminiscent of Heart, but with an understanding and acceptance moving forward. It was happiness mixed with being scared.

Shay and I never were in a relationship but we kind of did things that people in a relationship do...

My thought process when it came to relationships at this time was to be guarded, and I tried not to take what she said to me too seriously. I just tried to enjoy the ride, and I figured something would mess things up eventually.

At times, I wanted to post pictures up of me and Shay so that Heart would see them. I knew she had to have been stalking my page, since I was looking at hers as she was smiling and hugging up with another guy. But I chose not to since I knew that such behavior could blow right up into my face since karma is a bitch.

A good morning text message with a scandalous and very flirtatious picture attached was how Shay was. Then we would keep talking throughout the day, evening, and then night until we both passed out, or until I faked that I passed out at times.

She talked sweet to me when I stayed silent on the phone, drifting off to sleep, but other times her niceness turned into coldness. Once no one was around to entertain her, she would hang up.

Phone sex of course was something we were BIG on. I don't even know how it all started but once it did, we never intended on finishing! It became a part of our relationship and lifestyle. Plus, it was something she had never experienced, so we stayed up for hours doing it, although this affected my sleep pattern and my mood.

Sure, it was fun, but it became to be too much.

"You're not talkative today. Did I do something?" Shay asked.

"Nah, I'm alright. I'm just in one of my moods."

"Oh, okay," she said, then went back to doing what she was doing and talked to her FAM, while I stayed on the phone feeling conflicted.

I never really knew how to take care of myself and to allow myself to have personal time away from people. I always tried to be on for everyone all the time. Then when I wasn't, I felt like that was no one else's fault but my own. "Hey," Shay said one day, "I'm headed to your area. Do you mind if I stop by to say what's up?"

"Ah, I don't know if today is a good day. Maybe we can do it next week or so?"

"I'll just be there for a few minutes, then leave."

"Aight, cool... head over." I replied.

It was still October, but a week or so away from November with that lingering cold feeling trying to take over.

I was reluctant at first because I usually like to be the one to set up where I would meet, plus this would be the first time I would be meeting her and at my fuckin' house!

I had never even met this girl out in an open public space yet, so I didn't get why she was in such a rush to meet up with me so fast. Especially since I didn't even live on my own.

Feeling shaky and anxious, I got up from my computer desk in the basement and snapped myself into the mentality of survival mode: "Fuck it! Whatever happens, happens!"

I got dressed, fixed up my room, and intoxicated it with the smell of Febreze mixed with some perfume I sprayed all over my bed sheets and pillow.

I said to my mom that one of my friends was coming over so for her to be cool. I figured I had all the time in the world, but before I knew it, Shay gave me a call back saying she was on the bus headed to my area and wanted to know where to get off. I gave her directions, then told her I would meet her down the street. She was freaked by the dark so we stayed on the phone as she walked.

"Your area looks so scary! Why are there so many trees and a dark path? You really want me to walk down this shit?"

Needless to say, she freaked out, but I told her it was okay and that I would meet her up the street and would let nothing happen to her.

I stood on my sidewalk talking to her on my phone, trying to calm her down. I crossed the road looked in the distance to see if she was actually coming my way...

Talking and commotion

I slowly started to hear something in the distance so I put my phone down and listened. It just sounded like someone confused and scared. I put the phone back to my ear and realized it was her! So, I walked up my street fast and made contact with her.

The first thing we did was hug each other, and I assured her everything was okay. Then we made jokes about how freaky it looks in the night around my area.

We walked over to my driveway and talked, she asked if she could come inside to get warm.

I introduced her to my mom. Shay walked over and rubbed her hand on my mom's back as a way to try to calm her down or something... I guess it was something she learned from the school program she was in. Although it did kind of calm my mom down, my mom probably thought to herself, "Who the FUCK is this girl?"

We headed downstairs and talked for a bit. Then she said, "Hey, let's go to your room."

In my head, I wasn't really ready for that and didn't want to make anything go down, so I kept us in the basement for a couple more minutes before we eventually headed to my room...

Door opens

"Oh my god! This room smells so damn good!"

I was glad she liked it, but the whole time I was thinking in my head of what might happen. I had this broken-down heater in my room I rarely used since it was pretty much a fire hazard, but Shy wanted me to turn it on since she felt cold.

I asked Shay if she wanted anything to eat or drink but she declined my offer so we just stayed in my room and talked.

Nice and quiet with bursts of communication then back to silence was the vibe in my room as she played with her phone. I sat on the right side of my bed while she sat at my computer chair near the bottom of my bed. She was pretty shy.

"Nothing's gonna happen," I said to myself since she seemed a bit uncomfortable. I also wasn't going to push anything to happen since that isn't my style, plus I wasn't really in the headspace for anything.

"Ah, I'm so tired." Shay slowly made her way off the computer chair and crawled into my bed.

I asked if she was okay. And she told me she was fine but wanted a massage, so I started to give her one.

Ten minutes later, we started to undress while I kissed her from her neck down to her chest, belly button, then down her thighs until I made my way back up to her... (laughs) world!

By the time we were done having fun exploring each other for the first time it was probably about three or four a.m. Everyone was asleep in the house. When she left out of my room, it was dark, but luckily she had one of those flashlight apps on her phone. It might not seem like a big deal now. But back in two-thousand-and-twelve, for me, it was.

From that night on, we went on to have more adventurous "fun" throughout the week as well as having phone sex.

"Ahhh, ugh, mahhh."

Weeks had gone by, and Shay and I had become much closer because of our "fun time". "Baby, are you okay?" she said while I tried to talk to her with a toothache I seem to have developed out of the blue. I was miserable, I couldn't speak properly, and I felt stupid while talking so I didn't want to see her or anyone else.

"Do you want me to come over?" Shay said.

"No, nooo, I don't want you to see me like this, and I'm not even lookin' nice. I look like a rapist." I was in jogging pants with messy hair and facial hair that was growing too much.

She insisted on coming over and kept saying that it was okay and that she wanted to take care of me, but I let her know, "Hey, no sex, no... nothing, I really can't, so if you come over, we're just gonna watch TV, aight?"

She promised to behave so I agreed to let her come over.

We were in the living room and it was dark with the TV being the only thing lighting up the room. I was taking this opportunity to chill on the main floor of our house since my mom wasn't home. And my dad stayed upstairs in his room smoking weed like he usually did during the evenings so it was all good.

Shay and I were wrapped up in a quilt feeling cozy, watching TV, and that was exactly how I liked it! But what ends up happening? I felt Shay's hand slowly reach down to my dick, rubbing it... my first reaction was to laugh. Then she kept doing it and I progressively got turned on and hard.

Even though I was turned on, I still didn't want to go to my room because I wasn't in the best of shape and felt like shit, but Shay being Shay kept trying to instigate something sexual with her body language. Finally, she said that "let's go to your room" bit she always did.

Hours before she came over, I had ordered chicken wings from a pizza store I won't mention. While eating those wings, I became sporadically sick with a headache and became extremely weak and a bit dizzy. So by the time Shay came by, I was in a very strange state of confusion.

When we got to my room, I started to feel more spaced out and sick, so I said, "Let's just cuddle, I don't feel like myself. Warm me up."

With all that being said, and with how I was feeling, Shay went ahead and did the unimaginable. While holding each other, this girl took my clammy hand and forced it in her pussy! That made me feel sicker since I couldn't understand why a girl would want to do that, especially to a dude that's sick.

We stopped doing stuff after I progressively became sicker and headed to the bathroom to see if I could get anything out of my system.

Shay eventually left as I got more spaced out, and I literally lost touch with reality as the minutes went by.

By the next morning, I couldn't tell if I had even slept or not…

"Wow," I said out loud. I became extremely dizzy once I tried to position myself to try to get out of bed. The more I tried to focus, the more out of it I got.

I spent thirty to forty-five minutes in an upright position and tried to get out of my bed to walk over to the washroom but found it to be so hard.

I somehow managed to get up and make it but who knows how.

After I came back to my room, I started to hallucinate. I moaned and said, "Did Shay's pussy do this to me? Is it that potent? Ahhh…"

For most of that day, I might have eaten crackers and sat upright on the corner of my bed as I looked out of my window, but I was a zombie and was incoherent, and too far gone with a pounding headache.

My mom was still away because she was staying with my sis for a while. My pops never really knew how sick I actually was. "Man, just lay down," was all he said, then went about his business.

When nightfall came, my mom called the house to see how everyone was doing. My dad told her I was sick so she wanted to speak with me. After finding out how spaced I was, she asked if I wanted to head to the hospital. My reaction and response was "no" but she took it upon herself to three-way a health hotline to have them talk to me. Based off of what I said and how I sounded, they sent over an ambulance.

"Okay, Mr. Marshall, which hospital do you want to go to?"

I mumbled and said "Ah… take me to Scarborough General! I don't want to go to Centenary."

I was in another world and it all seemed like a dream. I was so out of it all I said to them was "no sirens on my street, I don't wanna make a scene."

When they finally came, it was so hard for me to get myself dressed since I didn't know what was going on. I stumbled while heading downstairs and to the front door.

The paramedics nonchalantly walked into my house with their gear. They tested my vital signs and temperature. Once they read my temperature, one of them said "holy shit", looked at one of their crew, and rushed me in the back of the ambulance and drove to Scarborough General.

While in the back I had no idea of what was going on...

When the ambulance finally stopped and the doors opened to let me out, I felt like I was in another city. It was all dark yet calm outside, but the paramedics already walked ahead of me towards the hospital doors. Meanwhile I could hardly balance or keep up with them. Then they finally clued into the fact that I might need some assistance.

They got me a wheelchair yet had me roll my incoherent black ass to the pre-waiting room area then left me to fend for myself.

I waited until my number was called, then I got my blood drawn and waited with everyone else, laying semi-lifeless in my wheelchair. I wanted to use the washroom but I couldn't balance myself so didn't bother.

After some long ass, double digit minutes of waiting I finally made my way into another room, but it was just another pre-waiting area and it was PACKED! It had bright lights and light green walls all around.

I must have waited there for ten minutes, then finally got in.

I had arrived at the hospital somewhere around eight-thirty p.m.

The doctor on call that day finally saw me and I stated my case. He said, "Yup, you definitely have food poisoning. We're going to have to put you on some IV bags to get you hydrated, then take it from there."

I didn't get to tell him my head was pounding like it got hit badly, but a nurse later helped me with that once I spoke to her.

I was put in a temporary ER room and laid down with an IV stuck into my right vein until I blacked the fuck out. I was in and out of sleep, but man, it felt so...nice! And I hardly had any idea of what was going on.

When I woke up out of my daze, I took my jacket off... and slid myself down and off the hospital bed and sat on my wheelchair. "Oh fuck," I said while freaking out because I never used the washroom since I was there.

I felt like time was against me, and ticking fast! My IV was connected to my wheelchair so I didn't know what to do. I opened up my door looking for the nurse, but she wouldn't look in my direction, so I closed my door and just sat there on my bed...

Thick gushing noise and sound

My stomach started to turn along with me feeling a lot of pressure in my bladder, then I helplessly shit myself while sitting on the hospital bed. The pressure was so great that my shit started to shoot out of my ass and was forced to gush out diagonally up and out from my pants and past my ass cheeks like a fountain that wouldn't stop!

Shitting in public was always a fear of mine and I think most people's too! But once it finally happened to me, especially at the hospital, it didn't faze me much and I think I was too far gone to even care anyhow.

I was amazed more than anything I think, just knowing that my mess could shoot upright the way that it did. I was about to get up but stayed there as I said "fuck" and continued to shit myself and even crouched on to the ground pulling my pants down until I was done.

When I was finished, I was wet all over with a stained shirt and pants and my room had a stench of sickness. My hospital bed along with the floor was painted brown.

I stayed spaced like that for a while until I kicked back into survival mode and thought of what to do.

Since I had a sink in my room, I rushed over to wash my hands, then took my shirt and pants off to wash them in warm water along with cleaning myself off with paper. I had nothing else to wear, so I put my soggy clothes back on as if nothing had happened, and the smell of food poisoning and shit kept lingering around me.

When I opened the door, I finally saw a nurse, so I called out to her. All I said was that I needed to use the washroom. I mean the state of my room was self-explanatory so I figured she would without a doubt say something, but this nurse was so desensitized, to the point that all she said to me was, "Did you get a sample?"

"Um, no," I told her, and I guess they wanted a sample to see what might have made me sick.

She disconnected me from my wheelchair and hooked my IV onto a long staff so I could walk around freely, which I liked way better.

"Ahhh." The pain in my stomach made me want to head to the washroom again, so I rushed down the hallway in a brightly lit ER area until I found one. And what happens? I started to gush out again and didn't even get a chance to sit down on the toilet! That's when I said to myself, "Fuck, how many times must I compulsively do this before they kick me out?"

Wiping myself with my IV and staff all around me was no easy task, but I managed to do it, and can you believe that after all that I still had to go one more time? I tried to clean up a bit before giving up, and then I slid out from the bathroom in a sneaky way, thinking that no one would notice.

When I walked back to my room, I saw a yellow two-sided sign with a red triangle in the middle that said "cleaning in progress". I turned away and acted like it wasn't because of me.

Since I had no more room, I just chilled with my IV by the nursing station and waited for my busy doctor to come racing back in my direction so I could speak to him. "Hey excuse me, how much longer do I have to be here? Are there more tests? Or... do I just head home?"

"You have to finish two more IV bags before we let you go, okay Andrew?"

I was thankful for everything they did, but hearing that made me gear up and mentally prepare myself to stay longer. "Ah really? Cool!" I said.

The IV bags were pretty huge, but I'd rather be safe than sorry, you know?

Mentally I had checked out hours ago. My shirt and pants were musty and wet with a lingering smell of shit since my ass had decided to attack the peaceful room so I just wanted to make sure I was okay to head home.

Since I knew I had to stay for a good hour or so before my other two bags would be done, I walked around with my IV looking around at my surroundings. There were so many people coming and leaving, with some in worse shape than others.

I left the main ER area and walked into the waiting room and looked around at all the people that needed attention. I felt sorry for them. I turned right into another hallway and sat on a chair and thought nothing but blank thoughts.

This stylish, young looking mom came over with her twenty-something year old daughter and sat beside me, which made me feel self-conscious because I knew they could obviously smell the shit. Their conversation was about the daughter spraining her ankle again, but what was even more interesting about their dynamic was that the daughter might have been transgendered, which struck me as interesting since I never saw that in person before. Being the person that I am, I was going to ask her about it, but I stopped myself since they probably weren't up for shitty conversation.

The longer I waited, the more I felt myself getting cold from my damp clothes, so I began to feel nasty. Then my mind snapped and I said to myself, "MAYBE I SHOULD HAVE ASKED FOR A GOWN!"

When I asked the nurse for a gown, she simply opened up this closet like it was nothing, so I took two!

I went into the washroom and changed but left my damp pants on, then went back into the waiting area to look at the clock. I assumed it would be at least two a.m. or so in the morning, since I had arrived around eight something at night. But to my surprise it was now ten-thirty a.m.!

"The fuck?" I said. I had stayed up for the whole night! But since I really had no concept of time, it didn't feel like it at all.

My IV finally finished. I called my sis and she came to get me along with some fresh clothes. My mom came along too. I asked for extra strength medicine for headaches and we headed home with me passing out again.

After two and a half weeks and two extra visits back to the ER at Scarborough General Hospital, I slowly got back to feeling like myself again.

During this time period, the pain I was experiencing in my mouth from one of my teeth actually turned out to be me desperately in need of having a root canal. I had to take medication to clear up the tooth infection while experiencing symptoms from my food poisoning.

I got a referral from Scarborough General for the pain in my teeth. I had to head to this strange doctors' office that had a strange vibe since everyone in the office knew the deal about the place except me!

"Sir, are you okay? Are you sure you're okay?"

"Um, yeah … I'm okay, I guess."

They kept asking if I was okay, and reassured me that I was okay, and were very calm as if they were prepping me up for something crazy! Then the doctor came out and patted me on the back to comfort me some more as if they were gonna send me off to hell.

When it was my time to see the doctor, I went in with caution. The first thing out of the doctor's mouth was "Where's your referral? Do you got it?" with a thick Jewish New Jersey/New York accent.

I handed it to him and showed my health card, and as I did, he said, "Andrew, I'm just making sure, and you know what they say, No Lunch No Meal Ticket," with a smile on his face as he moved around with a fast-paced motion.

He looked like a character from a TV show, five-eight, and a medium build, with grey and black hair. He wore khakis and a plaid shirt with brown casual shoes.

"Andrew, open ye mouth." I reluctantly and slowly opened my mouth, ready for him to do something which I would have reacted to. Then it all dawned on me. "Ah fuck, I'm at an oral surgeon's office!"

"Close ye mouth. Andrew? As much as I would like to do something? I can't because I see nothing wrong with your mouth. Here, take this." He wrote me up a prescription for pain then told me to call him in a week, but within that time I saw my own personal dentist who found out what was going on.

Sex, pain, ambulances, hospitals, shit, drugs, more doctors, dentists, more doctors and sex...

All within the span of the month of November, two-thousand-and-twelve. Crazy.

By the time December settled in, Shay and I increasingly started to talk less and less. I didn't want to call and run her down because I felt as though there was really no point, and I felt that the more involved with her I would have gotten, the more she would have hurt me.

Ring-Ring-Ring

"I swear to god! I will stop calling you so much, why do you let me continuously keep calling you!?" Shay started saying that to me after a while, but to be honest? I loved it, and didn't want my emotions hurt, so I somewhat kept at a distance. Plus, she always called first.

Things were getting rockier with Shay's family life, and she kept talking about splitting from town and vanishing without a trace. Which freaked me out! I mean, as much as I tried not to get too emotional with her, I was concerned. Fuck, it seemed like I was the only one who gave a shit about her at times, but she seemed to get off on making someone, anyone worry about her. It made her feel wanted and acknowledged, I guess.

A week went by without us talking so I sent her a text, but all I got back was "don't text me". I said "huh?" Then: "Get rid of my number and don't text me." My first reaction was to be mad, but I stopped myself from texting anything crazy back to her. I said, "Why do you play so many games? When you're ready to stop playing games then you can hit me up peace!"

My phone rang five minutes later and who was on the line? Shay! "Oh, you think I play games, huh? I see, okay... okay, good to know..."

"Nah, nah, I'm just sayin' like I don't know what's going on and you text me all that out of the blue? I thought we were good!"

She then told me that her "friend" took her phone from her and was messaging everyone on her phone, which sounded stupid and immature to me. She told me she might be heading to NYC for Christmas and would call me when she got back.

"I'll call you back, okay?"

"Aight, cool," I said to her.

All that interaction let me know that she might be talking to another guy, and a younger, insecure guy at that, since it seemed like he was trying to eliminate and X out as much of the competition as possible.

By the time Christmas came and went, I knew she might be back in Toronto. I waited two and a half weeks for her to call me back, but she never did. So, I cracked and called her but never got an answer. I left that situation as it was and carried on with my transition into the New Year.

After ringing in the New Year by drinking coolers and chatting with people through text and online, I just left everything behind, and had a "whatever" frame of mind.

CHAPTER 9

2013

*T*he beginning months of two-thousand-and-thirteen were pretty crazy! In January, it was too, too, too cold outside, but I was also getting used to being outside of the house more during the week. Being out of the house at least once during the week was a dream and a goal, so if I got out two days within the week, I felt like I was rolling. It almost didn't seem real or like I deserved that much freedom!

By February, Funky and I started meeting up downtown again like we used to back in two-thousand-and-eight/two-thousand-and-ten. One day, he wanted to buy some clothes and wanted to chill so of course I was down for it.

When we met on that day, I remember thinking it was going to be pretty cold out since it was always cold at that time. I wore my usual heavy wool blend jacket. But the joke was on me because it turned out to be twelve degrees outside. Which made me sweat like crazy!

We went up and down Yonge Street, Bloor, then College and then Dundas. Until we hit up a local coffee and donut shop so we could roll up the rim to win!

I kept looking at Funky and started laughing because this kid grew his hair all the way out. Before we even met that week, he had warned me that I would be cracking up from seeing how much hair he had. I was used to him having low hair since he was a skater and I didn't take it seriously until I saw it!

"Are you Jewish?" I said to him while laughing since his hair had big curls in it. Then we both laughed. I think he might have said, "Maybe, I think I could have some of that in me, way back though..."

His ethnicity was Polish and German so it wasn't too far off from the truth.

After chillin', talkin', and relaxing at this shop for a bit which was new and kind of interesting for us, we headed south, then deep into the Eaton Centre to look at clothes. He was always OCDish about that shit and what he wears, so it was jokes to witness it. If I thought I had OCD issues, then he took it to a whole new level!

With all the confusion going on, we still actually managed to finish all that we were doing, then headed back up north past Dundas. We got some rum and liquor from a nearby store, then headed further north back to College Street to sit and drink in a food court.

We got plastic cups, poured each other equal shots of rum from a medium sized Appleton Rum bottle, and kept it going. Again, we were laughing and talking about bullshit, with everything being nice and fun. This was shit we always talked about doing over the phone but never had the guts or social skills to pull off until now. The whole time while I was taking sips and shots of my rum, I didn't feel a thing and wished we had bought more as we hid our drinks from security.

Forty minutes later, and still... "Nothing". I felt nothing!

"Let's go," I said, but he didn't get up fast unlike myself. As I got up and raised myself, it was as if everything fun from life just hit me all at once!

I was buzzed as fuck! And loved it! I started to laugh as a big smile got slapped onto my face. "Yup, that shit hit you hard, you're feelin' it!" Funky said.

When we first sat down to drink at this food court, we noticed a shitload of security and a whole bunch of high-scale looking hot girls coming out of luxury cars but heading to the condo entrance instead of the mall, so I assumed they were going to a high-society party with coke, sex and a whole bunch of assholes who were ready to indulge. But hey, more power to them is what I thought.

Now Funky finally got up, so once we both started to walk we both FELT the buzz from what we drank! And after looking at those girls while being buzzed, we both felt like walking the streets on a mission to find a party of our own!

Heading up to the street and now walking across Yonge and College heading north all felt like a dreamy and hazy movie sequence.

Street and crowd noises

"Hey, where's the party girls!?" I screamed out in a happy way once I saw some attractive ladies. Funky kind of did the same but for him? He REALLY wanted to find a party! In the past, we had never really followed through with trying to find a party because of obvious reasons, but all that was gonna change today!

It was very cold by the time the evening came in, but we were happy. Pretty ladies, the city lighting up the streets for blocks, and everyone that was out just seemed damn happy and wanted to find a party just like us!

As we got even further north, we mistakenly headed into this rich area, so we walked along the side streets following the music until we found this semi-small club that had little stairs going down to a door. We randomly went right into the venue.

We... just, "stood there" with bags in both of our hands and me wearing a winter jacket with some of my hair grown out, and Funky with his long ass hair, feeling clueless. A few of the girls there made us feel like we didn't fit in.

That's when the hostess for that club – who was very sexy by the way and looked identical to Tony Soprano's daughter Meadow from the TV show *The Sopranos* – walked over to us and said, "You guys look lost." Which was her way of saying "Maybe you should leave." We didn't really care, though. We left, but all we wanted was is a place to chill and party!

We headed back onto the street and kept walking west until we crossed paths with this girl who seemed like she was simple and a plain Jane just like us. "Are there any bars around here? We need a place that's cheap!" Funky went on to tell her.

She was this cute, innocent-looking white girl dressed in a dark jacket and black tights, with dirty blond hair. "Oh, you guys want a place that's really shitty, huh?" She said it in a giggly type of way to let us know she was having the same dilemma herself.

She gave us names of places to check out, though, so we thanked her and kept heading west as she continued east. By this time, mentally we were destroyed! And forgot all that she told us. We ended up on a main street and saw a grey cat that we called over. At that split second, we decided to find a cab to see what we could find further south since the people there were more our crowd.

It was damn cold waiting for a cab. Once we got in, we asked him where the spot might be tonight!? He looked and sounded east African and mentioned we should hit up a bar near Queen and Spadina. We laughed and made jokes while heading down there, and one thing I know for sure is I was glad I got some heat on my hands, but got really anxious as we got very close to our destination.

The lineup for the bar looked crazy! And I didn't know if I really wanted to go in because of fear, but I waited in line just like everyone else, plus Funky was there with me. We cracked jokes, and others in line cracked jokes along with us, but we all wanted to just get inside badly. Especially some out of towners.

After waiting outside for thirty minutes or so, they slowly started to let people in and wanted to see ID. We smoothly made our way in after that to the darkly lit bar with mischievous evils and all the music, which got me off. We played the background and stayed to the wall. Chairs were lined up along this narrow passageway, with the actual bar being on the right. We ordered some shots of whiskey. Between the both of us, we probably had eight shots combined, which only helped smooth out our buzz even more.

Feeling so nice and carefree, we risked it and made our way deeper into the back of this bar where they had some live music. Funky headed to the washroom to piss his drinks out so I was checking the girls out.

I became brave, so I walked over to this long-haired brunette girl. She was on her phone which I thought was odd, so I asked her what was up. But she shot me down and didn't say much so I shrugged it off and walked away.

Then I saw another girl minutes later, a small-framed blond girl. I walked up to her and asked how her night was going. And where might everyone be going after the bar? You never know what's what at bars sometimes, though, because right after joking around with her, this juiced up white dude in a leather jacket with a buzz cut who seemed like he was trying to prove himself got right into my face and said, "So, what's up?"

My instincts kicked in at that moment in time and the first thought I had was not to let this guy prove himself... "Lemme calm his ass down." So, I took my hand and leaned in towards him as his eyes and body were all fired up and did what Shay once did to my mom. I placed my hand on his back and calmed him down. It was crazy to witness because this dude went from a ten – wanting to rip my face off – to a calm four and being peaceful in minutes.

Once I got to stabilize his ass, I repeated myself and said, "So, where's a good place to go to chill at?"

"Oh, um, maybe down the street? That might be a cool place," he said. So I said "cool", gave him a fist bump, then walked off.

"What the fuck was that all about?" Funky said. He watched it all go down once he got out of the washroom, and had been waiting at the corner just in case anything happened, ready to clock this dude in his face.

I told him the details of what happened as we made our way out of the bar and headed west till we finally got to the known medium-sized lounge everyone kept talking about. The cover was five dollars, so we were more than willing to head in.

Walking through those doors was like heaven and everything dreams were made of. All we heard while walking in was is James Brown. The atmosphere was nice and dim and sensual with good people around us.

There was a pool section in the back, the bar was to the right, and left of the bar was the dance area with "funky" lights and a projection screen playing randomized clips going with the music and DJ. Can you believe after all that we drank, we had the nerve to drink even more?

The theme of the night was eighties/nineties retro music, which I was cool with, and for someone who was locked inside of his house for so many years? I sure as hell wasn't too picky! Funky and I got right into the action on the dance floor. Then a MILF started to take notice of Funky and started asking him questions which he couldn't hear over the loud music. I danced with a group of girls.

Smells Like Teen Spirit by Nirvana came on and fuck, Funky went BAT-SHIT! This crazy white boy flung his hands up and plowed through the crowd without a fuck to give and it was a sight to see. We stayed until closing time, which was around two-thirty a.m., then headed out like everyone else. Funky was drunk as hell by this point so I had to pull him away from the small group outside so we could eventually head somewhere else.

"What happened to that girl?"

"Oh, her?" one of the regulars said. "Yeah, she's here all the time and loves getting her hands on fresh meat."

There was also this gothic looking girl in combat boots wearing a stylish short skit with a revealing top. She had her face covered in black and white makeup looking like a skeleton. I told her that I wanted to dance with her but was too shy. "Really? Aww, that's so sweet! Maybe next time if I bump into you," she said.

When Funky and I finally left, we headed west until we found a Subway restaurant to eat at. I felt out of my mind to the point I was wiggling and planted my face on the plastic counter with the bread and squished my face.

This kid that was working that night seemed like he was around our age and asked us where we just came from. We told him just up the street so he went on to tell us how he and his dad are into the club business and how they own fifty per cent of these crazy clubs in Toronto. He gave us his card.

There was another cool dude working there that we chatted with too. They were fun and happy and loved seeing us act like happy drunks as they wished us a goodnight.

It was cold and dark, and now there weren't as many people outside as we walked along the street heading west. Funky was still drunk and said "moveee" as we walked back onto Queen Street.

The buildings, the street, the emptiness, and the winter night brought on feelings of nostalgia and reminded me of the crazy cold nights I had when I was younger, but it also felt like I did all of what I was doing with Funky in another lifetime since it all felt so familiar.

Even though I was good with holding my liquor, I was surprised I didn't even pass out by this point. And I was also taking a mood stabilizer which intensifies the effects of alcohol, so I was really shocked. We must have walked from Queen Street all the way to Dundas West Station, which took us an hour and twenty minutes. Then I hailed down a cab and headed back to my hood in Scarborough.

This crazy new experience gave us both a different type of high, and from that point on, we wanted more, so we always kept talking about going back and doing it again! Within two weeks, we coordinated to head back down to the same area, replaying everything we first did, like drinking in the food court. I even talked to him about Shay while showing him some of her beautiful pictures that tripped him out, which made me feel good.

Just like the first time, I thought I was Superman, but the rum hit me like a fuckin' train once we started to walk, bobbing and weaving through buildings and alleyways to avoid traffic. We came across a drunk guy who only had on a t-shirt. He ended up following us to whichever party we were going to since he left his own screaming.

"Okay, the party continues, onward!" I said as me, Funky and this drunk guy walked down the street with cars honking, cheering us on. Then before I knew it, the drunk guy just ran off out of nowhere. I always wondered what happened to him. As for Funky and myself, we went back to the same bar and did the same things we did the first time around.

Good music, people doing coke, me and Funk going downstairs to the washroom to piss seeing people make out, more coke in the washrooms, and us drinkin' beers in the stalls.

"This has to be a DREAM! None of this is real!" I kept saying to myself because it all felt so damn fun with everyone... Funk got all crazy again and started dancing nuts, but then he started hitting people and stepped on a bouncer's foot more than once, which pissed the bouncer off.

By the time the party was over, that bouncer, who was this six foot tall black dude, cussed him out but he was too incoherent to understand much. So I stepped in and said, "Listen, if you have a problem, I apologize, but just take it up with me, aight?"

"Excuse me?" he said. "Listen, this is Canada! When you step on someone's shoes, you need to say sorry and show some respect!"

So I said, "Cool, alright, well on behalf of my friend, sorry."

When the club closed, we decided to head east this time until we hit Queen and Spadina. Along our journey, we saw other cheerful partygoers who wanted to know what was going on. But what made things more interesting was we bumped into these two white kids that kind of looked like street kids. One was a slim but semi-stocky ginger with wavy hair in a short-sleeved jacket, and the other was this lanky kid with a pointy nose and eyes that popped out who wore khakis.

"Hey what's up tonight? Where's the fun?" the kids said to us. I was in a cheerful mood so I told them to enjoy their night.

These kids started acting strange, though, and one of them randomly said, "We wanna learn how to fight! Can you teach us?"

I laughed and said, "There's so many beautiful girls on the street and everyone's having fun, why fight?"

That's when the kid with the bulging eyes said, "Well, I plan on getting into the drug trade in the future so I gotta know how to fight."

Funky was having no part of the fuckery so he walked off and scoped out girls and kept asking where the party was at. Then we all kind of drifted further east until we connected with another group. Within this other group I spotted a likeminded, level-headed guy like myself and told him that the kids with us wanted to fight. We both laughed.

Then I told the kids that this wasn't the eighties anymore, and if they wanted to end up on the news because of gun shots? The level-headed guy I recently met basically resaid everything to them that I said. Then he turned to me and said, "Where are you from?"

I said, "Scarborough."

"Ah, true, I was born and raised out there."

From that, we bonded a bit more, then we both said to these kids that they might want to get into boxing. Then we laughed as the group went on its way, but these kids were still following us.

After analyzing these kids for a while, I wondered if they were just some university students who had drank too much. I asked one of them what they were studying. He quickly said architecture but it didn't sound believable to me. They kept following us so I kind of felt like they were my responsibility, at least for that night, that is.

It increasingly got colder as we walked along the street, and I just wanted to get warm whereas as Funky just wanted to find any after-hours spot. We passed a Chinese restaurant, which wasn't too unusual since we were in Chinatown although the fact it was open and packed after two a.m. was crazy to me, but I just wanted warmth really.

"You guys want anything? It's on me, man!" the kid with the big eyes said. I gladly accepted since I don't pass up free offers easily, but Funky on the other hand was like, "Nah, I'm good."

Then both kids started talking about coke and eight-balls. A Somali kid happened to be standing around and heard the whole conversation.

"What do you want? What do you need?" he said while he slowly walked up to us with a smirk on his face. Now I'm from Scarborough and I'm also a big guy, so I knew how to handle myself. I said, "Yo, I'm not a part of this."

With a devilish smirk, he just watched the kids talk about coke and money, and they were saying all the right things in order to get themselves jacked, but I wasn't having it. Inside of the restaurant, we ordered a big meal that I was more than willing to take part in. The Somali dude was still around and gave these kids a secret word. He told the kids to speak to the waiter and give him the secret word and he'll hook you up! Now for myself, I was just there for the food and planned on leaving once I was done.

We sat near the door and I was facing the restaurant and the Somali guy just stood there waiting for them to say the word. Then after a while, the bulgy-eyed kid gave him twenty dollars. He looked puzzled but smiled in that same devilish way, then shook his head and walked off.

"Hey, I don't know when I'll see you guys again, nor do I plan to, so whatever," The bulgy-eyed kid said while paying for what we ate.

Twenty minutes later when we were getting ready to leave, these kids freaked and said, "Oh my god! Did that guy take off with our money? Did we just get robbed?"

"Don't worry about it, man, let's just go," Funky and I said to them.

After that we left and crossed the street, and at that moment, Funky and I were ready to call it a night because of all the craziness that took place! But these kids got all mesmerized and excited since they finally saw the after-hours club they kept hearing about and wanted to go inside.

"Do you guys wanna come? C'mon man! Let's celebrate!" they said.

"Nah, nah, we're good, man, you go and enjoy yourselves and get home safe."

They insisted that we come with them though because, according to them, we looked out for them and protected them throughout the night. But as they headed inside that was the last time we saw them… and it was funny, it was like seeing boys turn into men in a way all in the span of a night.

Weeks later, we ended up dead Centre in front of that same club and contemplated going in, but not before walking down the street and ending up in this dingy, fucked up, sadistic looking hotel that was right beside the club.

Drunk and out of it, we walked to the front desk of this hotel and saw this Indian guy who seemed like he was the owner. "Um, can we take a piss?"

"Sure," he said, so we headed down the dimly lit, checkered tiled hallway as the vibrations of House Music consumed the floor.

We took turns pissing clumsily as fuck, then decided we wanted to head into the club once we were outside. We saw this regular looking white guy with a trucker hat who was from out of town who urged us to come inside. He was high out of his mind and told us that he left his girlfriend behind since she didn't want to come for a second time.

One look in his eyes and you knew he was on some shit, appearing as if he'd seen a ghost, but still carried on a regular conversation with us. He tried to tempt us, but we didn't follow, and that was when this cute, blond girl came out of the club to get fresh air. She looked at us and asked, "So, why don't you guys wanna go in?"

"Meh, we're not too sure yet," we said.

"Here, take some of this," she calmly said while passing us some of her drink, and for a split second, I wondered if something was inside that would make us slip deeper into another reality.

She was a slim and curvy girl with a Russian accent who looked like a model, and she kept trying to convince us to come in. She said, "If you come inside, I'll dance with you…" After hearing that and knowing how hot she was, we were pretty much sold! Passing through the lineup and into the actual club made the other lounge that we always went to seem small-time!

The music was banging and thumped right in your chest within this industrial basement, and what I liked compared to the other times we passed by there was the music was actually good on this night.

It was dark down there so it took a while for my eyes to adjust and for me to scope out the scene a bit so I could get an idea of what types of people were inside.

The crowd was mixed with people from all different walks of life: Chinese crews playing the left, Black crews playing different corners doing what they do, and everyone else just off in their groups doing their own thing. Funky got his thug on way before me in no time, though, since I was observing the atmosphere. But after everything was cool, I did my gangster shake as I kept looking around, and as we were having fun, who did we see? That same Russian girl, so we went over and started dancing with her.

We saw a couple of other girls from outside that were now inside too, like this one black girl that kept appearing on the dance floor with a cowboy hat on and leopard skin-tight pants, with deep chocolate skin. I never had the balls to dance with her but Funky did...

She disappeared shortly afterwards, though, and Funky spent the whole night looking for her with his drunk and now high ass, not realizing that she had already left. Meanwhile he was doing circles around the club. After a long while, we found some seats and chilled, but he got up to look for her again! While this went on, I pulled out my phone to record the craziness until he came back. I knew life could be fun, but never knew it could be that fun!

We chilled for an hour longer, then I finally said, "We gotta go."

We headed to the front. As we opened the front doors, like a mafia movie, we got shot with light that blocked our eyes as if we were vampires!

"What the fuck?" Our eyes were sensitive to the light and we turned away. It was nine a.m. on a Sunday with the streets alive and active, looking nothing like the night when we went in. And what was even more twisted was that people were still trying to get into the club as we were leaving!

We crossed the road, got some food from a nearby convenience store, then headed to the nearest bus stop to head to the nearest train station.

"Who the fuck wears white shoes in the fuckin' winter? What the fuck is that?" a forty-year-old mentally ill homeless white guy randomly said to me while looking at my shoes. Then he had the nerve to ask Funky for directions.

Although it was now morning, we were still fucked up from the night before, so by the time we finally made it to the subway station, I screamed at Funky from the opposite platform. "You need fuckin' help! You need to reevaluate your fuckin self! Get help, dude! You're fucked up!" All while eating an egg sandwich and drinking water.

Train noises

I was pretty gone and heard House Music playing as I looked down the train tunnel, and I even told Funky to go and fuck himself as his train came. Then mine eventually showed up. As I got on, I spread my body out and passed out off and on until I got home at ten-thirty a.m. and slept.

CHAPTER 10

The Spring

Phone vibrates and goes off

"… Hey… Um, what do you think about me working for a while?"

"Huh?" I said.

"You know, being an escort, what do you think about it?"

It was Sky messaging me out of the blue, asking me about my thoughts in regards to her getting into the escorting life. I asked her where this all came from, and why do it now? She gave me some reasons and added that she's always been a sexually aggressive person.

Sky and I always kept in touch off and on through text with our conversations dissolving as fast and as intense as they started, but regardless, I always thought about Sky and wondered about her well-being. When she told me she wanted to do all of that, I didn't judge her since that wasn't my style. I basically said, "Well, yeah … go and do you and be smart! And don't do dumb shit!"

"Okie :)," she said in her text message back to me. Then I opened up about freaky sex blogs I had in the past as my way of letting her know that what she was doing wasn't that abnormal.

"Damn! I know the most interesting types of people!" she went on to say once I disclosed all that to her.

"When would you… start?" I asked, so she said, "I don't know? Maybe the weekend."

I never told or expressed it to her but my heart kind of dropped because I didn't really want her to go out there to do it – hell no! During this time, I told Rebel and Sky both about the crazy nights Funky and me were having, and Rebel came out with us once but left early since she had to be up in the morning.

My relationship with Sky has always been an interesting one though … I knew so much about her but so little at the same time. By the time it hit the weekend, she told me she wanted to work. I felt nervous knowing that she might be doing her … "thing", which I kind of and kind of didn't wanna know about. But she later let me know nothing happened that weekend.

She did, however, start weeks later and let me know about it. She told me that one of her first clients was someone that she knew, so, in her own words, she thought it was going to be awkward, but it actually turned out to be pretty chill. We often traded ideas of what we wanted to do in life, and one day I let her know that I thought she was very social yet antisocial at the same time. "Damn that's crazy how you can tell because that's how I actually am."

I mean it was easy for me to tell… since I never really met her again but we text messaged each other all the time. Because of certain aspects of her background, I didn't find her behavior to be that odd at all, though. It was kind of fitting. She always called me by my nickname which I loved, and we had a lot in common in terms of demons we were struggling to deal with, and we were both hypersexual people! Ha!

She knew about Shay and never really thought Shay was good for me. Sky and Shay actually went to the exact same school but Shay never knew any of that whereas Sky did.

Sky and I always talked about writing, and maybe writing a book about certain aspects of our lives. We always encouraged each other to just go for it! So, hey *"Sky"*, here's looking at you, girl! *You're next!* We both went at life at a different pace, though, and with that being said, I always thought that maybe sooner or later we might actually run into each other. It is what it is…

By the time the spring of two-thousand-and-thirteen came along, I started playing with this camera I got in two-thousand-and-seven/ eight. I never really used it aside from a couple times with Funky. I kept taking test shots from inside of the house and tried different angles and experimented with the manual settings, and anytime my sister came over, I would take shots of her as well as my newly born nephew to see if I knew what I was doing. And by doing this, I became more confident.

Sessions with Dr. Pierotti were still going on, and we were making breakthrough after breakthrough! Seeing her in two-thousand-and-twelve was obviously good, but at this stage, it was all about getting out of my house more than twice a week, and building some type of structure around my life, which scared the shit out of me!

The fact that I got out a couple of times and partied was a good enough pattern and structure, I figured, but I still wasn't used to the regular day crowd. Taking the train was still a lingering issue for me. I also started talking about school and social work since I felt like that was what I was meant to do. The school I wanted to go to was in an area I hardly frequented. The routes to get there involved train lines and other forms of transit I NEVER really used, which scared me!

Taking the train was highly uncomfortable for me, so I usually stood and made sure to face the window so that others couldn't really see me and so I couldn't see them. For me to get to this particular school, I had to get to this station called King Station, which was something I wasn't used to or did, so I wasn't havin' that!

Dr. Pierotti knew how much I wanted to go to school and how much I wished I could simply go on the subway and go through all my obstacles. Talking about going to school was all I did at a certain point. Literally! And the more I talked about it, the more out of reach it seemed at times. The only actual way I could keep this goal alive and fresh in my mind was by calling occasionally to ask about the Social Service Worker program and their Community Worker programs over and over again.

After one session too many where I talked about going to this school, Dr. Pierotti crossed her legs and put her pen in her mouth, pondering what we could probably do. "Hmmm..." Then out of nowhere, she said, "I have an idea ...Why don't you turn this into a game? Collect transfer stubs from different places until you build up the confidence to go to King Station!"

When she first mentioned it, I was skeptical and had no idea how I would pull that off. But I said, "Sure, I'll try it." She sensed my doubt as well as how unenthusiastic I was so she told me that she wanted to see me with some stubs by the next visit, I guess in order to encourage me.

That? Scared me! Not only was I given a task, but I actually had to complete it since that was the expectation. Those similar to me know all too well what pressure can do to people like us!

After my session was done, I decided to head home from downtown. I kept questioning myself within that space of time, asking myself, how will I ever be able to pull any of this off? I didn't think I had it in me to do any of this at all and felt like I'd just let my doc down. I was scared of failure, too, which I thought would make me look double stupid in her eyes and in mine...

I didn't make much of my week after that session with Dr. Pierotti, and entering the next week getting ready to see her, I thought of things I could probably do to help me out.

Oh shit, I thought, why don't I go out with my camera? I stuffed my camera inside this cheap black messenger bag I bought while hanging out with Funky during the winter and crazy clubbing nights. My sessions were usually on Mondays at around two p.m. so I made sure my bag was packed with my camera whether I would use it or not. Or till I had the nerve to use it! When I saw Dr. Pierotti, I surprised her with the camera I had in my bag.

"Wow, what are you gonna do with that?" she said, so I told her that I planned on taking a couple of shots.

She was just as excited about it as I was, so she suggested that I head to a park in the area called Queens Park where I could get some good pictures. This park was located near a university, too. But I wasn't too sure about it since I never really been there on my own. Once our session ended, she encouraged me to just head out and shoot! So, I got up from her comfy, light brown sofa with my messenger bag strapped around my shoulder and told her I would see her next week. I smiled as I headed out of her office and outside.

Stepping outside felt good since it was spring, bringing fresh air and warmth and everything transitioning into the beginning of the summer. People were no longer rushing to where they needed to be and instead they strolled on the street feeling relaxed.

Since Rebel had recently started her first year of university, she was always on the go around the same time that I was, so it wasn't unusual for us to bump into each other. All we really had to do is is text one another.

I got a call from Rebel around three p.m. but didn't pick up, then a text saying "Hey!!! Where are you? Are you downtown?" We usually met up after my sessions like a ritual but I felt like I had to be alone for the day. I sent her a text message back saying, "I'm good baby I think I'm gonna chill out a bit on my own, cool?" She figured something was wrong since it was rare for me to do this, but my intuition told me I needed to be alone for a while…

There was this spot I happened to find by chance located at the southeast corner of Bay and Bloor. I would usually sit there to kill time during rush hour. I hated the packed trains during the rush, so this slowly turned into a place where I could just relax and watch cars and people pass by.

Feeling out of place and uncomfortable, I looked at my messenger bag, slowly unzipped it, and felt for my camera without taking it out. As my hands touched the cold hard metal casing of my cam, I instantaneously got struck with anxiety! So, I took my hand out, sealed my bag, and waited for about seven minutes.

"Fuck it" I said, while slowly getting up to make my way to Bay Station across the street. I made my way to St. George Station, then south to Museum Station, which was where I got off.

Confusion

Everything looked unfamiliar and unusual around me when I found myself upstairs on the street level. Without hesitation, I took my damn camera out, turned it on, and then took a picture of the Museum Station sign halfway up the stairs.

Walking all the way and being fully exposed to the street, everyone around me and all the cars passing me, I said to myself, "I made it," while clinching onto my camera like I was gonna break it! The ROM (Royal Ontario Museum) was in front of me, crowded with people taking in the sights, while university goers headed south down to Queens Park.

Once I took that first shot of the Museum Station sign, I didn't intend on stopping. I casually made my way down to Queens Park while looking left, right, backwards, and forward. Walking with my camera with people noticeably seeing me felt DIFFERENT! Holding my cam helped in a way, though. It made me not focus as much on people or really care about them since I was focusing on getting the right angles and shots around me.

I made it to Queens Park Crescent. The entire park was located directly in front of me, and all I had to do now was cross the road to get there. I crossed the road, making sure not to get knocked down by any of the fast cars crazily whooshing back and forth past this big, giant roundabout.

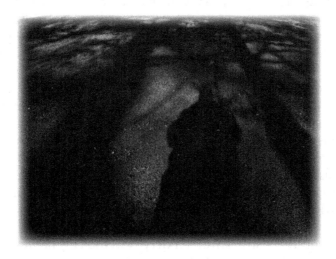

In Queens Park when I was shooting

Finally making it across and readying myself to enter the park, I noticed a guy taking pictures of this older and very beautiful looking woman. I assumed it was his wife since he was making her do a whole bunch of poses, and from the looks of it, she was getting off on it just as much as he was.

"It's a nice day out, huh?" I casually said to them while making my way over and sitting in a nearby seat.

"Yeah," the guy said to me, but he didn't seem pleased with me talking to him. He was slim with balding brown hair, and he spoke with an accent. He sounded French to me. His wife was a slim, brown-haired cutie with a curly boy cut.

They kind of ushered themselves away from me once I got there and started talking to them. They didn't seem to be too friendly, but the way that I saw it, it was still on with the show.

Entering deeper into the park was fuckin' scary! There were people on my left, on my right, and dead in front of me. The closer I got, the harder and faster my heart started to throb.

"Oh fuck, a squirrel!" I positioned myself and took some shots while this squirrel and its friends were having a rave in the tree.

Dr. Pierotti specifically wanted me to get a shot of a squirrel in a tree, so I was happy that I actually captured the moment.

Everything started to seem like fun – up until I slowly started to not feel right and unsettled.

"Okay, I'm a big, black dude that's anxious in a park near a university with students all around. Do I standout a bit too much?"

I found a place to sit, and the longer I sat there, the more negative my thoughts became. I felt boxed in, stuck and stranded. I didn't know what to do, so I pulled out my phone and started playing with it, not knowing what I was doing but just wanting to appear busy. I felt like turning back and going to the subway station, but going forward symbolized courage and progress whereas heading back meant failure.

"Act now or forever be fucked!" I repeated in my head three or five times before I said "fuck it!" out loud and pushed forward into the park, weaving past people and other obstacles.

I was so happy to be out of that situation and I felt victorious at the same time. I could have turned back but didn't since forward was the mission!

I fixed my bag, shook my shirt, and brushed my hair, hoping to rid my body of the insects that decided to turn me into their new home. As I kept walking, my speed picked up, and then I felt for my camera, ready once again to snap some more shots.

Sunset in Queens Park

Making my way out of the park, I was now walking onto Queens Park Crescent East heading south. I noticed a couple of people walking my way but really didn't care at this moment because I had all the confidence in the world from what I had dealt with a few minutes ago.

All this walking, all these events, and me being all by myself to experience them did something to me... I started to think clearly! I started to feel like how I had felt when in NYC ... all my thoughts started to decompress, slowly making me see, feel, and process my current life and situation.

Near the end of the roundabout, the road met with Queens Park Crescent West, with a U-turn kind of road in front of it connecting all together. College Street and University Avenue crossed paths up the street from where I was, with the Legislative building behind me.

I hung out there for fifteen-minutes or more and took more shots while my mind raced with all these clear ideas of what I wanted to do with my life and how to execute other plans I had in mind.

Snap

I remember taking this one shot at the Legislative building, with the sun and trees all around which made me feel proud because here I was being active and doing things in a freeform way with no one to stop me. I got to the main intersection of University and College, looking at all the traffic, and again I said "fuck it" while taking shots, not letting anything stop me! I took a picture of the stop walk lights, then proceeded straight into the road when it was safe, making my way over to another section of traffic islands

Funk and I used to pass this area but we had never really stopped here, so I was kind of in shock at all the things that were around. This was also known as the hospital district in Toronto because there were so many hospitals.

Trees I saw while taking pictures while thinking
of my friend that passed away

Cars were going north on my left and south on my right as I walked to this hidden island that was like its own park. There were homeless people I happened to bump into when I was there, too, since I guess they know the best spots in the city really. I passed one hospital that has been etched in my memory all too well since one of my big brothers from my hood who pretty much helped raise me passed away there from cancer. I sat at this concrete bench they had along this mini-island and just thought about life and death, his life and me walking along this route fourteen years later taking pictures.

"Life is a trip!" I said to myself, while a homeless dude laid out on the bench beside me stayed lifeless only to move when he was convulsing...

"Do you need help!?" I asked. He opened his eyes, looked up at me, and then closed them, so I got up. I took a picture of the blooming tree that was there and wished my big brother farewell before I walked off.

I kept going until my body noticeably became very weak, then I started getting headaches with my body getting shaky. At first I got mad, thinking it was impossible for my anxiety to come back after all that I had done, but I quickly realized I hardly had anything to eat! By this time, it was ten p.m. and dark out, with the city lights flashing everywhere. I was getting dizzy because of lack of food. I tried to look for a place I could eat at while still being on the mini-islands but couldn't find anything, so I called it a night and headed home.

When I Took A Picture of the Moon From Taxi

Getting all the way back to Toronto's east end was a blur, but I do remember taking a taxi from Kennedy Station. While on my way home incoherent in the back, I noticed there was a full moon, so I took a picture of it with my last remaining bit of energy and before my battery shut off. Then I passed out. Luckily for me, the driver knew me and where I lived, so there was no issue in getting me home.

Two days later, I finally uploaded my pictures to my computer and thought they wouldn't even look good, but most of my shots looked nice! Anytime I look at those shots I took in the spring of two-thousand-and-three, I think about the journey, the events, my friend's passing, and me turning into another person simply because of what took place on that day from beginning to end. The boost of confidence from my adventure made me want to head out a lot more so I could eventually get new and interesting shots ...

Me: Look what I have?

Dr. Pierotti: Oh, what is that?

Me: I think you might know...

Dr. Pierotti: Oh! Amazing! I gotta see!

A week had passed and I was back in Dr. Pierotti's office sitting in the comfy sofa, excited to show her the pictures I took which I turned into a DVD for her. I gave her the DVD, then she placed it in her laptop quick time to see what was on it.

"Oh, my god! These pictures are pretty neat," she said. I wasn't that comfortable with compliments, especially at that time, and I didn't really know what to say. I just nodded my head while not making eye contact.

"Oh, and I have this." I went in my bag and showed her a shitload of transfers that I ended up collecting, and I think I even went a bit too overboard, but yo, once you pop you just can't stop.

She asked me how it felt being out there while taking shots, and I told her how therapeutic it was and how clear it made me feel. I said "Yup, I know why people head over to the park now!" and laughed.

"So, what's next!?" she said with a big, pleased smile on her face.

"Take more damn pictures," was my reply.

Conquering some of these fears as well as doing things I truly loved and enjoyed made me want to see if I could get out there to take on even more!

Forcing myself out on my second or third days was always the hardest because it was so unnatural. I used to stall for long periods of a time, not leaving my house until three or four hours after I decided it would be a good day to go out, even after I had already showered and dressed.

I made it a duty to pack food inside of my messenger bag and always made sure I had my camera packed inside with me. It was all about taking those nice shots, and I think having a packed bag gave me a sense of comfort. Downtown was mostly always the destination. Since there was so much I was doing down there, it only made sense, plus I was the most comfortable around there because of my sessions.

One day, when I got downtown, I just stood around like a scared child gripping on to my bag, but I still managed to make it to this park which wasn't too far away from where my doctor's office was located.

Train passes

Right in front of me, the trains heading north and south would pass. I took a picture of one of them as it passed directly below me heading south. I waved and screamed as the train operator smiled and honked his horn at me.

To the left of me, there were three construction workers fixing up a soon to be condo. I screamed at them and asked for pictures, but two of them were camera shy and backed away as I said, "It's cool, ha-ha-ha." When I backed away, I randomly saw two cute girls lying on a sheet together. At first I thought they were resting, but they were making out. "Do you mind if I get a shot of you both?" I asked.

"Not at all," they said. We exchanged information afterwards so I could send them the pictures, then wished them a happy afternoon.

"Damn! What's going on today? I'm glad I came out!" I said to myself as I happily strolled out from that park to head down the street to get some industrial shots.

In little to no time, I got right back to Yonge Street, snapping shots north and south, stopping every few minutes to gather myself and to let the adrenaline subside while I asked myself where I should go from here? I started to walk slowly, not knowing where I was going, and happened to discover a few secret locations of mine that I still use to this day!

One of these special secret places put me at mid-level with the city. Finding this place was perfect for me because I got into the habit of testing out camera shots and tricks up there, and I would eat there, pondering both life and sub sauce.

Being up there seeing some of the city made me develop an obsession with rooftops, too! I wanted to find bigger, higher, and better buildings. Within the timeframe of two weeks or so of me going out on this "second day" that became my third if I was lucky, I came across a security guard that I got to know since we always saw each other in and around the area.

She knew of my obsession with rooftops all too well since I wasted no time in telling her and often asked if she could get me up to the rooftop of the building she oversaw patrolling.

"You like building tops huh?" she said to me, then told me to come back to that same building within a week in the evening and she might see what she could do, while giving me a firm handshake.

After about two weeks of me not really going near her location since I didn't want to be a nuisance, I decided to head back to see if she could sneak me onto the rooftop of her building. Weeks back, she had stressed to me to come after five p.m. on a specific day if I really wanted to get to the top, so this one day of the week is when I came.

Doors open

When I walked through the front doors and got close enough for her to make out who I was, she had a look of displeasure on her face.

"Ah, you really wanna go up still?" she said.

"Yeah! Of course, I mean, you only live once, right?" I said back to her.

From that point, she quickly went into military mode and said, "Okay, let's do this! But follow my lead, okay?"

So, like someone who was scared but excited at the same time, I quickly said, "Okay!"

"Let's go," she said quickly as I followed her lead. "Oh, and one more thing. Hide your fuckin' camera! And if anyone sees you? Let them know you work here, got it?" "Yes!" I said.

We headed onto the elevator and up to the highest floor, which was fourteen or sixteen stories up.

Elevator opens slowly

She got out first, walking fast, so I did the same. "Ah fuck!" she said but only loud enough for me to hear. "Why are there people still up here?"

We passed a huge, long kiosk. I pinned my eyes on her, following like my eyes had built in infrared.

We made it down to the end of the hallway with me almost being out of breath. At that point, I figured all we had to do was is walk through a single door then we'd be home free, but nope, I was wrong!

She opened this door, and through this door was a staircase. We headed up two or three flights of stairs until we got to another door... that looked odd...

This door seemed to be heading to the attic. She went in as I followed once again. What I saw as I walked through made me feel like we went back into the nineteen-fifties or sixties and got stuck! It was industrial looking with bad lighting, steam, industrial noises, pipes and cold hard concrete!

We did a couple turns then walked straight while bobbing and weaving our way past pipes and sharp corners until we got to three staircases with another door in front of them.

"Are you ready?" she asked me.

"I'm cool, yeah," I said, so just like that, she went ahead and opened up this door and...

"What the fuckkkkk?" came out of my mouth.

In shock and looking around like someone who was high for the first time, I slowly stepped through the door. We were finally on top of the roof.

"Wow, the city," I said while overlooking it from left to right and in front.

"Yup! This is the city!" She put her hands on her hips as she looked outwards proudly and comfortably like she'd done this sixty times over. She stood closer to the edge than me.

I slowly positioned myself beside her, then got my camera out and started snapping shots of the city while smiling like a madman! Out of nowhere, she said, "Yep, see that building down the block? They used to let people go to the top, but since a couple people jumped to their death, they don't do it anymore."

We stayed up there for a good thirty minutes taking in the view, talking about how beautiful the city is and suicide...

Roof Top With Guard

"If you think this view is amazing, you should check out the CN Tower! Have you been there before?"

"No," I said.

"Well, you really need to go there if you're into amazing city views, nothing compares to that place!"

I took one more shot for the road, then we left, heading back through crazy obstacles.

"Yes! We did it!" I said to her all crazy once we got back to the front lobby. I reached over and hugged her. She smiled, hugging me back, and for a few minutes she slipped out of her Security poker face persona and was a real person, but just as fast, she went back to being professional.

I thanked her again, then left.

That same week I posted some of those rooftop pictures to one of my social media profiles, leaving some to wonder where I might have taken the shots.

That was a fun day.

Since I was on my photography high and did not plan to come down anytime soon, I ended up walking around Nathan Phillips Square and Toronto's City Hall weeks later to capture what was going on. As I walked around, I was careful and cautious, making sure not to get myself in too deep with the crowded sea of people there. Because I wanted to avoid the commotion around the square, my senses just told me to look around to find an escape. I noticed stairs and walkways that led me up and around this miniature driveway and path which got me to the top of the square.

Once I was finally at the top, I took my camera out and snapped shots with breaks in between admiring the city view while standing right there at City Hall. The top section had a pebble-like fence or border I could lean over and rest my elbows on. To my left was Bay Street so I watched people pass. I was on a high so I giggled while getting more shots, and even screamed at a businessman to pose for me since I saw that he himself was taking shots.

Shadow picture I took of myself while taking pictures

Since he wasn't too friendly, I turned back to my right and saw people having fun and couples trying to sex in public.

While I was looking around at everyone, I noticed this guy making his way in my direction and his body language seemed as though he might try to talk to me. When he finally made it up, I cued myself, waiting for him to come over to try to sell or fraud me out of something.

"Hey there," he said. "Can you help me out? Where can I get some good food?" He held a map of Toronto.

"Um, cool... yeah, just... go up the block and you'll hit the spot," I said to him, then broke off from the conversation.

"Can you help me?" he said again, so I said "sure" and walked him up the block.

I told myself to disengage from him after helping him and just said, "Good luck man, enjoy our city." I still didn't trust him since you never really know being in the city, and I was waiting for his opening line where he would try to sell something to me, and that's where I would have said "peace."

He wanted me to head down another street with him and I did this and didn't see much harm in it since it was out in the open... but something REALLY seemed off. While walking, we carried on casual conversation and he asked me if I had any siblings, about my parents, and how Toronto was. To me it just all felt like he was fishing for information so I kept my answers short and sweet while trying to break away, but he still stuck to me.

He was an East Indian guy and he told me his name was Vivek and that he was from Dallas, Texas, and also that he had lived in Chicago for a while.

"Hey, Drew, let's walk further," he said while being relaxed and calm, but I still suspected him of something. We started heading further down a side street away from all the busyness and my heart started to beat. I figured I might have to punch him as it seemed like he lured me where he wanted me.

I slowly started to clinch my fists and waited for him to make the first move, then just like that... he turned around towards me and...

"Let's head back," he said, leaving me in shock but glad nothing had happened. After that, I thought to myself, I better get out of here quick! But I didn't really see him as a threat anymore.

We headed back onto the main streets and walked along Dundas until we made our way into Chinatown. Then he said, "Oh the Chinatown in Chicago is way bigger."

I said, "We didn't even make it down the main intersection yet, hold on!"

"Wow, now we're talkin'," Vivek said once we made it to Dundas and Spadina. He was taken aback and in shock at how big Toronto's Chinatown actually was.

We walked along south on Spadina until we made it back to Queen Street and City Hall. Then Vivek started saying he wanted food, but something from Toronto.

I was losing my patience and running out of options for him when we happened to pass a Pizza Pizza. I said, "Here, man, this is the best I can do!"

"Do you highly recommend this place, Drew?" he asked, and I said, "This is what's around so you can eat here!"

He opened the door, and I motioned that I was going to leave, but he said, "Wait, you can leave after we eat."

"Huh? I don't have money, man, and I gotta head on my way," I said, but he insisted that I eat with him!

At that moment I kind of gave up and said to myself, "Hey, if you're gonna have someone kill you, at least they want you to have a full stomach. Fuck it, have a pizza and die, you took some pictures, you're good, man."

We waited in line to order, then he said, "Drew? It's all on me, don't worry about it!"

Like that, he pulled out his credit card to pay. Again, I figured I might as well get whatever the fuck I want since it might be the last thing I'd eat...

After getting our food, we sat in the middle of this pizza place and gradually started talking a bit more about each other. He revealed he was actually a professor in Dallas and that he was up in Toronto for a convention. We started talking about science, religion, God, and the need to be good and loving towards others on this planet.

"So, Drew, what do you do?" I was comfortable with him at this point so I disclosed to him that I was dealing with a lot and trying to get my life together. And that I wanted to go back to school or try improvisation at The Second City Training Centre. I'd wanted to do that since two-thousand-and-five but wasn't in the right frame of mind back then.

His face lit up when I talked about academics and he tried to give me some tips on how to make sure I got accepted into college since that was a fear of mine.

He gave me tips on how to smoothly get into whichever program I wanted to, and even went as far as giving me his contact information so that he could encourage me.

"Well, as much as I don't want to admit it, Drew, we do measure ourselves by our accomplishments. So yes, please do go!" Vivek said.

After we finished eating, we got dessert, talked some more, and then he told me he had to rush back to his hotel. Then he thanked me for showing him around before he left.

"Are you serious? You guys talked about science, religion, he treated you to food, and you're just telling me now?" Rebel said as I talked about what had happened with Vivek the day before.

I also ended up getting caught into a video shoot with these guys who were making a hip hop song. I also saw this black girl who was a photographer taking shots with intense flash of a hipster.

"Damn, I wish I had a camera like that. I'm here taking pictures with this ghetto camera, man," I said as a joke just to open things up for conversation.

"Oh, yeah, if you wanna get good shots, you might wanna get a good camera, something over a thousand or fifteen-hundred," she said while taking pictures along with her assistant.

Her demeanor and tone of voice made it seem like she was an arrogant hotshot, so I slowly walked off and shrugged my shoulders. I mean, sure, I could have told her I took over four-hundred plus shots that same day that came out great but didn't want to ruin her high or her ego. And after walking off, I ended up taking shots in the dark at night which she figured only her camera could do.

Photo of a Building in West End Toronto

A Shot I Took at Night

"You're crazy," Rebel said to me while we were both on the phone as I headed into Funky's west end area near Dundas West Station.

I called her to let her know I had finally gone to his area to give him a surprise visit. While scanning his area, I used all the information that was around me and took advantage of it.

"Who are you?" two Portuguese girls said as they passed by me in the lobby of his building. I said I was waiting for my boy.

"Oh, where are you from?"

I said, "I'm from Scarborough."

"Oh my god, I used to live out there. I'm so glad I'm gone. I hated it!" one of them said.

When they walked off, I headed up in the elevator and walked around until Funky finally picked up his phone and met me downstairs at the corner of his place.

Squinting my eyes, I saw this figure in jeans and a whitish t-shirt getting closer to me. It was Funky! We laughed then gave each other fist bumps. He took me on a tour of his area as we talked. He showed me the ins and outs of how he gets around, and I understood his logic since we dealt with the same hardships. I took shadow pictures of us both, and we managed to make it back to his place. But as to how we parted ways that night? Who knows? One thing is for sure, though. I'm glad that night happened. That's my dude right there.

Funky and I

CHAPTER 11

Exploration

*H*appy, excited, and hopeful, yet feeling somewhat doubtful, I sat back in Dr. Pierotti's sofa and talked about picture taking, the interesting run in with Vivek, and meeting up with my boy Funky.

"Wow, you're doing even more, it seems!" Dr. Pierotti said to me with her usual enthusiasm. I thanked her for always supporting me, and then we got into talks about me wanting to head over to The Second City Training Centre or conventional school.

Second City and regular school were things I had casually talked about in the past, but it was just a thought since I believed that I was too destroyed and destabilized. After my session, I headed out of the clinic and right to my secret location, which was four major intersections away. I looked at the city with a sub in my hands while I thought about what I wanted to do with my life.

Sure, my camera was packed inside of my messenger bag as always but something felt different this day. I still loved taking pictures but I felt like I needed to do more with my life, aside from taking shots, then going home to enjoy them.

Later that day when I finally got home, I made a list of things I wanted to do and a list of things that needed to be done! My list consisted of going to The Second City Training Centre, hitting up two luxury car dealerships which I made test driving appointments with, and placing an elegant ad online so that I could take exotic pictures of lovely ladies.

I was doing so much that I naturally started to grab a hold of my life again. All these pieces of my life had dropped on the floor as if I was a full mirror that broke into jagged pieces of glass that I had to put together again. I was ready to mend myself back together. Strangely enough, when I was having all these thoughts, Rebel asked me if I wanted to go to Second City to see a show, I said "yes," of course. When we got there, I wanted to sit up close and personal. During the show, the improvisers picked on Rebel, and I and had us in tears from laugher, and while the show carried on I watched and knew for sure going to Second City was something I wanted to do!

By the time we left, I had a headache from the laughter and tears. I turned around and took a picture of The Second City sign since it was another victory for me. A week later, the two luxury dealerships I made appointments with called me to confirm that I was coming in. One of my appointments was on a Tuesday and the other on a Thursday. I was excited as usual and told some of my friends that I was going, and that shocked a lot of people leading them to think I was crazy.

The first one I went to starts with the letter "L". I headed to their downtown location to do a test drive around ten-thirty or eleven in the morning. From Scarborough, I raced downtown to this nice, classy, and kind of posh but stylish dealership with nothing but glass that made up the exterior. Walking up to the front desk, feeling VERY uncomfortable, I let them know what my name was and that I had an appointment.

"No problem, Andrew, Vans will be right with you!"

I said thank you, then sat down in the waiting area with everyone else, but didn't feel like I belonged at all.

"Do you want a drink?" one of the receptionists said. They gave me a bottle of water with the luxury name on it. I can't lie, I felt important at that moment!

Fifteen-minutes seemed to have passed before a medium-built brown-haired white guy that looked six feet tall came walking up to me. "Are you Andrew?"

I said, "Yes I am."

He smiled at me and said, "Follow me, sir."

As we walked, we talked about the models I was interested in. One was a hybrid so I asked questions about it as we walked over to this elevator that looked like it was straight out of a Mission Impossible movie!

We headed to a ridiculous height, then we stepped out into this huge room with a few cars at different corners of the room.

"Do you have your license?" Vans said.

I said, "Oh, I don't actually drive! I just wanted this experience so it could motivate me to want to drive! I hope I'm not wasting your time, but I wanna feel how these cars are."

Startled from what I said, he said, "Don't worry about it. The only way this is a waste of my time is if you weren't even interested in our line of cars at all. I'll show you everything you need to know! Sit in the passenger side."

I jumped in the passenger side as he hopped in the driver side, then we sped off, going down ramps until we hit the streets with traffic in every direction. All I could say was "Wow!" Vans had a big smile on his face as he shifted gears and turned corners.

"So, Andrew, tell me a bit about yourself?" he said.

So, I paused for a moment before rapidly speaking. I was straight up and honest and said, "I'm screwed!" Then I basically said I was trying to get my life back together and would love to own a luxury car one day, but needed education first.

"Hey, I completely get it! And it's good that you're thinking about your education right now and that you're trying to make a difference, so that's the first step," he said.

"How did you get into this line of work, man? You must feel lucky to come into work every morning," I said.

Vans said, "I've always been into cars. Back home in British Columbia, I used to drive up and down a dirt road. After high school, I got my Bachelor of Science degree, then applied for a salesman job here in Toronto. I've been at this gig ever since."

"Are you serious?" I said to him. "How did you just randomly pickup and move over here like that?"

He simply told me, "While growing up, my mom always put different types of food on the table. At first when she tried to get me to eat different things, I was apprehensive about it and afraid. But she looked at me one time when I refused to eat what she gave me and she just said to me, 'how will you ever know if you don't try?'"

"That moment has always stuck with me, which is why I am always willing to try new things, Drew."

"That's really inspirational," I said to Vans.

We eventually turned around and headed back to the dealership after testing the car, and it seemed like we had a damn good conversation. On our way back, I disclosed to him how tough it has been for me the past couple of years. He let me know how much he loved how motivated I was, and before I left the dealership, he gave me his card and encouraged me to continue my path and to never stop!

As for the other test drive appointment, as the day approached, I felt an uneasiness since I felt like I might be wasting someone else's time being as I didn't plan on buying a car, nor did I have a license to drive. I felt that it would be in good character to email the salesman from this other dealership and to straight out be honest with him about my situation.

The email went something like this...

Dear Tanzie,

I really would like to see and test out that luxury car I am scheduled to drive in a couple of days at your dealership, but to be very honest with you? I do not have my license and do not want to waste your time.

If you do not have free time available in order to show me the ins and outs of how this car performs it's cool, but if you do however have free time that is cool as well.

I hope to hear back from you Tanzie.

Speak soon!
Drew ;)

Within twenty minutes, Tanzie got back to me and I already assumed it was a no go before even opening my email. To my surprise the email said, "Thank you so much for your honesty, Andrew, and I would be more than willing to help you. Let's make our appointment for Wednesday of next week instead of in a few days. Sounds good?"

I quickly replied, saying, "Let's do it!"

By the time next week came, I had another appointment with Dr. Pierotti and told her about how I went to the first luxury dealership.

"You don't drive, though. How did you do a test drive?" she said in a confused way.

"Yeah, I know ... well, I just got the salesman to drive me, while I sat in the passenger seat!"

That was when she looked at me and cracked the fuck up! She asked me if I really did all that?

"Yep, and I plan to go back to another dealership in a few days!"

"I see. Well, I'll have to hear about how your second visit goes." She laughed and wrote down her notes as most therapists do, then she smiled.

The day of my second test drive was finally here. Similar to the first dealership, this one was located downtown, so I took the same route.

While walking in, I took a deep breath then noticed it was kind of crammed in the front because so many of their cars were on display, with the back of the dealership set aside for repairs.

"Hey! You're Andrew, right?" said a crazy energetic Asian guy with spiked hair wearing a slick business suit.

"Yeah, that's me," I said.

"I'm Tanzie, and you wanted to check out that car you've been drooling over, right?"

"Yes please!" I said to Tanzie. He told me to wait outside then vanished.

I eventually walked out and stood at the side of the road wondering if he had stood me up, then...

Car noises

Feeling stupid, I just waited at the corner with my hands in my pocks not knowing what to expect. Before I knew it, this car pulled up right out of the blue with Tanzie in it! He looked over at me and said "get in" with a serious look on his face.

Once I got in, he requested that I fasten my seatbelt. Then he pressed on that fuckin' gas pedal like he was on a mission! This fuckin' Asian was possessed! He swerved through traffic like it was his favorite pastime and like he had no fucks to give. He looked over at me and saw that I was freaked out. He said "What? Am I going too, slow...?"

With a devilish look on his face, he shifted the car into a higher gear and cut through more traffic, then shifted again!

"So, Drew, what cars do you like?" he asked. I told him I had gone to another dealership the week before, but then he cut me off and said, "Why you want that? BE-A-MAN!"

Then he shifted the car again with an excited look on his face that I slowly started to mirror since I started to enjoy it all too! We then headed on the highway going faster, but then gradually made our way back to the streets then back to the dealership. We drove through to the back to park and went inside until we got to his sales desk.

"So, Drew, what do you think?" Tanzie asked.

I said, "Well, within a year or two, I might want this car."

His "BE-A-MAN!" statement along with the whole driving experience really sold me on everything. I mean, Vans was amazing, but Tanzie? He was on something completely different, as if he drank energy drinks for breakfast.

Tanzie lightly laughed at my response then said to me the model of the car I like might be gone within a year and phased out since they change their designs so much. During his demonstration, I remember turning to him and saying, "You know so much about cars! Where did you go to school? And how did you end up working here?"

"School? What school?" he said with a puzzled look on his face while passing every car on the road like a racer.

Tanzie and Vans were both working within the same industry, but the individual pathways they took were completely different. But in the end, they both had the same "drive", pun intended.

I told Tanzie I wanted to head to school so I could afford a luxury car and he said, "Why?" I realized he was different and had a hustling mentality, which was good! Because that's how you get towards your dreams sometimes.

Before making my way out from this dealership, Tanzie hooked me up with a big brochure for the car model we test drove for some inspiration. Then I headed out and slowly made my way to the main roads. While walking, I had to take a serious piss, and luckily for me, I saw a gas station. I ran in and asked for their keys. The bathroom was traumatic, but once I was relieved, I kept it movin'. I stood at the corner of the street and felt another big sense of accomplishment as I looked at the city.

I went into my messenger bag to get my camera out to take a few shots of the cityscape that was in front of me before I let out a big sigh of relief.

As I walked, I found myself slowly entering the area where the school was that I wanted to attend so desperately but never felt like I had it in me to go. The area was busy and it was around lunch time, so there were more and more people coming. I started to see further down the block the more I walked, and I felt like I might run into someone I might know. I was on the opposite side of the street from the main entrance to the college. And then — "Records!" I said out loud. I happened to walk in front of a used antique store with furniture, used records, and anything else you could think of.

Record collecting has always been a passion of mine since I love new samples and songs and because of my love for music creation, so I couldn't pass all this up! Flipping through the record crates they had in the front, I by chance happened to discover *Boz Scaggs*. I was looking for that *"Lowdown"* song. But I discovered something even better, the whole damn album!

In shock, I kept looking at it, thinking this couldn't be real. Then this older white dude with greyish facial hair who looked like a biker stopped dead in his tracks and said to me, "Heyyy, is that, um, Boz Scaggs!?"

I shook my head and said, "Yup!"

He smiled and said, "Fuck, he's great and you have good damn taste! They don't make them like that anymore. Pick that shit up." So, I did.

Before leaving this store, I headed to their basement to do some more record snooping. To my surprise, they had a whole surplus of records that I gave up on going through before completely leaving the shop. Dead Centre in front of me was the school I always wanted to go to but avoided much contact with, but it was all by chance I was here today.

My nerves built up, and I eyed down the school thinking of what I wanted to do while being there, and how I would go about functioning within a school environment. I stepped right on the curb while looking at the school, thinking about my life and how much it could instantaneously change simply from me attending this college. Then, just like that, I raised my foot off the curb and placed my Boz Scaggs record in my bag, being shocked it fit inside exactly. I turned away from the College and walked off with my body language saying "fuck it" and me even saying "fuck it."

A week later I talked to Dr. Pierotti about everything, and I mean EVERYTHING, that happened within those couple of weeks. She especially loved it when I told her the Tanzie story. I let her know that my experience passing the college and not actually going in might be a sign, and I was battling between going there or Second City anyhow, so this kind of made my decision easier.

Second City had drop-in classes every Monday around five or six p.m., until eight p.m., for anyone who wanted to "test drive" how their classes can be. I expressed to Dr. Pierotti how I wanted to go, and maybe all that I had been doing prepped me up for this.

"Screw it!" I said to Dr. Pierotti, "I think I'm gonna go, man!"

She got excited and said, "Yeah, why not!?"

My appointment was on a Monday at two p.m., and drop-in classes were on a Monday, so being that I was already pumped and really wanted to go, I headed out of her office then got something to eat before jumping on the train. I passed stations I never get off at until I got to St Andrews Station, which was funny to me since that's my name.

I headed west, passing all types of people and making my way through the crowds. The closer I was getting to The Second City Training Centre, the more anxious I became. I remember becoming physically sick to my stomach with every step I took. The Centre was located near King and Peter Streets. I crossed intersection after intersection until I finally had everything in my sights – which is when I had a full-on anxiety attack.

My body became shaky as I waited for the red light to change. Once it did, I crossed over and made my way through The Second City doors, then down the stairs heading to the front desk to ask where I needed to go for the drop-in classes. They directed me to head down the hall. The room was empty with me just inside there, but not for long since more people started to show up.

Some of us carried on small talk until the room was packed, and then we just sat there waiting for an instructor.

"Good evening everyone!"

A hip-looking, post-punk rock chick came elegantly walking through the doors of the drop-in room. She requested that we all move the chairs that we were sitting on to form a circle so that everyone could see and interact with one another.

Since I had been the first one to arrive in the room followed by a Middle Eastern looking guy that referred to himself as Paris, we got to bond quickly and took out most of the chairs for others to sit once they came inside.

Me, Paris, and the few others who came early all sat within the same area. Our instructor went around asking each person what their name was and a few details about their lives and why they chose to come to Second City. This one Indian kid who sat far away but directly in front of me said that he was an orange out of the blue once it was his turn to introduce himself. When my turn finally came, I just blurted out, "Hi, my name is Andrew Marshall. I have Social Anxiety and Bipolar Disorder, I am bisexual, and deep down, I am a lobster! I belong nowhere else except for here!"

The room went dead silent, then slowly people started to laugh, but Paris? He laughed straight from the start, bursting into tears, and no one really knew how to respond to what I said. Lobsters are an obsession of mine. That was why I mentioned them, and as far as the whole bisexual thing? Bisexuals make great DJs and are skilled at making great pie.

When it was time for Paris to introduce himself, he did it in a smooth, slick manner while telling everyone he wanted to try his hand at acting. Once we were all done with introductions, our hip instructor told us to ditch our chairs. Then we paired up with a partner to play some improvisational games. Scared as fuck, I paired with Paris as we were instructed to play a game where you looked into the eyes of your partner and did everything they did and vice versa, which they called "Mirroring."

After a couple of games, then some more games, we might have gone for a fifteen-minute break before returning for MORE crazy games. Before we all knew it, it was eight p.m. Our instructor told us we could leave or we could wait for an hour to participate in the weekly show called *"Monday Mashup."* Me along with a couple of others agreed to stay around to get something to eat until show time.

Paris and I and a girl I am now good friends with went up the street to a salad restaurant along with four other people. We formed a big sitting area outside since it was the middle of the summer, August to be more specific. We asked questions about each other and asked one another how we enjoyed the drop-in class.

This one guy with us seemed like a typical playboy type of guy, and I figured he had no issues with anything. But he came out and said that one of the main reasons he decided to do improv was because he wanted to gain some confidence for him to be able to pick up women. Just when I found that out about him, he asked me why I wanted to do improv? I paused as everyone waited for my answer, and I slowly said, "I just wanna be a jack ass and make a fool of myself to make people laugh."

The playboy looking guy and Paris got uncomfortable by my answer as if it really threw them off. Playboy kept looking at me as if I was fuckin' nuts! I have to admit something about not fitting into what they wanted to hear really got me off. When we finished eating, it was nearly nine p.m., so we cleaned up and rushed back to the Training Centre to be able to catch a seat in the drop-in room that was now transformed into a medium-sized stage.

Before show time, people were encouraged to place their names on pieces of paper inside of a box so that their names could be called throughout the show. Anyone called would participate in whichever game they chose to play on stage.

"Welcome!" the host said. The hosts were usually one of the Second City faculty instructors and they each had different styles and energy they always brought on stage.

As the night went on, everyone who put their name in the bucket got called up to play games. I wondered when my name was gonna be called, and as I thought about it, they finally called me up to go on stage! With my heart beating crazy and my body filled with adrenaline, I ran up to the stage to partake in some of their games that I knew little to nothing about since improv was all new to me.

We played this game where they would turn off the lights then turn them back on after a few minutes, and then talk about your pose and everyone else's as if they were describing a picture from a vacation spot. I remember being there on stage with the lights shining in my face and me sweating like crazy. But those show lights called me and felt addictive. Can you believe it? After all that, it did nothing except boost up my confidence even more! In September, I placed a couple of ads on some popular posting websites since it was something I had eventually wanted to get around to doing.

I made postings for nude modeling and so-called regular modeling, but I say so-called because what's regular modeling? Within a day, I got seven responses, which led to even more as the days went by, to the point that I stopped counting. Half the responses were from girls who instantaneously wanted to become superstar models within a day, and their egos were so big that you could touch them just from the emails alone…

Throughout all the responses, there were two emails that stood out the most. A girl named Sophie Rose caught my attention since she came off as being chill and laidback, and we clicked on the same level so we messaged back and forth. It didn't take long before we exchanged phone numbers for us to communicate beyond emails. Sophie wanted to have some erotic pictures taken, and I wanted to take erotic pictures to build up my portfolio and to maybe leak some pictures on to one of my sex blogs.

The other girl I messaged back I shall refer to as Cray. It's kind of strange and somewhat scary how much our intuition really doesn't lead us astray because, although everything seemed okay, I was reluctant to connect with Cray. After going against my gut feelings, I eventually called her. We talked on the phone and everything seemed fine, then we set a time to meet up within the next few weeks at my office.

Me and Miss Sophie Rose instantaneously clicked first, so I wanted to meet with her a week before meeting up with Miss Cray. I let Sophie Rose know where I wanted to meet her, which was at a nearby coffee shop around Yonge and College, then after we could head down to the food court if she was cool with it. Remember where Funky and I used to drink? Well, this was the exact same place! Except I treated it like an office space at this point since I did most of my business down there. *smiles*

Wednesday the next week at four p.m., I made my way down to the coffee shop since we both agreed to meet there. I was looking all around to see if I would spot out a girl that fit Sophie's description, and constantly checked my phone to make sure I didn't miss any of her text messages. We did exchange a few text messages to let each other know what was going on, so I just leaned on the side of a wall checking out my environment until I spotted her.

I freaked out wondering if she would find me because I never really gave her a clear description of how I looked, then I freaked again hoping she was okay with how I would look.

After twenty-five minutes of waiting, I saw this girl come up the escalator that looked like her and really? It was her! Because there's only one Sophie Rose. As I watched her make her way towards me I tripped out because she seemed unique.

She was five-four with blonde, shoulder length hair and tattoos on both arms, her legs, and her thighs. She looked like a pinup model, and she was just so CUTE!

We greeted one another once we both got closer. The look on her face was shock since she hadn't known what I looked like. We shook hands and talked for a bit then headed down to my, um, "office" in the food court to talk some more. We sat near the outskirts of the food court, which was where my professional office was located, with her facing the food court while I faced away from it as we stayed seated at a table designed for four people.

I had my messenger bag with my laptop inside since I started carrying my laptop with me almost everywhere I went. I took it out as we casually started to talk, then connected it to my phone so that we had access to the net and so I could show her the blog I'd been working on.

"Tell me a bit about yourself," I said to her, and then she went right in and talked about herself and how much she loves the art of photography. She even mentioned that she went to school to study art so all that blew me away! While we spoke, I couldn't help but think about how amazing she was and how I didn't measure up to her at the time. She treated me like an authority figure though and I didn't get it.

"Oh, I really need a photographer! So that I can put a package together for some of these adult agencies," she said to me, and I was down for the cause, man, and really? She was already a star to me.

We agreed to shoot by the next week in the evening at her place and to take it from there. By the time the next week came, I went ahead and confirmed the meet-up with Miss Cray to see if we could discuss how we'd go about things. Then I got ready for the shoot with Sophie Rose.

With me going through my camera gear, and making sure my

laptop was okay, and double checking everything before the actual shoot day with Sophie Rose, I noticed I became increasingly more anxious. I was wondering how I'd react to having a beautiful, fully naked woman right in front of me while I took shots of her. Would I be okay? Would she be okay? Would I know what the fuck to do? This would, after all, be my first nude shooting and I wanted to make sure it would be chill.

Semi-rested, tired, and worried, I slowly got up out of my bed the day of the shoot. We had decided to meet around four or five in the evening, so since I got up in the morning I had plenty of time to worry! I brushed my teeth and took my usual shower where I discover most of life's deep mysteries and where I psychiatrically evaluate myself as well as the actions of others. I then finished up, dried myself off, and headed to my room to dress.

I double checked everything I needed. Bag? Check! Laptop? Yes! Camera? You're not leavin' it! Batteries? Charged, locked, loaded and secure! "Oh, where's my USB cables?" Ah, they're over in my pouch! Ah! My memory stick for my camera! How could I forget that? Pack that in crazy!

Once I was packed, I double checked myself and everything I needed since it was almost time for me to leave my house! Sophie lived in the west end and I didn't mind traveling that far, especially for a crazy shoot. But she didn't live far from where Funky lived so it made me not worry as much about traveling.

I got to Kennedy Station and hopped on the train, leaving my dear east end of Scarborough until I got off at the right stop. From there, I took a bus then sent her a text to let her know I was in her hood. She sent me a text saying she would meet me soon, then ten minutes later just told me to walk halfway down the street to meet up with her.

Walking along, I didn't see anyone, but slowly I started to make out this pink figure, pink hair, pink sweater, and I think she might have had light blue jean shorts on. We hugged, then she took me back to her place. Once we arrived at her place, she welcomed me straight in!

"Damn, wow!" I said in shock looking at her place. I was amazed at how decorated it looked! It was painted mostly green all over with a few posters on her wall. Then out of nowhere this cute cat came out from hiding. Sophie said, "That's my baby, his name is Tank. I call him Tank because he always runs into things. He's dumb as bricks but fuck I love him! Ha-ha-ha."

After being introduced to Tank, I asked if I could use her bathroom and she said, "You don't need to ask. Go right ahead!" I'm glad she was cool with it since I had to drain my shit badly. Standing in the bathroom and aiming right at the toilet as my piss rushed out, I observed the bathroom since it was pretty unique. Then I cleaned and composed myself a bit.

Nicely calm and ready, I left the bathroom and walked by a poster she had on her wall that was hard to miss. The poster said, "RELAX, IT'S JUST SEX!" with a picture of a girl with her arms and hands tied up bondage style...

"Damn, can I take a picture of that?" I said, and she said, "Sure, go ahead!"

After taking the picture of her poster, I went into my bag and got the rest of my gear all set up for our shoot. Then we talked for a bit longer about how we'd shoot.

"Cool, alright, I'm ready," I said.

She said, "Okay, well let me slip into something a bit more comfortable. Nakedness!"

She speed-walked to her bathroom to get herself ready so I sat there looking at my cam and watching Tank AND thinking to myself, "Okay, this is the moment of truth, let's see how I handle this..."

Five minutes later, she stepped out of her bathroom walking elegantly towards me with nothing on looking as naked as possible with a devilish grin on her face!

"Dayum!" I said out loud, followed by, "Oh my fuckin' god! You're beautiful!"

"Well, thank you, kind sir," she replied. Then? We just started taking pictures.

From calm to straight out passion, everything changed in the span of seven seconds as the mood and energy went from one to one-hundred!

She posed, I aimed, she grinned. "Oh lawd dayum! That's a nice shot," I said.

"My god! I love your fucking energy, Drew," she said as she laughed at how energetic I became.

"Hey, wanna hear some *Jay Z?* I have his new album," she said.

She turned on her stereo with the music bumping and the energy intensified even more.

After taking a few shots in the far-right corner of her living room, I noticed all these different pictures on her wall so I asked her about them.

"Who are all these people?" I asked.

"Oh they're my friends."

The wall was white and had a big obvious sign above the pictures actually saying "friends". I don't know how I missed that.

We commenced to shooting and she went back to posing as we talked in between, with *Jay Z's The Holy Grail* playing in the background on her stereo which set the mood perfectly as our energies fed off one another.

From the beginning to midway through our shoot, I kept praising and complimenting her on how beautiful she was, and how cozy her place looked. I even stopped a couple times to take it all in and said, "I wish my place was like this, this is so inspiring!"

Sophie looked at me at that moment and said, "Hey! Your house is your sanctuary! You should be waking up feeling amazing and inspired every day."

Then I said, "Well, I'm at home in my little room, ha-ha-ha."

"So! Decorate that shit to bring your mood up! So that you're motivated and inspired!" She said.

I actually wanted to have more teasing like shots whereas Sophie wanted more straight up and out sexual shots since her growing fan base already loved her for that. We balanced it out, though, and eventually moved to the centre of her place to take more pictures.

Looking dead centre in her place all I saw were shoes all lined up on her shoe rack. "Yup, I'm addicted to shoes, and I told you I wasn't joking, I really am obsessed with the colour pink." The top and third row of her shoe rack mostly had pink high heels on them.

We took some pictures of her in front of her shoe rack, and pictures with her holding up her cute cat Tank, then we stopped to think of some other creative ideas.

Out of nowhere she screamed, "I know what to do!" She ran off looking for clips, then she ran off looking for something else, then finally came back with clips and three flowers that she managed to slip on to her nipples and one on her bottom sweet area.

Excited and mesmerized, I continued to take more shots, and even got more confident in saying what poses I wanted her to do. She eventually even said to me, "You could touch me if you want, you are after all a photographer." I went up to her and guided her once, but in the end, I just wanted to be a gentleman.

Three hundred plus shots later and with my camera battery on the verge of dying, we decided to call it a day. We were both happy with how our shoot went and we were eager to see some of the pictures, so after we both placed her furniture back to where it needed to be, I yanked my laptop out and sat down on her couch to connect my cam to transfer the pictures to my laptop.

Sophie sat right beside me during this whole process and once again she was elegantly naked, and I've never seen someone be as comfortable like that before in my life. It was cool and different. Once I was finished uploading the pictures from my camera to my computer, we copied them over to a memory stick she had. We went through the pictures and loved them!

Sophie asked, "Hey, did you eat anything? I'm about to eat."

I said, "Nah, but I should head back home to eat something."

Then she casually said, "Hey, if you wanna come and eat with me, it's all good," so I said, "Sure!"

She went in her room to dress herself in the sweater she had on earlier and some black pants I think. We eventually packed up, left her place, and walked down the street until we hit up a chill local pub that she recommended. I felt out of place there since I didn't really eat out a lot back then, but since I was doing a good job at continuously fighting against my anxiety, I challenged myself and did what I wanted to do!

We sat facing each other at this booth big enough to seat six people and carried on with our conversation talking about shooting and the industry. Minutes later, a waitress came over giving us two menus so we looked in them, but I was thinking of getting the cheapest thing since I knew I was broke.

Then our waitress came back assuming we were ready to order. Sophie ordered the works, getting a pretty nice meal. By the time our waitress asked me what I wanted, Sophie said, "Don't even worry about it, this is on me."

I said, "Are you sure?"

And she reassured me, saying, "Don't worry, I got this!"

We waited for a few minutes then our meals came along, and all I was thinking was "holy fuck" since we had some big plates with amazing food. She even got us two full pitchers of beer.

I loved it! And I loved her. If she was tryin' to seduce me, she was doing a damn good job!

Throughout the night, we gradually got into deeper conversation revolving around relationships, hurt, love, passion and following our dreams in life. Every word and sentence that came out of her mouth at that moment in time was heartfelt, hitting me like a dart.

When we finished up at the pub, we slowly walked back to her place talking some more about life, and I couldn't complain, man, the beer was all up in my system so I was feelin' NICE!

The streets were deserted and everything was calm and quiet since it was late. Our conversation started getting crazier the closer we got to her place. When we finally got to her place I stopped, then she stopped… and then…We hugged! With her thanking me for my help, and pointing and directing me to where the closest bus stop was, which was right across the street just up the block.

While waiting at the stop, the whole day rapidly flashed before my eyes and I cracked a smile. By the time I made it to the nearest train station to head east back into Scarborough, I was barely even conscious since all my energy was gone. This was another day where I didn't even remember fully how I made it back home, but what I do remember is by the next morning I was looking at a whole bunch of text messages from Cray since she had been trying to get a hold of me while I was with Sophie Rose.

Cray and I decided to meet over the weekend, and the place of our meeting/interview was of course down where my lovely office was. Now while I was going through all the motions getting myself ready to meet Cray, something still seemed off and my intuition kept warning me of danger. But I kept brushing it off.

"Let's keep this professional with no weed or any touching, okay?" Cray said to me in a text message, so I replied and said, "Relax man! Take shit easy… just be cool…" So there I was again waiting at my office, but instead of Sophie Rose, it was Cray I was waiting to meet.

Scanning left and right while putting my head down to look at my laptop, I didn't see anyone coming my way, but just like that, she seemed to have appeared heading straight for me. Although she never really knew how I looked, she seemed to know it was me. We both greeted each other by saying "hey!" She got some food from the nearby grocery store then came back and popped the plastic lid to her food open and ate like she hadn't eaten in a long time. Then we talked about shooting. Most if not everything was going fine while we talked, so I just went with the flow.

After talking for a bit and feeling like we clicked, I told her that we could definitely set up a day and time for our shoot. She said, "Sure, that sounds cool! But, um, let's take some shots now."

I didn't like the idea of shooting right away, but she persuaded me, saying, "C'mon, we'll just do a few, okay?"

"Aight, cool, fuck it," I said.

We headed up to the main floor then out to the street and into a parking garage, going up to the third or fourth level since her car was parked there. We made our way to Cray's car which was parked in the back. The closer we got, the more uncomfortable I felt since I wasn't feeling the whole vibe.

We both got into her car, then we both started talking. "You want weed?" Cray said, so I said "Nah, I'm good, I gotta be focused while shooting."

Then she said, "Well, I need this before doing any type of shoot."

"Cool, do your thing," I said.

It wasn't a big deal to me, but I found it to be a bit odd since even hours before she had been stressing how she wanted no weed to be involved and how professional she wanted things to go. As Cray lit up, we talked about weed and bullshit while she held onto her spliff, taking deep pulls here and there after every long sentence.

Laughing

After a couple of pulls, it seemed like the weed hit Cray pretty good because she let out this "Ya, I'm trippin' the fuck out" type of laugh. After that, she said, "Um, are you ready?" So I said, "Let's see how the weather is and if we can do it up."

She put out her weed, then we drove off, hitting Yonge Street heading south until I let her know of a good location to shoot at. I directed her to head north so she made a U-turn and did a couple of crazy maneuvers until we eventually got to the spot and found parking. As I escorted her to the location…

"Wow," she said, and I felt all proud and happy and said, "Yup! This is it!"

We both stood there for a few minutes, then we both loosened up. Once she found a safe place to put her bag down, we started taking some shots on the fly. When she became more comfortable and confident, she slowly took her jacket off as we took more pictures.

We spent the whole evening at this location taking pictures until it got dark and chilly. Then she offered to drive me back home, being that it was late. While driving home, we had a pretty chill conversation but something still seemed and felt OFF! My senses were going crazy warning me of danger but everything appeared to be okay. As Cray dropped me off, I assured her that I would upload our pictures and would send them to her, then we hugged and she drove off, heading home.

When I got inside I said "hey" to my mom then got something to eat, then headed straight to my room to upload and process the pictures to my laptop so that I could send them to a file sharing site. While flipping through our shots I became excited about how they all came out, so I took a picture of one of them on my phone and sent it to Cray. Minutes later, she responded with "what are you doing?"

So I said, "I'm fixing up our pictures as they're being uploaded and wanted to show you what we did."

"Why are you looking at my pictures? What are you doing?" Cray said, so I told her to relax and calm down.

I let her know that all the pictures would be ready for her to see by the next day since I was too tired to get it all done that night. I closed shop down and passed out after that.

Waking up the next morning, the first thing I did was is grab my phone to see who messaged me or what calls I might have missed. Surprise, surprise, who messaged me all crazy? "Cray", of course, and she was asking about her pictures and accused me of stealing them. Being that I don't like mix-ups or miscommunication, I called her then and there and said, "What's up with you?"

Cray then said in an angry voice, "Do you think I don't know what you're doing? You're trying to take my pictures! Don't take advantage of me, I will not be taken advantage of! You won't use me!"

Everything went from calm to chaos in a matter of seconds. I remained calm since I naturally am that way but hearing her cuss and raise her voice a few times finally made me click! "What the fuck is wrong with you!? You need to get yourself checked the fuck out! You're not right! That ain't right!" I said, then hung up on her.

Feeling confused and with my high from shooting Sophie Rose killed off, I told my dear Sophie Rose all about what just happened.

"Huh? What the fuck is wrong with this girl? She's crazy, you don't need that type of negativity around you, you're a sweetheart!"

"Besides, the female body should in fact be celebrated," Sophie went on to say.

By the time I had all of Cray's pictures uploaded and ready to send over, I wrote a full-page email to her expressing how crazy I thought she was and to let her know she needed to check her personality. I let her know that I was willing to talk it out but we never did, at least not then.

CHAPTER 12

The City

"**D**rew... hey... Drew! I heard you went to Second City to check out their Improv program. I've heard of it too and I'd like check it out with you soon if you're cool with that."

"The fuck? How did you know?" I said.

It was October at this point, and Sigz always seemed to be around right at the perfect times off and on social media. We both agreed and decided to head to the Monday drop-in class since he wanted to see what all the rave was about. We arrived at Spadina Station around the same time so that we could head down together, but we never actually saw each other until one of us decided to call the other.

I think it might have been me that called him. Then I remember seeing this cool guy leaned up against the wall nonchalantly taking his phone out to speak. Once we both figured out where we both were, we smiled then connected as we both hopped on the five-ten street car to make our way to The Second City Training Centre for our Monday drop-in class.

While on the street car heading down, we caught up and he asked me in detail about how everything ended with Heart and I, since he knew about all that took place during that time. We also talked about music and I kept asking what tunes he might have ready for release? When we finally got to our last stop, we made our way down the street to the Training Centre and the actual studio for our class. With our studio slowly getting packed, our instructor finally made his way in, jumping and bursting with energy! Our instructor was none other than the fun, energetic and inspiring Ken Hall!

His hyper ass had me and the rest of our drop-in class going! After doing our drop-in class together, we both decided that it might be cool for us to register at the same time to partake in the first level of their improvisational program. My mentality around that time was to do everything on my own, but it helped a great deal knowing that I now had an ally to take on this whole new experience with.

There was also a beautiful, playful and positive soul from drop-in and we naturally became closer to one another since we were so similar to one another, so we exchanged numbers and kept in touch. Kesha was her name and she was a high-class girl from Scarborough with another side only few got to see. We by chance happened to meet up for Monday Mashup a few weeks later with me going up on stage with some others. I tried to get her up too but she just watched until we both eventually left.

Making our way outside and walking to where she was parked, she turned to me and said, "So, when's the last time you got crazy?"

And I said, "Um, it's been a while."

We both became quiet as we crossed the street and knew fully well what was on our minds, so we laughed. When we finally made it over to the parking lot and to Kesha's car, my mind was blown away because true to her style she also had a classy luxury car! I looked at her ride in amazement and might have even cursed a few times, then again once my first curse session was done.

Kesha laughed while I was trippin' and just smiled and said, "Get inside, silly, let's go for a cruise." I ran over to the passenger side and hopped in, and then she took off with us cruising up and down the busy downtown streets. She saw how animated I was getting which got her acting up too, so she pulled the windows of her car all the way down as she sped up!

Feeling energetic, hyper, and up for anything, we headed away from the downtown core and further into the west end until we found a quiet street close to the lakeside. What did we end up doing? We, blazed out of course, and with that being my first time in a while of smoking up, I tripped out hard! Laughing, dancing, and then I freaked out getting a few panic attacks before sliding out of her car onto the ground. And then dancing in the middle of the road as she laughed her ass off!

I can't lie. I tripped out hard, so she made sure I was alright and got me home in one piece and demanded that I called her the next day so she knew I was alright. Everything was in slow motion, and then I was stuck in the kitchen for twenty minutes since I couldn't comprehend how to get out, but I eventually made my way upstairs then passed out.

The first day of our beginning Level A class started at six p.m. Our room filled up with all these new and interesting faces. One of the main thoughts I had before heading into our first real and actual classes was "How will I function being in a room filled with nearly twenty people?"

Getting outside and finally attacking and achieving my goals rapidly was becoming commonplace, but dealing with others in a room for more than two hours? I had no idea how that was going to be. Similar to the drop-in classes, as people started to walk into our assigned studio, we all naturally started to talk and handed chairs out to one another being helpful, and just like the first time around our instructor made a bursting entrance.

"Hello everyone! My name is Marjorie and I'm going to be your Level A instructor," she said.

Marjorie was this crazy, spunky, stylish, energetic brunette who was of course an Improviser but also a Comedian as well.

One of the first exercises Marjorie got us to do was turn to the person we were seated next to and talk for five minutes finding out about each other, then introducing that person to the class. Me and Sigz purposely sat away from each other to challenge ourselves even more, so the person who I sat beside happened to be this girl from NYC of all places. We talked about NYC and Montreal since she had a lot of friends there, and I told her that I talked to a girl from NYC.

Being that I sat right next to Marjorie, she automatically chose me to introduce my classmate first. My god, my heart was beating so fast, and I think my throat became dry and even cracked a bit, but I managed to do it. My classmate returned the favour and gave me a pretty neat intro too. There was also this chill animated artsy kid in my class that I later referred to as Party, since I gradually found out that he was into the party scene and was free spirited.

When it came to class though, I never really knew what to expect since whatever was going to happen would indeed happen, and I felt powerless. It felt like I had little to no control over anything that took place.

As the weeks went by, I began to feel a bit more comfortable and stable with my routine since I felt like I had a pretty good handle on things.

On Mondays, I went to Second City for my Level A Improv classes, and on Tuesdays I now had sessions with my doctor, and Wednesdays were the same thing depending on the situation, then Thursdays were a free for all with Friday being an either-or day.

I let Dr. Perotti know about the progress I was making while in my first ever improvisational class and expressed to her at times that I really didn't know if I was cut out for it at all. I wasn't used to being in large groups since I had isolated myself for so long, so getting back into the rhythm of things was interesting to say the least! Having someone talk to me and then me having to respond back to them while others were talking, listening to what someone was saying, remembering what they said to me and then doing this repeatedly with different classmates all within ONE session of class was overwhelming.

At times, I felt stupid and slow since it really did take me longer to catch on to things, but it wasn't that I was slow. It was just so much sensory overload coming at me all at one time, and this was something I was definitely not used to. But even though this whole new experience had me filled with feelings of uncertainty, Sigz and I started chillin' out more during these times and hit up a couple of parties where I got to meet a few of his other close friends.

With October gone and November on the verge of ending and us not even being aware of it all because of how busy class was, a few of us from this newly formed crew decided to venture out to a huge party on Friday night. We waited outside in this huge lineup that stretched over a block. I had enough and told some of the people I was with that we shouldn't wait anymore. We slowly walked up and through the lineup casually until we got to the front and acted like we were there the whole time.

When we finally got inside of this party, we waited again but not too long. Then we headed straight for the dance floor where I witnessed so many different smiling and happy faces. A lot of these interactions felt so new to me ... it was like that party scene straight out of that Joaquin Phoenix movie *Two Lovers*.

I tried picking up two girls with one of them saying "respect" to me for coming up to her since no one else did during the night. She also said that even though she had a man, she found it to be pretty odd that guys weren't really talking to other women being that it was after all a singles night. It was a fun night though, and a kick off to other stuff that would be happening.

By the time Christmas holidays were getting near, one of my friends suggested that we should probably hit up a strip club. And I mean, I was down for it since I didn't go much but anytime I went, I never regretted how much fun I had.

Since I was getting out a lot more, I gradually reconnected with a lot of old friends while getting to know the new. They were all getting mixed in together, and out of this mixture of friends came a sub-group which I refer to as the Secret Social.

The Secret Social really came about after being out with a few friends who expressed how curious and explorative they were, and by talking more, we eventually found out how much we had in common. The dynamics of our group was simple … to have as much fuckin' fun as possible with no judgement and to see how far we could push the envelope.

One of our first missions I guess you could say was when we headed to the strip club during the Christmas holidays. I wanted to head to a different club that I knew but we all decided on a better one. Me and three other members from our Secret Social crew headed out that evening to the strip club: me, two other dudes, and one of our girls.

We synchronized everything so that we would all meet at Dundas Square at the same time. Once we all met up, we hopped on the train and headed westbound until we got to Kipling Station. While on the train, we talked about how crazy the night was going to be and what we were gonna do once we finally got to the club.

Once we finally made it to the last station, we went to the taxi stand so that we could catch a ride to the club. Once we caught a cab, our cabbie knew where we wanted to go so he wasted no time and floored his car speeding off into the night! The ride seemed like it was taking forever, so the longer it took, the more negative thoughts I got. Before any of those negative thoughts could take hold, we ended up making a hard right coming off the highway, then onto the street, then to our destination with our cabbie wishing us a good time before he pulled off.

The outside of this club made it seem like an exclusive place. As we entered all we heard was smooth R&B, freaky Hip Hop tunes, and seductive House Music. We all walked slowly and let our eyes adjust to the dark light so that we could make our way to a table to sit down and situate ourselves.

With most people who go to strip clubs, the first thing they really wanna do is find themselves a place to sit so that they can be relaxed, opposed to standing up looking clueless and confused. So, there we were, a few of the Secret Social sitting down, listening to music and watching some lovely ladies dancing on the stage. The girl in our group was excited as she complimented a few of the dancers, taken aback by what she saw and loving it.

While watching what was happening on stage and looking into the crowd every now and then, I noticed one dancer gradually making her way over to our table but I played it off like I was ignoring her and didn't see her. She eventually made her way to our table though and introduced herself.

"Hey, I'm Lexie," she said. She shook all of our hands and got our names. Then she looked at all of us with her hands on her hips and said, "Okay, between the four of you, who's the horniest?" Simultaneously all four of us pointed at each other as if we were drawing guns on each other ready to shoot, so she laughed.

She was about five-six without heels on, light brown skin, long brown hair with these big brown exotic cat eyes that spoke crazy shit when you looked into them, yeah … she was pretty.

She sat on my lap while we all started to chat, but I was freaking out over it the whole time since I wasn't that used to being in such close proximity with a girl like that so quickly. On the outside, I seemed cool, but on the inside my heart was beating with my hands getting all sweaty and I KNOW she had to have felt how fast my heart rate was going! Maybe she thought I was just excited, but my hands were clammy as fuck.

"So, do you want a dance?" this Indian princess said to me all happy and flirtatiously … and I said, "Nah, I'm good, ha-ha."

But she persisted, saying, "C'mon have a dance."

I said, "Nah, I'm really good, plus I don't have the money for it. If I did, I'd go up with you, but I don't."

So, she backed off and said, "Okay, fine, but if you want a dance, let me know."

Before walking off, she pulled her right bra top open and said "Do you wanna suck?"

I laughed and without hesitation I reached over and sucked on her nipple, which triggered me to instantaneously become demonic and horny.

Still sitting on me and smiling after I sucked on her nipple, she said again, "So, do you wanna go upstairs for a dance?"

I said, "Nope! I'm good!"

The look on her face after that was a mixture of disappointment and looking at me as if I was trying to take shots at her ego. She gave me a stern but friendly stare and said, "C'mon, let's just have one dance, okay?"

"Sure," I said, reluctantly feeling like I was doing her a favor way more than she was ever doing one for me…

Now all happy, Lexie said, "Take your beer and follow me."

I got up from our table and followed her through the dark

mysterious atmosphere until we reached the stairs, then step by step up the stairs I went as I let her guide me to where the dance would take place. Upstairs was dark with single and full seats. I didn't know what to do or expect since I had never taken things that far at a strip club, so I continuously scanned the area until she said, "Okay, here is cool… relax and have a seat."

We carried on with small flirtatious talk once I sat down. Then she sat on my lap, hugging and holding me as if she was my girlfriend. We must not have talked for long because once the music started she spontaneously went into seductive mode.

Getting up then doing a full spin with her back now facing me, she slowly pressed herself back onto me as she twerked her body while using her left hand to reach behind to feel me as this all happened. Her crazy big brown exotic cat eyes seemed more intense to me once she spun right back around to face me. She sat on me like she was ready to fuck.

"Are you enjoying this?" Lexie asked with her voice sounding all soft.

I said, "Hell yeah, this is pretty fun," in a relaxed tone.

She kept flirting and dancing on me as I laidback kissing her a few times on her chest, lips, ears and neck while telling her how lovely she looked. Both of our breathing intensified, then while still being on me, she said, "Do you want a blow job?"

So I said, "Nah, I'm good…" but she insisted and didn't listen to what I said. Before I even knew it, my dick was out with a condom wrapped around it faster than I could say, "I was born in nineteen-seventy-nine!"

Enjoying it all as she went down, I didn't know what else to really do so I took my beer and drank it slowly as I watched her. Minutes later, she grabbed my right hand and placed it on top of her head, directing me to apply pressure, pushing her head up and down and back and forth … all I could say at that moment was "damn".

Three songs later and she was wondering how come I didn't or couldn't finish. She became excited from it all though and said, "Damn! You can last pretty long. We need to fuck."

It was all trippy to me, because little did she know I was too in shock to finish. But I guess it worked out in my favour.

We ended up leaving the dancing room and I got her number on the way back downstairs while only paying for one or two dances. She told me to give her a call. Then I returned to my group of friends with a smile on my face, telling them I would tell them the full story later, all while the condom was still wrapped up on me.

Before leaving, our lady of the group happened to get a lap dance from a girl she liked, but that's a story for another time.

Two weeks after having all that fun at the strip club with the Secret Social, I decided to text Lexie to see if it was her number and to see if we could hook up for some fun.

"Hey, what's up, it's your freaky friend from the club from a few weeks ago. I hope this is Lexie," I said in text in the hopes that it would really be her.

Fifteen-minutes later with no response, I figured I had the wrong number. I was going to delete the number, but then I got a text back saying, "Hello, yes this is Lexie, and I do remember you! How are you? *smiley face*"

I went from being happy and hopeful to feeling let down, then back to hopeful since she actually got back to me. "Um, would you like to chill out for a bit?" I texted right back to her and she followed back by saying "sure!" I told her that I wouldn't mind meeting downtown around four-thirty in the afternoon if she was cool with that, but she gave me fair warning that she didn't know the city that well.

I got myself ready after that, taking a shower and making sure I was looking my best and smelling nice. I even went ahead and booked a hotel for us near Yonge and Bloor so I made sure I was out of my house by three something in the afternoon.

When I finally made it on the train to head downtown, I felt all this pressure in my head and felt dizzy. It was like a mixture of high levels of anxiety and blood pressure, maybe, but it didn't feel good. I almost felt like passing out as the train I was on made its way into the core.

Once I got off the train at Yonge Station, I headed up Yonge until I got to the hotel I had booked. I entered the main entrance of the hotel and went to the front to check myself in. They gave me the keycard for my room, then I went upstairs.

I walked off the elevator and through the halls until I reached my room number. I vividly remember opening the door then turning on the lights and getting a wicked flashback of Heart and I! The smell of the room, the way everything was arranged, and the general feel of it all was reminiscent of us. I can't lie man, it hurt! But I tried to snap out of it quick because that wasn't my reality anymore.

Leaving the room quickly and heading downstairs to the front entrance, I looked at my phone to see if Lexie got back to me. She sent me a text saying, "Oh, fuck! I don't know about this Toronto traffic and streets! Am I going in the right direction?"

I said, "When was the last time you came down?"

She basically told me it had been a while. So, I gave her directions as best I could and looked out for her coming. While I waited for her, I paced back and forth wondering if she understood my directions, but then I got a call with her screaming on the other end telling me she was close. Then she pulled up in her car so I jumped in, riding around with her until we found parking.

Right after we found parking, we headed into the hotel and straight to the room I got for us. Seeing Lexie outside of her element was interesting. She was crazy, chill and hyper all at the same time! But for her, it just fit and added to her cuteness. When we finally got to our room, she tripped out at how fancy it looked while I sat on the edge of the bed. She turned around slowly doing a three-sixty, taking in the room. Then she put her jacket and purse on one of the desks and calmly sat right beside me.

"So, what's up?" Lexie said with a crazy smile.

I said, "Ah, nothing. It was nice outside today, man."

I was more laidback and wanted to take things slowly since this would be our first time doing shit. I even told her that I wanted to take things a bit slowly since I knew she was in a faster mode than I was.

"Okay," she said in a cute way, then she backed off, allowing me to talk more, giving me space, or so I thought...

Right when I was in the middle of talking about some bullshit I don't even remember, she eyed me down, smirked, and then jumped right on top of me, cutting my bullshit and getting the party started! She pinned me down on the bed, making out with me. Then I just clicked! I rolled over, making out with her as my wallet and keys fell out of my pants, but I didn't care. I just threw them off!

As for my glasses? They vanished too, but the only thing that was a priority at that moment in time was her. I laid her on the bed, made sure she was comfortable, and then went downtown. It was only fitting being that we were downtown.

"Holy fuck! Shit! My God!" Lexie moaned and screamed like a mad woman! During our downtown session, and I loved it! But I also wanted her not to make so much noise, so I kept talking about it which was odd. While she was enjoying herself, all she said to me was, "Who the fuck cares if anyone else hears? We paid for this room. Go crazy! Baby!"

When she said all of that, I thought to myself, "Yeah, she has a point!"

That's when I just let loose and enjoyed everything more. After pleasing her for a while, she returned the favor, then jumped on top of me like someone trying out for an Olympic cowgirl team. Being who Lexie was, she didn't hold back. Similar to our experience in the club, it took a while, a long while for me to finish, but at least I can say as a gentleman I let the woman go first, if you get what I'm sayin'.

When we were finally finished, we cleaned up the place, found our stuff, and left. I walked her to her car, then we both drove out with her dropping me at Bay Station. We did this maybe two more times. The last time started off with a crazy passionate kiss along with some other things. After that we lost contact, and really it was my fault since I didn't text as much.

I ended up telling Sigz about some of what happened, but by this time it was the middle of January and we missed the deadline to register for our level B improvisational classes. I was also worried about how I was going to pay for my classes since I didn't really have a lot of funds at the time, but through quick researching and observation I found out that Second City had scholarship programs. All I needed to do was is write an essay stating why I thought I should be granted the scholarship along with giving some background information on myself.

Being that I had some extra time on my hands since I wasn't doing the first term, I used this to my advantage and started writing an essay and kept tweaking it. I worked on it when I was happy, sad, suicidal, a nervous wreck, not hopeful, sleep deprived, and when I was sick!

Around this time, a lot of my writing skills naturally developed into me wanting to write to companies that I bought things from. Clothing companies, car companies, computer and electronic companies and so on. I eventually realized that I was writing business proposals and wasn't even fully aware of it.

I've always been an expressive person, and being that I had some blogs where I posted and exposed what was going on in my mind, that's probably what led me to want to write more. It's funny how you can be doing nothing but then a lightbulb just goes off in your head letting you see the obvious that has been in front of your face for the whole time, but you were too occupied with too many distractions to ever notice, see or realize.

There was a certain big and tall clothing company that I decided to write to, but not only did I decide to write to them, I decided to make them a full-on booklet with pictures of me modeling their clothing. At the time, I figured my idea was too over the top and wouldn't work, but I love challenges so I went ahead full on into the idea anyhow.

Writing over and over, editing and coming up with the perfect delivery and letter and booklet? All felt pretty stimulating to me!

When you're down and out, that little spark inside within you that wants to do better and that wants better for yourself is all that you have and can rely on at times. This is the spark that most suicidal people try to feel before Xing themselves out. To me? If you can visualize it? You can fuckin' do and be it! In most cases when everything is taken away from you, these are the only things that you have in order to make yourself get up in the morning and function.

I'll share some of the essay I wrote for Second City right here...

"Use Your Strengths, Exploit Your Weaknesses"
By
Andrew Wayne Marshall

Hello and good day, my name is Andrew Wayne Marshall and I have a lot of interesting things to say, I hope to be considered for your scholarship, as I write this letter to you I can feel myself becoming a bit excited, and throughout this letter I hope to give you a better understanding of who I am.

I am involved within the Arts and making people laugh is a part of my dear heart, doing both the Second City Improv and Comedy courses is something I would enjoy most definitely, and as my two choices a perfect chance to inspire others while I dance with grace throughout classes offered at Second City.

Since I suffer with Mood and Anxiety Disorders I know Second City would help me greatly, not only do I get to socialize and meet new people but I could possibly find a lovely lady friend who might date me, happy days would fill up as they come, my self-esteem would also boost up into the sun, and then I would continue on being pretty happy but could you blame me?

Because of my experiences with mental illness I would like to help out others such as myself with issues that are serious, and not only them but people in general who are also dealing with emotional issues and/or problems, without a doubt I do relate to their pain, not only have I seen the dark end of the tunnel but out into the light is where I stay and remain.

Second City Improv and Comedy writing courses would help bring me closer to where I would like to be, and that's an inspirational comedic speaker people can hopefully relate to and aspire to want to be.

I started with small steps, and see my dreams slowly coming to reality, the only thing that is stopping me are issues I have financially.

Throughout my fight and struggle on this path to become better, I spent a lot of money on taxis due to lack of mobility brought on by my Social Anxiety, needless to say I raised up my debt, and I am in the process of paying off used credit, so offering me this scholarship would help me tremendously.

I will be saving needed money, which is number one, that can be put towards a business startup fund, and then on to another phase of my plan to help/take over the world through laughter and away I go I shall be happy. ☺

With this essay, I got accepted back into The Second City Training Centre and granted access into four different courses.

Term two was in March so Sigz, and I made sure we were ready for it and registered. The day before our first official Level B class, I remember being anxious to the point I became sick to my stomach and then got food poisoning. I couldn't and wouldn't let that stop me from going down to the Centre though.

A few hours before actual class, I headed to a drug store to get some Pepto Bismol before heading to class. I drank it up in the washroom and let out all the sickness I needed to let out, then proceeded to our assigned studio.

And just like the Level A class, waiting around for the instructor to come while seeing new faces and greeting people was how Level B was.

"Hello, everyone! I'm your Level B instructor!" What the hell? It was none other than Marjorie from our Level A class!

Sigz and I looked at each other and were relieved that our instructor was someone we already knew, and she was happy to see us along with some of the new faces. But they weren't really new faces to her since they did her Level A class, they were just new to us.

We all got to know each other a bit throughout our classes, and I really felt like I was on the verge of having a nervous breakdown being as how I felt like I had to keep myself together and not show too many signs of my Anxiety and Mood issues. One day after class I waited until everyone left and I talked to Marjorie about it just to let her know what I was dealing with, and you know what? She was more than understanding plus she knew something was going on with me, which made me pretty happy.

The dynamics of our group kept getting more and more interesting as we all got to witness how we all were with one another. Near the middle of our course, we started to connect more and warm up. Now, nearing the end? That was when there was this crazy insane energy that seemed to have come out of nowhere, but really, it was just all of our love and energy for each other being expressed on the exact same level to one another.

It's a known thing that everyone gets to perform on stage at Second

City once you reach Level C, so we talked about that a lot and we always wondered how it would be. I mean, the only stage time we ever got as a crew was doing five minute games on stage at Monday Mashup.

Luckily for us though, we had our classes on Mondays so right after, Mashup was most likely the spot.

After surviving Level B, me along with most our crew went over to Level C for term three, which was around May to June. While this class was going on, though, I signed up for a new class they had recently developed called "Improv for Anxiety," which was ran by an amazing dude named Cameron Algie.

The anxiety classes only had a Level A to them, and I did them on the weekends, but once I was done and in Level C, they rolled out with a Level B for the anxiety classes which I did and LOVED! My anxiety crew was just as important to me as my regular class crew, and I loved mixing and meshing with both. Sometimes though I was up, then I was down, then up, then down… and I don't know how some took that or if they understood that.

In the Level C classes, our group became close, and that artsy kid who I first saw in Level A was now back in our Level C class. I was more than happy to see him back. A girl from our class who I'm referring to as Cathleen was one crazy bitch! In Level B, she was a bit shy but became this hyper energetic crazy girl by Level C, and there was no logic behind it but I loved it! She always used to say the most random things and not knowing or understanding how funny what she was saying was!

She was this cute crazy bitch from Cornwall, a town a couple of hours east away from Toronto. Being in the city really seemed to fit her personality because she was turned all the way up! All the time! Well, she had downtimes too, which is where we got to bond a lot more and I loved it just as much!

There was also this beautiful girl in my class that was the splitting image of Abby from that comedy show called *Broad City*. To me she is Abby since she's pretty much her twin. So, if someone from *Broad City* happens to read this, please get at her, or me!

There was this Vietnamese guy in our class too that always seemed to hold our improvised scenes together. I don't know how he did it. But he had a real damn talent at doing all this improvisational stuff. As for myself? I was randomized and did my own thing! I don't know if I really fit into any one scene properly, I just had a fuck it and go mindset, and being that I was all over the place to begin with, I tried to use that to my advantage, I guess you could say.

Our instructor for our Level C class was this well-known and respected improviser named Frank McAnulty. I loved his style because he encouraged everything that we did, and somehow found the magic in our fuckery!

I did a lot of fucked up, strange and straight up uncomfortable characters along with another homie...what was neat about this other crew member is she really pushed it and did the strangest characters that you wouldn't expect a female to willingly have the balls to do. But she did it. Everyone from our crew had their THING though, which is what made our group so special.

Heading to classes every week finally led us all down to the wire to our last few classes. We knew that we would have to perform for our Level C graduation and kept freaking out over it since it was all a new experience for us. I guess just like mostly everyone in my group, I was afraid of looking stupid on stage and messing up, but in the end, improvisation is all about making the best of what you've got and what you get while on stage, which is where the true magic and nature of improv comes out to shine.

In class we played many games, but one of the many games I kind of hated was this game where six people take the stage and are broken up into pairs of three. Within the pair, one would be the reader of a random book while the other would have to justify lines that were read or would have to act them out.

When it came down to our actual graduation day, you already know what game I got stuck with! We all assembled near the back hallway of the Training Centre and saw who was going up at what time and who was doing what. We took about two pictures, then waited until it was our time to hit the stage. It might have been a Sunday in June around five p.m.

We were all scared at that point, but I tell you there's no better feeling than walking on stage being in front of the crowd while they cheer for you! It was encouraged to tell friends and family members about our graduation show, but some of us didn't want anyone to see or to know when we were performing. We did this improvised singalong that we had rehearsed earlier which carried over to the next person until it got all the way down to the end of the line, then back to the person who started it. Then our show started.

I don't remember if I went on during the first half or the second half but it was somewhere in between that...

When an Improv show is going on, the audience can throw out offers telling you what or where you are, so me and my team member we were placed in New York. When my team member read the randomness from the book she was given, I put on a hardcore New York accent to make people laugh... some got it, but others didn't, ha!

After everyone got to do their set, we all walked off that damn stage feeling invincible! We ran out and screamed and did freestyle raps on the corner since we were accustomed to doing so after class anyhow. We hugged, kissed, hugged some more, laughed and were on a high. So, we continued with the high energy leaving Second City and celebrated! Oh, and Rebel actually came out to watch and support me too! *kiss*

We took to the streets like madmen and madwomen marching away from the intersection of Peter and King as we acted up yelling at cars and getting all cheerful and crazy until we found a place to eat.

There was a restaurant we found, so we chilled there to get some food, then talked a bit before heading off and following the sounds of the thumping music and vibrations we heard that evening! It was chaotic with a whole bunch of things going on. Clubs opened on the left side, on the right side and before we knew it? We found out where all the music was coming from because we walked right dead centre into the shit of it!

The Much Music Video Awards were taking place, so we all decided to stay and be a part of it. The music, the people, the energy, and their energy on top of the energy we already had from being on stage, doing our show and the crowd receiving us – well, it just made us feel good!

I started feeling the energy so much I started rapping again as my crew cheered me on. Then Sigz danced up with a few cute girls and Cathleen was getting crazy with the other girls from our crew. I think I even wrapped my arms around this girl that came our way and kissed her on the cheeks then smiled.

As the award show was dying down, we headed further up the street since we were on Queen Street and wanted to head closer to Dundas Square. I don't know how and I don't know why but they were giving out cereal boxes of some chocolate flavoured something. It was neat though because while all this was going on, Sigz had his boom box so all the girls and even some guys walked along the street with us as if we were the main people you'd want to be around.

This one guy casually walked up to us and asked if we needed any coke or weed, but we let him know we were aight. Getting to Dundas Square seemed like it took forever. But once we finally got there, it made all the difference in the world. The girls were already at the Square but me and my Vietnamese homie were on the other side, where I got into a freestyle session with some other rhymers on the street that he recorded with his phone. Then after about twenty minutes of that, we broke off and headed to the Square.

"This is the most fuckin' fun I've had in a long time, man!" Sigz said to me while smiling and being happy.

We all took to the stage they had at Dundas Square and danced until we couldn't dance anymore and then called it a night. As to how most of us even got home that night? I don't remember. It could have been by train or by taxi, but either way... we got home safe!

CHAPTER 13

Living it Up

*A*fter our graduation and celebration, most of our Level C crew wanted to take a break for the summer holidays, which kind of broke the crew up into splinters with some people such as Cathleen heading into Level D. I didn't want to stop so I enrolled into another Level C class where I reconnected with people from my Improv for Anxiety class.

I mean, Level C was cool and all, but some of us really took a beating so we wanted a rest, and others such as myself felt like they might need to take it over again. Cathleen heading right over to Level D was ironic being as how she was the one out of all of us who wanted to do Improv the least! So, that just goes to show you how easily things can change.

Doing classes with my Improv for Anxiety crew who were slowly being integrated into the regular Level C course was cool, and I felt comfortable in class with them. It was a mixture of people from two different classes mashed into one but felt pretty warm. Cameron Algie ran this Level C class, and as usual with his classes, we got to sit around in a circle afterwards to talk about our feelings and what we liked or even hated about class, which was cool.

I also enrolled into Second City's Standup Program around this time since it connected with everything else I was doing and wanted to do. Level C classes were on Sundays in the evening, and my Standup Classes were on Thursdays in the evening. The comedy group was small with just twelve to thirteen of us in the group and I loved how that was! On the first day when it came time for us to introduce ourselves, my voice cracked since I was that anxious, and most of us came with pad books, pencils or laptops. I came with a pad book at first.

My comedy group reminded me of the bad or renegade kids at a school no one else wanted to really be around. They were a group all on their own and made their own rules, so I felt like I belonged with them a-hundred-and-ten per cent.

After class, we'd leave as fast as we could to head up to this open mic night at Spadina and College named The Cage. We slowly started to find out about open mics in and around the city, so Thursdays at the Cage after class was just the routine.

Although I loved my whole class, two people that stick out the most, were, Danny Adhim and Matt Baxter. Danny had a way of keeping our group together and made everything function while being caring towards everyone. Matt is like my brother from another mother. He expressed to me how he dealt with Anxiety, Mood issues and ADHD so we had more than enough topics to cover, PLUS he wrote rhymes and freestyled just like me.

Danny was the first openly gay dude I really started to become close with, and what made him even more unique was that he was a brown Guyanese dude. Since my other crew took the summer off, Sigz always had parties he himself put on, or parties he heard about and got tipped off to. He usually would tell me and others from our group in advance about them so that we could all go.

"Yo, Drew, there's gonna be something sick this weekend, you down?" He left me an audio message on the social media site we used, so I responded back in text saying "sure!"

Cathleen was supposed to come along that day too but she couldn't since she'd volunteered to help with some of the Improv festivals happening that day. Me, Artsy and Sigz went to the festivals. Afterwards, we left and headed down to the beach by taking the streetcar all the way down to the end of Queen Street. Artsy brought two of his cute lady friends along with him, so that was pretty cool.

By this time, it was evening, and once we got off the streetcar, we walked further away from the main beach area then snuck through a broken fence heading down a steep rocky hill. I swear I nearly broke my right leg since I was seconds away from almost hitting a big rock but it all seemed worth it once we got to the bottom, which led us back to a safe and calm restricted beach area.

It all seemed so peaceful with not a lot going on, so, as we started to walk left along the coastline, I turned to Sigz and said, "Are we in the right place? You sure the party is happening here?"

"I don't know... we'll have to see," he said as we both kept walking. Along with everyone else, we looked onward trying to make out if there were people partying in the distance.

It was quiet with nothing to hear except our voices. Then we noticed a bonfire but we just assumed it was some randoms doing their thing. As we got closer, the sound of music was faintly heard and increasingly got louder until it smacked us in the face, making us know that "yup" we were definitely in the right place!

People dancing, a big ass bonfire, the lake in front of us and banging music with lovely girls all around! What else could we ask for? We danced all the way into the night with a full moon appearing right over the lake, dancing in groups and randomly dancing with different hot girls as the DJ switched from House to Drum N Bass, to Hip Hop, then back to House...

We stayed all the way until the end and then decided to make our way home along with everyone else, once mostly everyone started packing up their shit and started to leave. It was probably one in the morning at that point.

Most people from this party headed west along the lakeshore and tried to make their way back up that same crazy hill that we all went down in order to get to this party, but honestly? From the time I came down that hill, I had no intentions of going back up, so while the party was going on, I was thinking of ways of how to easily make it out of this place once the party would end.

Me, Sigz, Artsy (who I now called Party) along with his two cute girlfriends naturally headed east, but everyone was gonna turn around to head back with the crowd...

I said, "Hold up! Hold up! Maybe we can keep travelling east to beat all that hill bullshit and we'll find an easier way to bypass everything."

"Cool, let's try it," Sigz said and everyone else was cool with it too.

The more east we went, the more disconnected from the main party crowd we got until we were eventually left on our own. It was dark and chilly and big water patches surrounded us. As we walked we just wanted to get the fuck out from where we were. We came across another bonfire with randoms that had a dog that chased us, so we ran like fuck speeding over to another area that kind of looked safe, where there were trees but there was nothing but darkness and dog piss. Since it was the night, it all looked like the gates of hell.

Confused and running out of options, Sigz said, "Maybe we should just head back." But while he said that, we all happened to look up through the scary darkness and noticed stairs that looked like they were magically put there specifically for us.

I don't remember who agreed or didn't agree, but we all decided to head up this old looking wooden set of stairs that had sections of it missing. Well, I know I was one of the people to say let's go up ... ha!

Heading up was freaky! These stairs kept going higher and higher and it got to a point to where I started to say, "Yo, maybe we should head back down." But everyone else at that point wanted to keep heading up since we had already gotten this far.

When we finally reached the top, with nothing but a freefall underneath us if these stairs ever gave out, all we encountered was is a metal barred gate.

We looked at each other, and I don't know if anything was really said, but there was just an unspoken understanding that we weren't gonna turn back now and that this was our out! Our freedom! If we could just defeat this wall, freedom would be on the other side!

After standing in front of this gate for a couple of minutes, we decided to let the girls go over first. Well, they agreed to go over first so that they could scope out the environment. We helped boost them over one after the other so that whoever was over first would help the other get down, and it worked!

"What's over there? What's over there?" Me, Party and Sigz kept saying to the girls. The girls ran off then came back and said, "Fuck! There's stairs!"

Excited like Underground Railroad slaves, Me, Party, and Sigz took turns hoisting each other up until we got over. Now, Party went over before Sigz and I and everything was cool, but then it was my turn. At first, I felt confident about it as Sigz held me up and as I pulled myself up, but after a certain point, I called it quits.

Party saw this and was like, "Nah, nah, you're almost over man!" and like nothing, he leaped back over and helped Sigz push me up! To this day, I don't know how they managed to raise me up but I eventually pulled myself up and with their help I got over. Well, almost! See, I got stuck on top of the fence then lost my sense of surrounding and had voices on different sides speaking to me.

"Go over, go over!!! You can do it! You can do it! C'mon Drew!"

You know those moments you sometimes have when you really need to put your mind into a do or die moment? Well, this was one of them. I tried to realize where I was, then looked towards the bottom and said to myself, "Fuck that drop looks pretty far down," but again, this was a do or die moment. So I said to myself, "The longer you stay here? The scarier the fall will seem, so make your decision now to drop and brace yourself for the fall."

And just like that, I let go and closed my eyes as I tuned everyone out... then saw nothing but a flash of bright light as my body impacted the ground. Silence, that's all there was... just silence for a couple of minutes. Then the girls ran over to make sure I was okay and not dead. As I opened my eyes, all I saw was a concrete ledge inches away from my eyes and I noticed I was bleeding from my forehead. To this day, I still wonder what would have happened to me if I landed a bit closer to that ledge, it's scary.

After that, Party made his way back over and then Sigz followed as I dusted myself off. From that point, we proceeded to go up the little stairs our girls discovered, but once we went up, it led us into the back of someone's house, so we crouched our bodies running and ducking like ninjas then one by one ran out into the open so it wouldn't be too obvious that a group of people were running around.

Before we knew it, we were out into the open and back to civilization. Party being the crazy he is stopped for a second before we completely ran off and calmly took a picture on the driveway of the place we ran from posing with the car, so, I ran over and posed with him! Then and only then did we finally leave, walking until we found Queen Street again.

In the end it wasn't so bad, we just left with me having a forehead gash and a limp that I laughed off.

The next day I planned to head over to my Level C class but got a message from one of my friends from Improv for Anxiety that he was stuck in the hospital. This dude's name was Jobim, and we kept in touch since we had similar interests. He also had mental health issues and I tried to be there for him as a support whenever I could.

"Yo, Drew, I'm in the hospital, can you come?" the text read on my phone, so I said, "Sure man, fuck it! I don't think I'm going into class anyhow, I'm too out of it." I mean, my intentions were to go to class but I was running late.

I found out Jobim was staying at the exact same hospital where I tried to get admitted, so, headed straight down.

When I got near the hospital, I figured I might as well get something to eat before heading over, and even got something for Jobim. I got both of us chicken sandwiches and maybe a donut or something before making my way to the hospital.

Entering this specific hospital was interesting because it was far from my first time ever being there. As I passed the front lobby I saw some of the "committed" patients walking around, then made my way past the cafeteria. I had a lot of good and bad memories of this hospital since I knew it all too well and usually ended up there at times when I felt like ending my life. I also did group sessions there so I was far from a stranger.

Jobim let me know that he was located on the tenth floor and again, in knowing this hospital I also knew that floor a bit. That floor was where individuals who were dealing with acute issues such as psychosis were placed. There was really only one way in, and one way out, and this was all controlled by the staff who worked within the main control room which was in the centre of it all.

Taking the elevator to the tenth floor then getting off, I saw exactly what I expected to see, the main control room with a few of the nurses in there, so I walked up to the speaking window and...

"Hello? I'm here to see one of my friends since it's visiting hours," I said calmly.

The nurse asked me, "Okay, now who are you here to see?" in a cheerful uppity manner. I told her, and then she buzzed me in, electronically unlocking the doors then directing me to proceed right through the doors.

Walking through this section of the ward was different for me because I had never come this far. As I walked past the different patients, it was trippy, scary, sad, funny, fucked and a real eye opener all at once.

Most of the patients were heavily sedated, so it was like walking among zombies who had no idea what the fuck was going on, and the ones that weren't as sedated would be playing games, watching TV, or running up and down the hallways.

The nurse told me which room Jobim was in, so I slowly walked the hallways getting to his room, hoping to not see him in the same state I saw others in.

Walking down the halls, I counted the room numbers and tried to look inside all the rooms. I slowly made my way to his room, which took me a while since he pulled a trick and used a towel to cover his window so people couldn't look inside, and he had covered the room number so I couldn't find him as fast.

Getting up to the door, I knocked, not knowing what to expect, then he just opened up the door all happy smiling and said, "Yo, Drew, what's up man!? Come in! Come in!" I sat down on his bed and was greeted by one of his other friends that came to visit, and he seemed like he knew the mental health system all too well himself.

We all shot the shit and talked about girls, then he and his other boy that came to visit him started debating about what colour his friend's earphones were.

"Drew, Drew, Drew! Seriously, what colour do you think these headphones are?" Jobim's friend anxiously asked me.

I said, I don't know man, whatever. Maybe it's red and maybe it's a mixture of red pink, I calmly said, then I started laughing.

"Oh, c'mon get outta here with your diplomatic shit!" his friend went on to say to me, let's call him Allan. I call him Allan because he reminded me of a young Woody Allen: he looked like him, and sounded like him, he had the glasses, the style, everything, but he was only sixteen!

For a sixteen-year-old, he seemed pretty assertive, but I reminded myself that people who have dealt with the mental health system sooner or later have to become VERY assertive. If not, the system will pretty much take advantage of you, and will eat you alive and throw you in a grave.

So, for a sixteen-year-old to be that mature let me know that he was introduced to the system at a very EARLY age. Which was sad, but on the flipside manned him up quick at the same time and I could relate. After their debate, I asked Jobim how he was doing. So, based off of what we talked about, I decided to head to a nearby convenience store to get some Red Bull to sneak inside for him and a couple of others since they were heavily sedated.

While doing this, I wondered for a moment if he had just called me down for me to sneak shit in for him. But in the end, I figured it was all good since we were boys and he was in a way worse place than myself so why the fuck not? His friend came with me, so when we came back, I bypassed being checked by Security, headed back to his room, and gave him the gold. There were two other dudes with us now and they seemed REALLY bad off, so we passed some of the drinks over to them too.

We all kind of sat in a circle and I watched these sedated souls go from being doped up to being a bit more coherent and cheerful. Jobim turned to one of his boys and said, "You're feeling that now huh?"

We all looked at this guy waiting patiently for his response, then he raised one of his eyebrows up fast and smiled to indicate to us that, "Fuck yeah ... this shit is waking me up now." We all laughed and went "yaaaa!!!."

Minutes after that his sixteen-year-old friend said he was gonna leave and might be back the next day, then after a while the other dudes who were in the room left, making it only Jobim, and I in the room together.

At that point, we got to talk more personally about things that were going on and about shit that was going on with me. I joked and said I should be at my Level C class but it was aight. After an hour or so, I told him I might dip out, so I wished him well then left his room, walked through the hallway observing everyone and everything, and then got buzzed out, took the elevator to head down to the main floor, and left the hospital.

Since it was later in the evening by the time I left, I decided to go for a little stroll to process things and to think about my own life. Being up there with my boy made me realize how much freedom I had and how much of a good job I was actually doing for myself, so I told myself not to come down too hard on myself when things don't go my way.

I also reflected on how it was entering the ward. There were so many people up there that looked like dead people walking, or defeated soldiers, and code emergencies that happened but nothing too serious. Most of the patients just wanted their freedoms back and revolted when given the chance. Seeing my boy like that in that type of environment was fucked up, so all I kept saying to myself was, "This dude has to get better! That's not cool!"

Weeks later, it was back to my grind and business as usual. After seeing my friend in the hospital, I went to attend my regular Level C classes to connect back with my crew.

"What the hell happened to your forehead?" One of them said all shocked. I laughed it off and said I was at a crazy party. They told me to be careful but then another one of my dear classmates saw what happened and basically said, "Wow, I don't party that crazy, that's nuts."

Since my Band-Aid looked a bit too obvious. And with someone cracking a joke that maybe they need to make Band-Aids for black people, I made sure to go to the store right after class to get the clear type. In and around this time I was also fine tuning my booklet for the clothing company I wanted to do business with and be a brand ambassador for. When I scraped my forehead, and bled from the fall I had from the beach party, having good presentable pictures was all I mostly thought about.

"Oh my god, is the cut okay? Is it bad?" was all I frantically kept saying before me and my crew parted ways that night, like I was some damn model, but it was all good.

Writing to this company was one thing, but making a booklet for them was another. I had little to no experience with making booklets so wanted to place that responsibility into the hands of someone who knew more about this than I did. I was also on the hunt for a photographer around this time, and found it to be funny that a photographer such as myself found it to be so difficult to find someone else.

After getting referred to three people through friends, I decided that I might wanna go out there on my own to see if I could find myself my own picture taker. I never was and am not one for complexities so I simplified the whole process by randomly giving my local camera store a shout and taking it from there. And would you believe? With that simple reaching out, that's all it really took. When I called, I told them I was looking for a photographer, so they told me to call back later and to speak to a girl named Joanna, so that's exactly what I did.

When I called back, I got a hold of her so we talked briefly. Then she told me to send over the stuff I wrote so she could get a feel for what types of shots we should take. I sent my written material to her, she got an idea, and we worked it from there deciding on a time and place to take some shots.

Joanna and I decided to meet downtown at Dundas Square to take some shots, then to take it from there. The day we had scheduled slowly turned cloudy so we rescheduled, which worked out for me because man, I was tired the day she wanted us to shoot.

The day of our official rescheduled shoot was the perfect day though. Everything was on point! The weather was warm, it was sunny, and the sky was clear and blue with hardly any clouds. The idea that I had was is to take at least three different sets of shots so that I could showcase myself wearing this specific company's clothing. I wanted to showcase it in an urban area since I saw little to none of that on their website, in their store or in their marketing at all.

It seemed to obvious that making your company and brand appear more urban and hip would be one of the first things you would do since hardly anyone knew of them in the first place, including myself! My sister had pulled up to their store one day by mistake. As usual I took the taxi then the train from Kennedy Station all the way down to Yonge and Bloor, then headed southbound to Dundas Station to meet Joanna at Dundas Square. To speed things up I already had on what I wanted us to shoot, with me just having a few of my other things inside of a bag.

When we both finally met up, it was cool. We talked for a bit then we headed back to her car since she forgot a lens, then we headed back to Yonge and Dundas.

"So, what kind of shots do you wanna take?" Joanna asked me with her gear ready, locked and loaded.

I said, "I don't know? Something that looks victorious. I wanna look like I conquered shit ha-ha."

"Cool, alright well before we start I'm gonna get you to do something for me, okay?" she said.

I listened as she said, "WIGGLE YOUR BODY." So, I did! "Wob-wob-wob-wabaaa"

"Feel loose?" she said.

"Yeah, I'm ready to go man!"

She just said, "Okay let's go!"

She pointed her cam as I ran out into the intersection of Yonge and Dundas pointing at her camera as she snapped shots! Then she went to another corner and did the same thing. And "yeah" I loved it because this is the type of crazy shit I was into.

I was sweating like mad since I perspire a lot in the summer months, but it was all worth it and the shots came out amazing! Even though I thought the pictures were already good, Joanna fixed them up even more and sent them over to me a week later. I couldn't thank her enough.

With Level C going on, and this business letter thing going on, I still had my comedy classes that were happening but hardly had comedy material written. I quickly realized that writing in class while trying to retain information just wasn't my thing so didn't bother to write much, I just recorded what was said, but even that I never really used or listened to at all. I just wrote when I got home.

Evan Carter, who was a well-known and respected comedian, was our instructor for our comedy class and unlike many of my Improv classes, there was hardly any buildup, you just hit the stage! After a few classes, it was up to us to walk up to the mic that was set up in our room, turn the lights off, and have the spotlight shine on us as we went through with our routine in front of the group.

We all took our turn to go up sharing what we had, and honestly, it's true what they say man, waiting too long or being one of the last can kill you! I waited so long before going up, and as I did that I was dying inside with doubt, but once there were only three people left out of our group of twelve or thirteen people, I said "fuck it" and ran up as my class cheered for me in support as we did for one another.

"Wow," I said in a joking but serious way as I went up to the front of the dark class with only the spotlights on me. It was like a gunshot effect and you really don't know how surreal or insane something feels until you do it. I blanked out while up there because the intensity of the lights really threw me off.

I slowly went into my routine while shaking and blanked out so many damn times, then left the mic as my classmates encouraged me. One of my classmates even went on to say he felt sorry for me while I was up there when we ripped apart and analyzed each other after we all finally went up. Something about being on that mic drew me in though, and as much as I was afraid of it, I just had to be on it. I had to speak on that mic and I had to control it. That was how I felt and what I kept saying to myself.

Around this same time, I was getting myself ready for my Level C performance with my crew, and thinking about when, where, how and if I was going to even piece together an actual booklet for the company I wanted to get in contact with.

Everything was going so fast and made sense but at the same time made no sense since I felt like I was losing momentum in every other area. Whenever I spent too much time on one thing, I felt like everything else was slipping by...

"Will I make it? Can I accomplish all this shit that's in front of me?" I kept asking myself before heading to bed, or even sometimes on my way to my classes.

As classes carried on with everything getting closer to the actual days I would have had to perform on stage with my Level C crew and comedy class, things intensified even further. With my Level C classes, most of our class sessions turned into prep sessions to get us ready for the stage. Since I was doing Level C classes over again, it wasn't much of a big deal to me since I knew what the stage was like, but at the same time it was still nerve-wracking because it was all being done in a different style I was just getting used to.

With comedy classes, we ended up taking a trip down to the same club where we would be performing. The whole point of the trip was to see how comics were on stage. This club was just north of Yonge and Eglinton in Toronto's midtown. We got there early to have one of the comics who hosted there give us all a breakdown of how things worked in a club. Then we got to ask questions and then we all took turns walking slowly towards to the stage then standing there to get a feel for how everything would be for our performance.

As always, Danny had a presence about him so when he went for the stage, it all seemed so natural as if he was born to do it. I mean, I thought everyone looked damn good but Danny being the person he is just made it look right. When I walked towards the stage and stood there, I acted all crazy and smiled as everyone laughed. Then when I came back to join everyone else, they said that I had stage presence and that there was just something about me, which made me feel good.

Everyone had their own style though, and it just made our group what it was in the end.

By the time show time came around, we got seated in the front and got to see the host for the show who was a black comedian out of Cali who ragged on us for being in a comedy class in the first place. Then we got to see the headliner whose name was Slade Ham from the comedy crew *The Whiskey Brothers* out of Houston, Texas who also got to perform for troops in the Middle East.

Just from seeing those two alone in front of the crowd, I really didn't think I had it in me to rock the crowd like they did. After his crazy set was done and everything cooled down, we actually got to meet up with him after his show. Once he found out we were in a comedy class, he had this confused, puzzled look on his face. He pointed to the empty stage with the spotlights still on and said, "Listen, I know you guys are in a comedy class and all but, really? There's no substitute for that thing right there." He pointed at the stage and made sure we all got a damn good look, then he basically said, "Hit the damn stage man!"

CHAPTER 14

Make it or Break it

*W*ith only two weeks left and not really having much material, I buckled down and looked at all of my random jokes I had scribbled in my pad book that I carried to class sometimes.

From looking at everything I had laying around, it seemed easy and simple to piece it all together so I just did it. Right after that I kept reciting what I had until it was stuck in my head. Then I got a hold of Rebel that weekend and performed my material on her. I felt stupid and exposed knowing I would be saying my jokes right in front of her but reminded myself that, "Fuck, this is comedy after all! Do it!" She also encouraged me and said she wouldn't judge.

We used the front door to her place as the main stage as she sat on her sofa and watched me, and I purposely had my written jokes away from me out of sight to force myself to remember as many of my jokes as possible, especially under pressure. Everything was in darkness except for the front of her door with the light beaming down on me similar to how it would be like at an actual comedy club. I cleared my throat, took a deep breath as I composed myself and said...

"Have you loved someone so much to the point you wanted to X them out? Yeah, like... like, having a love that's so strong you figured you might as well just kill them since there was no other obvious place to go from there except down!? Yup, I love you, but since I love you so much you gotta die now..."

In shock, amazed and amused, Rebel put her hands towards her mouth covering it, so I kept going on with some more of my loosely written routine... but then stopped to try and ask her how I was doing...

"Are you psychotic?" She said, concerned since she'd never heard me get that harsh before with jokes.

I said, "Yo, it's comedy man! This is the type of shit that's in my head!"

Then she responded, saying, "Oh… I see." But right after that, she opened up and started saying some twisted jokes of her own AND even gave me advice and assistance with tweaking some of the sick shit I was saying! That moment right there I think made us a bit more comfortable in wanting to share and express how twisted our senses of humour were. Performing some of this material in front of Rebel and getting the reactions that I got really helped me. If I didn't get the chance to do that with her, I think I would have been more of an extreme nervous wreck. Thanks, girl, you helped me out so much…

Feeling oh so confident since I got to perform for Rebel giving her a sneak peek of what was to come, I still felt like I needed to fine tune a lot of what I wrote and wanted more input, so I met up with Marjorie during the week. I usually met Marjorie at chill laidback lounges she always seemed to know were fitting for whichever vibe to calm and chill me out.

We met once a week or whenever we could since she really believed in me and my vision, and most importantly, she saw my vision better than I ever did at times.

"Is this your truth? Did these things really happen, Drew?" Marjorie said while looking over my jokes after I built up the courage to share them with her.

"Yeah, for the most part they're coming from a place of truth, except for the last few couple of jokes," I said, but I felt kind of stupid for writing half of the shit I did near the end, I told her.

Marjorie always made it a point of duty to tell me to stick to my guns! But if what I was writing or expressing wasn't close to my truth in any form, get rid of it. While she looked over the routine I had, she worked like a computer crossing out and making a big X where my half-truths were.

She also helped me find out what some of my main strengths were at the time, which were being… Empathetic, Creative, Free Spirited, Determined, Outspoken, and Intuitive with a side of Crazy all rolled up into one! After meeting up with her, I reworked some of my routine and emailed it to my Improv for Anxiety instructor Cameron to see what he thought. Once he got back to me, one of the things I remember him saying was is how much he loved how vulnerable I got, which meant a lot to me. He also loved raw emotion and for people to be who they truly are.

Winding down to the last class with Comedy and with Improv, we performed in front of each other again and I just improvised my damn comedy set. I remembered half of it but said "fuck it" to the rest. My class went crazy giving me applause which then made others go up and express themselves in the same way.

One of my crew members even ran up to express himself too, it was love... and in my Improv class it was the same thing, as we did mock shows getting all goofy, feeling a sense of accomplishment having gotten through yet another level with each other and still being somewhat coherent enough to carry on. Our comedy show was scheduled for the weekend on Sunday in the afternoon, and Level C performance was on I think Wednesday, and this all took place within July. We did a draw for our comedy show to see who would go on at whichever time, and I was number five.

I vividly remember how debilitated I became and felt on Saturday. I couldn't move, I didn't want to talk, I didn't eat and I never left my bed, I just stayed there paralyzed thinking to myself, "Why did I do this again? Why would I put myself in such a fucked-up predicament?"

I hardly got any sleep the night before and stayed slouched in my bed all the way into the evening. I admit I even thought of not going at all, but once I am committed to something, I usually stick with it to the end.

Weeks before, Danny had made a Facebook event page to spread the word about our show so people would come out. He even got us huddled up together standing in front of our class mic to take a group picture for the main page of this group, so that added a lot more pressure plus put more responsibility on us to do this show!

It was one thought over to the next that Saturday, and that was half of what kept me in bed since I didn't want to confront anything, but slowly I thought about my jokes, my crew and banging this damn show out! In one shot I gathered all my mental and physical energy and pulled myself up and out of my bed! From that point on, it was game time for me, so I wasted little to no time grabbing my two-page routine and recited it over and over in my room while naked, with and without my paper in front of me!

Everything was cool, but the more I recited the more anxious I became, so out of desperation I told myself to drop everything and head to the basement to work out and pump some weights and do a few sit-ups.

"What the fuck?" I said to myself thirty or so minutes after working out. I felt looser, I didn't feel as restless since my blood and oxygen were circulating and my thinking was more stable! It was as if that was all my body really needed in the first place.

Really, though, I don't know why I thought of exercising out of the blue... I guess when you're desperate you'll find a way to calm yourself, but that all taught me a valuable lesson.

By the time I got back upstairs and got back into my room, I was super confident so I ripped off my clothes and recited my routine again being naked like a big black Superman with his chest out over and over again all into the night until I felt secure and very confident within myself and until I got tired! Then, wiggled myself into bed and slept like a fuckin' baby...

Alarm sounds off

Slowly coming out from a peaceful rest and not even thinking about my comedy show at all, once I turned off my alarm and looked at the time, I remembered I had some business to attend to. The show was three in the afternoon so being that I lived all the way in Scarbs, I had to time my trip just right as usual. I also had some time to work out and I figured why not? Since it worked the day before.

After that I had two apples then headed out of the house and to Yonge and Eglinton to make my way to Absolute Comedy to get settled in with my crew. When I finally got within the area where the club was, I crossed paths with one of my crew along the way, then we bumped into two more before making our way into the comedy club. As I entered the club with my other classmates, we were welcomed by a few others from our crew that already arrived before us.

"ARE YOU ANXIOUS!? ARE YOU ANXIOUS!?" One of my crew asked me, which was interesting because the day before, I had been a nervous wreck, thinking I was the only one feeling like that. Meanwhile everyone else felt the same way I did!

I told them I didn't feel anxious, and they freaked out, saying, "Huh? What's your secret?" So, I said to them I worked out before coming down.

It was interesting to witness how the dynamics of our group kind of changed that afternoon because for the most part during class, the cool, calm and collected people were now the ones on the verge of losing their shit. While the more anxious ones in class were now some of the calmer ones, and it was trippy to witness. After discussing the order for who would go on when and getting reacquainted with the stage again, as well as taking a look at the green room, we waited in the back of the club cracking jokes and watching the club fill up to capacity.

It seemed like it didn't take too long either. All I know is I looked towards the centre of the seating area then turned away for a while, then ten to fifteen-minutes later I looked back and it was half full, and then filled within twenty minutes.

Like any other show. we were encouraged to invite our friends to come out and support us and the show as a whole, so, unlike my first Level C performance, I invited Rebel, Sigz, Momma Chick aka Earla Dunbar, Paul and another undisclosed but close friend who brought her friend.

Our class instructor Evan Carter hosted our show so he introduced us one by one with the special request intros we gave to him before the show started. Now when it came to the green room, I don't remember if we stayed packed in there until we were individually called up or if we all left once we were introduced, but regardless we played the back of the club until we were called to the stage.

One of my crew Matthew Donovan was fourth to go on in our lineup, so since he was crazy and quirky with his jokes and had a style similar to myself, I relied on his performance to gauge the crowd to see if they would even respond to my type of humour.

...

One joke. Two jokes, then three and four more jokes were delivered from him as I watched the crowd's response as he went through his set. Matthew had a funny joke about pussy and Fiji water that only he could have come up with, along with him singing at the beginning of his set.

I crossed my fingers and clenched my fists and I looked on feeling like a soldier knowingly going into battle with no hope of ever returning or making it back home. My heart sank into my chest at this moment because it didn't really make sense to me that I would be going on next.

Looking towards the stage was intense because I kept thinking that I was a part of the audience, but in a couple of minutes that would all change and I would be the one they were looking at. I scanned and analyzed the club from the back and tried to think about how they would really react to me.

During the time we were in our comedy class, we had a supply teacher once that shared some of his experiences with us and mentioned some of the big names he and Evan got a chance to perform with.

Basically, with all the knowledge and memories he shared, he just wanted all of us to remember one small thing…

…

Before you go on stage? Breathe slowly counting to three, holding your breath in, and then say "fuck it," letting it all out – and hit that damn stage!

… "Fuck it!"

Matthew finished his set, leaving the stage, and Evan wasted no time when it came time to introducing me.

We created a simple path system so it wouldn't take us long to get on or off the stage, so once I breathed and let my fucks go, I marched straight to the stage from the back not having a damn clue as to what was gonna happen!

I walked up two or so steps with just a bottle of water in my hand and two folded pieces of paper with my routine on them facing sideways. Then I let out a crazy scream while rapidly pivoting myself so that I faced the crowd and just looked at everyone. The light was nice and bright on my whole face and body, but as much as it intimidated me, it also seduced me in a crazy, magical way.

While on stage, I made one side joke and the crowd went silent with nobody laughing at all. Once I witnessed that, I leaned into the mic and simply said, "That was a joke, you could laugh." Then the crowd laughed with me.

From that point on, I felt like I could maintain the crowd just as long as I kept my energy balanced. The feeling that I felt at that point in time was crazy, and half of my jokes were engraved into my head so I said them! One thing that was cool and interesting was the fact that I was naturally good with timing how and when my jokes would come out. If I didn't have any of that, I don't think anything I was saying would have come across the way I intended.

While performing on stage at most comedy clubs, lights at the top of the stage let you know how much time you still have: no lights mean you're good, but once lights start to flash, that means you need to wrap it up quick, and a steady light means you need to bounce asap! Halfway through my set while everything seemed to be going smoothly, I blanked out. I forgot everything I was going to say, so with no shame I grabbed my folded routine, glanced at it for a few seconds, then said my jokes again with even more confidence as I threw away my written piece of paper.

Near the end of my set, I basically told everyone to support people with Mood and Anxiety issues and to support anyone going through any sort of mental health related problems then ran off the stage to link with my crew.

Did I mention that because of Matthew killing his set I knew I'd be okay for the most part?

Joining back up with half of my crew and us all sharing our high from being on stage was insane!

I don't even know what order some of the others went in, but Matt Baxter might have been seventh. Although he had partied hard the night before, he still killed it. When it was almost time for Danny to head up on stage to do his set that we were all eager and excited to witness, I remember him standing right by the stairs to head down to the floor path that led to the stage and he was anxious as fuck worrying himself to death.

Seeing that made me get off the stool where I was sitting to walk over to him in order to help calm him down a bit. I feel no shame in saying I rubbed his shoulders to help him loosen up, then got him to do some fast, last minute breathing techniques that I hoped would help him relax. As he stood there in a daze similar to how I had been in that exact same spot thirty minutes before he was there, I gave him some words of encouragement and a fast pep talk. Then he ran towards the stage once his intro was done utilizing all his energy killing the crowd with his presence and jokes combined.

Danny always thought ahead, though, and already had his people in the crowd filming on the left, the right, and maybe even in the centre! I think he knew from jump that he was going to take the world by storm and shit, he did! And it all started there.

After his set, he came running off the stage and ran over to us and we hugged, man, and it was beautiful. We were all like soldiers coming over a hill one by one and waiting for our friends to safely make it over just like we did, but all we could do was is watch and encourage until they made it over. Sitting on my stool, I sat back and watched the remaining comics in our crew do their thing, and out of nowhere Danny came by being all joker-like and grabbed my leg, or maybe it was closer to my crotch?

Anyhow...

Once the show was completely over, all my friends that came out to see me came up to me telling me how much they liked my set, and it felt pretty good. One of my friends got me to stand back on stage and took some shots of me before we all eventually left the comedy club and went our separate ways. Me, Rebel and Sigz headed south to

Yonge and Eglinton to a pizza place and talked about a crazy party I missed before we all headed home.

Since I put so much energy into Sunday's performance, by the time Wednesday came around, I was pretty much burnt out to the point I really didn't want to do much, but that was the day of my Level C graduation show. Our show happened in the evening and I don't know how I might have looked on the outside, but inside, I was a damn wreck. My fellow classmates were freaking because this was after all going to be their first performance on stage...

Cameron noticed that one of our dear classmates was shaking like crazy from the anticipatory anxiety, so he got him to get on the stage first which I thought was insane, but Cameron always used to say to us that it was better to do something first and get it out of the way then to sit there and wait until your anxiety got worse if you were scared of doing something.

This same classmate and I were in one of the first scenes for the evening, too, and I thought everything he said was on point. As for myself, I don't think I was all put together for that show but then again, I was always the random wildcard within that group. Most of that Level C performance was a damn blur to me, and I tried to keep myself together enough to be mentally present until it was all done.

I don't know how I got through that performance, but I did... and with the help of my Level C crew that made all the difference in the world! With this show now winding down, we all agreed to head down the street to the local pub most of the Second City Crew usually went to after class.

"Oh my god, you guys were great! You were great!" It was none other than Cathleen who happened to emerge from the crowd of people to give me one of her crazy hugs as we made our way to the pub.

I hung around for a bit with my Level C crew, but I felt as though I couldn't hold on any longer and as if I was going to break down into tears. I let Cathleen know I was gonna head out, and abruptly let everyone in our group know that I was leaving. No one really knew what was going on with me at that moment, so how could anyone really know what was up? After that week, I got to rest a bit before Level D classes began, but I still felt unbalanced and I didn't have a lot of energy.

With all my successes, I had up to that point, all I kept worrying about was if I could even manage and get through a newer and higher class. I would have to wait to find out. With me waiting around until it was time for Level D classes to finally take place, I remember arriving early to class as I always did whenever I'm about to do something new.

It was funny and ironic, because it just so happened that Level D classes were going to take place in the exact studio I just had comedy classes in! It was pretty funny to me. Being that I was one of the only people in that room for a while, I think I might have taken some chairs out for others to sit in and then sat there in silence waiting for whichever instructor to come into the room.

My head must have been down but at the last moment I heard someone talking to themselves. I raised my head as they made a sharp right turn into the studio, then our eyes locked on to each other as our minds spoke to one another for three seconds. Who was it? It was fuckin' Frank McAnulty! My original Level C teacher. Although Frank loved me, I don't think he was ready to do another full-on class with my crazy ass.

We talked for a bit before he left to get some stuff, then one by one most of my Level C crew came into the studio and, similar to our Level C classes, we got shit up and popping in little to no time once Frank got back. Cameron had a whole new batch of new people for his Improv for Anxiety classes and was just down the hall from our studio, so he stuck his head in our class to make sure we were alright.

As our classes went on, I became more and more emotionally drained, so I started doing what had helped me out for my comedy performance — working the fuck out! I did this before class to loosen up and to make me feel confident. Building up the energy and being fearless enough to head to class was a war within itself, but I did it! And after classes were done, I felt good along with everyone else. After class I slowly developed my own little ritual of strolling on the streets by myself, processing how good class was and thinking about life in general.

I'd usually talk on the phone with my girl Soul around this time, seated on some concrete steps a few blocks west of Bay and King on the north side of the street.

I also used this time to think about how things would go along with me and the booklets I was putting together... the big and tall booklet specifically.

Similar to how I met my photographer, I also happened to meet another cool chick at another store who was going to help me. We talked, communicated and even met in person so she could show me what she put together with all the photos and documents I gave her. During our time going back and forth with each other, we slowly lost contact with one another since life... kind of happened, which left me back at phase one of trying to put a book together.

Feeling like I was stuck and not making much progress ever since Joanna and I took pictures, I came down hard on myself and somewhat felt like a failure. Level D classes were still going on and even though I felt like quitting every single time class was coming up, I somehow pushed myself to go through with it, and since I was consistently proving most of my negative self-doubt thoughts wrong, I always came out on top.

Frank always pushed and encouraged me in class and that made a big difference. He always seemed to like the crazy and wacky characters I'd play. Along with my classmates, I managed to go through and finish Level D and killed it with a big bang performance, and with one of my classmates singing her fuckin' lungs out, showing off her hidden yet beautiful talent!

This whole time, I was still feeling like I failed when it came to the booklet stuff until one day I put my foot down and decided that enough was enough! I grabbed the demo and mockup versions of the booklet that wasn't completed, examined and studied it, and remembered what program that girl used to try and make my book. I figured if I got the same program she used and followed her design, I'd have my own booklet within no time and then I would redo it all and make my own authentic version. Through that whole process, I actually learned a hell of a lot within a short amount of time, so I guess everything happened the way that it did for a reason.

I went through a shitload of revisions before even knowing what to do with these booklets, and while in the creative process of making them, I tried not to think of the end process because I had little to no idea how I was going to get them out as hardcopy books.

Pictures, PDF documents, putting pictures and text on the right pages... you'd figure it would all be so simple then, but it wasn't. Or maybe it was, and I was just too picky, but, I mean, I wanted my booklets to be perfect since I was sending them to a company to make a statement. And a personal and fashionable one at that. Eventually after a bunch of revisions, I finally built up the courage to call up my local business and printing store to ask them if they could help me out with making a booklet. "Sure, sure... come in!" the lovely voice said to me on the other end of the line.

Her name was Raina, and through trial and error, we finally got my booklets printed and looking oh so nice and crispy, which tripped me the fuck out. With no time to waste, I got around to sending them to the company I wanted to view one of my secret projects.

Ring-Ring-Ring, Ring-Ring-Ring...

"Hel...Hello?"

"Is this Andrew Marshall?" the voice on the other end of the line said.

"Yes, it is," I said back.

"Well, I'm calling from the HR department and I have your booklet right in front of me. This is pretty interesting," they said to me while flipping through my booklet.

"Thank you!" I said happily, then they replied "You're welcome. So... what do you want?"

I was caught off guard so I just said "clothes". "Okay, that's fine... now, what can you do for us?"

"Um...err, well... yes! I could help with marketing and branding! Stuff like that!"

"Interesting, okay well... look out for a call from our marketing department within nine or so minutes, okay?"

This all happened on a Tuesday or a Wednesday with my phone waking me up in the morning around nine-thirty in the middle of October. I was in a daze but once I answered my phone I went into game mode quick!

Even though I was shaken out of my sleep and confused, I was also filled with excitement so communicated the best that I could to this woman who was from the HR department of the clothing company I was trying to get in contact with. Once I got off the phone with her and waited for someone from this company to call me back as I was instructed, I finally got a call from someone within their marketing department and can you fuckin' believe that they wanted me to come in so that we could talk about their brand?

While talking to someone from the marketing team, we both agreed on a day and time for me to come into their head office for a meeting, which was around ten-thirty or so in the morning and scheduled two weeks from the time we first spoke.

I played it cool while I was on the phone with them, of course, but once I got off the phone and realized I was really going in for an actual meeting with them? I went into a panic! Because all I kept thinking about was how I was going to present myself and nail it since first impressions really do count at times.

It didn't take long for me to get over it or maybe I should say get past me freaking out before I went into thinking mode.

"That's it!"

I thought to myself that I could just write down all the neat ideas I had for their company and ways to help them improve. And since I had more time to think about what it was I wanted, I wrote some of that down along with ways I could help them out as well. By the time two weeks came around and the time for me to make a lasting impression was only a day away, I was shitting bricks! I of course talked to Dr. Pierotti about all of this, everything really, and even the head director to the clinic since he always gave me a lot of pointers.

The game plan that I had was simple. I without a doubt intended to go to the head office meeting with their clothing on me from top to bottom, along with my trusty messenger bag with ten or more printed copies of a list I made stating what I could do for them, how I could help, and what I wanted.

This period was pretty intense for a few other reasons too. I had just started up with Level E classes. This would be the final level and section to the short form Improvisation Program I was enrolled into at The Second City Training Centre. The stakes were high and I felt pressure no matter which direction I chose to look into. Level D had sixteen or so people in it, whereas Level E narrowed everything and everyone down to only twelve people in the group. The instructor I had for this class was the amazing Jason DeRosse who is a well-known and respected actor and improviser as well.

Waking up the day of the meeting was interesting, I set my alarm clock for seven-thirty in the morning and made sure I took a shower the night before along with packing my bag with an outline of what I wanted to talk about, accompanied with my demands written down. As usual, I taxied it to Kennedy Station then headed along my journey. This certain company was located in the northwest section of the city within the area of North York.

From Scarborough to downtown Toronto and then all the way up to North York, there was nothing but chaos, a sea of people and nonstop movement. I mean, I was used to seeing all this crazy shit in the afternoon or in the evening, but not in the morning since I rarely even got up to do anything around that time anymore. Feeling like I was pressed for time, I tried my hardest to jump on one train, then transfer and hop on to another, until I was on a bus headed further into the west end. I got off a few blocks from where we left.

For a few seconds, I felt like I was lost and not going into the right direction but then quickly realized I was dead on going the way I was supposed to, or just took a gamble hoping that my decision was the

188 | Andrew Marshall (Drew M)

right one, but once I slowly started to see a few other big name head offices within that same area, I felt like I was in the right place.

The decision I made was to head down this side street that seemed like it led to nowhere, but while walking along this side street I was sort of reluctant to continue further down since I increasingly thought I might have gotten off the bus a block or so too early, so at that moment I just stopped.

"This is dumb!" I said to myself while pulling out my phone to search for the full address and to see if I could get a picture image from the net of the place, and in doing all of this I slowly pulled the phone away from my face and realized I was standing in front of the head office all along. Since it was right across the street!

So, what did I do beyond that point? I waited...I stood there clueless in the fall chilliness and waited until it came down to the final minutes before I figured I should casually make my way to the building.

I increasingly also kind of felt uncomfortable being' this big black dude standing in front of a head office staring at it for more than fifteen minutes, so I figured I might as well go before Security came out of nowhere to ask me questions. Looking directly at this big head office, I crossed the road, then stopped as I got on to the sidewalk. I then slowly walked straight towards their big main doors and opened one of them.

Once I got myself past those doors, I was faced with another door. This one single door was somewhat like the first but in order to get beyond that point you'd need to get buzzed in, which is what I already knew since HR and the marketing department had already warned me about it and told me to basically buzz the front desk girl.

I stood there for two minutes observing these big windows all around me, then looked on my left since that showed a bit of what was happening beyond the doors. I then eventually buzzed myself in with the code they gave me.

"Ring-Ring-Ring, Ring-Ring-Ring*

The phone rang out until it went to the front desk voicemail, and I might have left a message but from that point on, I waited at the door and told myself to maybe try again within a few minutes.

Right as I was waiting, though, this stylish middle-aged white dude who seemed like he didn't have a care in the world dressed sleek and stylish in a grey business suit walked out of nowhere and opened the door for me with a smile on his face and told me to take a seat in the waiting area once I told him I was there for a meeting.

After introducing myself and shaking his hand, he vanished, and I walked over to the waiting area and sat on this really comfy and cushy black leather couch. Again, I started to observe my surroundings.

The floor looked like it was made out of marble or something resembling marble with the logo of the company on it along with a coffee table right in front of me. In front of me and to my left, there were stairs for people to go up or down in my direction. As I sat there and took in all that I saw, I honestly nearly busted out laughing because the thoughts that were going on inside of my head at that moment in time were... "Drew, how the fuck did you get your ass in here? You really did it? If you pulled this off, that's crazy, you need help, you sick fuck!"

I knew I had to compose myself and seem somewhat professional, so after joking around and laughing with myself for a few minutes, I got myself together and really, if I made it this far? I wouldn't wanna have someone from the marketing team come down to the waiting area to see a big black dude laughing with himself.

"Hey, I'm Crystal! Are you Andrew?" Right when I pulled myself together, this woman came out speed walking on my right side introducing herself to me.

"Yes, I am Andrew!" I said with a big smile.

"It's so nice to finally meet you. Come with me," Crystal said.

So I said, "It's nice to meet you too. And sure, lead the way!"

Crystal led the conversation of course and rush walked us past this door, that door, and before I knew it, I was fuckin' lost not knowing which way was the way out.

"Yea, this place is like a maze... ha-ha-ha!" Crystal said to me as we kept turning left, then right, then left again until we made it to this huge office space area with everyone on computers, then again left down this hallway which took us straight to the marketing office. Well, one of them, anyway.

This was my moment of truth and something I was thinking about over and over AND over again since I played out the scenario too many times in my head of how it would all be like... similar to death or sex. What I imagined was is over ten people in a room eying me down and asking me questions about what I thought and asking me about my booklet. Crystal led me into this medium sized room and told me to get comfortable and take a seat and asked if I wanted anything to drink but I said no.

"Okay Andrew, hold tight and I'll be right back and we'll start this meeting process, okay?" Crystal said.

So, with a smile, I said, "Sounds good to me."

I was stuck with my thoughts of what would happen next while I heard muffled mutters coming from the main work area and from another room beside the room I was in. I just stared at the big office table where I was seated and zoned out, then realized that there was a folder there with my booklet in it and a yellow sticky note slapped on the front almost like they were studying and breaking it all down.

Eight minutes later or so, I heard movement coming back into my direction so I tried to be as ready as I could ever be and braced myself for the unknown as the movement got closer and closer and...

"Hey, Andrew, I'm back! This is Nero and he'll be helping me with our meeting today, okay?" Crystal went on to say, and then Nero smiled at me, introducing himself as I got up and out of my chair to do the same. Then we all gradually got ourselves comfortable and seated with Nero on my left and Crystal on my right.

"So, Andrew, I want to first tell you that we're very impressed with the booklet that you put together for us. Can you tell us a bit more about that?" Nero went on to say.

I looked directly at him and said, "I love you guys! If not for your company, I would not have changed the way that I did. So, because of that, I would love to help you guys out." I also let them know they needed to have a stronger presence and to market to a hipper audience.

While I was talking passionately about their brand with a big golden smile on my face, I noticed that Nero gave Crystal a look... Now at that time I can admit that I was way too naive to the whole marketing world, but some of what I was saying in front of both these head marketers was like me indirectly taking jabs at Crystal and how she holds it down without me even knowing it.

"Oh, oh... yeah, well, we're actually doing what you are talking about, Andrew, we want to market it to those people and we are!" Crystal's fun and warm demeanor kind of changed up the more that I spoke with her having a counter statement for all the good I was saying and again I never really understood why?

Nero then stopped everyone from talking and said, "Andrew? I want you to know one thing, one of the main reasons why we even called you back is because you said our brand changed your LIFE. Now, that's golden!"

I let them know that I always went out of my way to mention their clothing and company to people on the street I felt would benefit from their store as well as observing people's style while I was on the street.

"Oh, Andrew we do that too," Crystal said with a big smile on her face.

The dynamics of our meeting at that point seemed like it was me talking to Nero, who was genuinely interested in all that I did and all I wanted to do, but Crystal seemed like she was holding onto and/or losing her job with each statement that came out of my mouth without me even knowing the true intensity of all that I was actually saying. We talked about a few other things and near the end of our meeting, Crystal said, "Okay, well, we're going to have to move a few things around, but, Andrew, if you're on board with us, we would like to make you our brand ambassador for our company. Sounds good?"

"That's amazing! And I'm down for it, of course," I said back to Crystal while getting up and showing off my jeans, shirt and even my jacket, which was all bought from their store.

One last thing I remember me saying while we were all still in this meeting room together was, "Oh, along with being a brand ambassador, I'd love to eventually help out within the marketing department as well."

When I said that, Nero calmly turned his head to Crystal without moving his body at all and gave Crystal another look. It was a look straight out of the movies as if to say... "Bullseye, you just got checkmated! What, oh what, shall you do, girl? This kid is coming for your job... ha!"

Soon after that, all three of us carried on with regular chitchat until I took the cue to end the meeting. I stood-up and thanked them for allowing me to come in and giving me the opportunity to become a part of their team. Nero shook my hand and thanked me for coming to the meeting, then made his way out since he had to split anyhow to take care of other obligations, but he let me know that Crystal would take it from there.

With Crystal and I now only in the meeting room, she thanked me again for coming in and expressed to me that they needed all the help they could get because their sales weren't going up. We slowly made our way out from the meeting room and she quickly said, "Hey, do you want to see a little tour of our place?"

"Sure, I'd love to, man. Show me how it all goes down."

This office was a crazy maze with small hallways leading into bigger, wide open spaces, and I even got to check out their newly built photo studio for all their models and press shoots.

After my tour was done, Crystal gave me her business card and told me to keep in touch, but also reminded me to catalog some of the clothes that I wore along with some hip words to say about them and for me to email it all back to her by the next week. They also warned me that if my social media was too crazy or politically incorrect, I might want to clean it up before we got things started.

On the performance side of things, my Level E classes were stressful as fuck with me eventually going into autopilot mode, which made me become more and more numb as the classes went by.

The first few classes of Level E were a cinch, but it got more challenging as it went along. I mean, a part of me liked that and viewed it all as a big hurdle I had to get over in order to prove things to myself and to those that were cheering me on to finish.

Some nights while I would be in bed thinking about class, life in general and other shit, I often reasoned myself out of not wanting to finish, but it's so true what they say about mind over matter situations because a lot of the time when I would feel like that or would lie in my bed thinking of the negative, soon after, I would envision my life right after getting over it all and how good it would all feel.

I can't even lie… thinking about me working with the clothing company and being their brand ambassador really got me going and made a lot of my bad days seem like it was all worth it, and that's the same for anything, right? If you sit there and think about how you will be like and how everything will go down to a T, it makes it that much more real.

The colours, the people, textures and even down to the damn smell!

With the brand ambassador stuff on the table, though. I had doubts and thoughts of if I was even cut out for it at all? But because of how much I had already done, it just made this seem like another challenge that I would take on and conquer. With the last level of The Second City program, the graduation show that we would perform would be done on the mainstage at the main Second City building. This was always at the back of my mind but I never tried to think about it much since there was really no point in frying my brain any more than it already was.

I looked forward to it but dreaded it all at once. It all seemed like a crazy time and after a while, I started to grow my hair out to rebel as if to say to myself, "Okay, you're in a rough spot right now, grow your shit out until you can defeat this!"

For the three or so classes we had left, we started up with rehearsals again and talked about how our performance would play out and did rehearsal after…rehearsal. Fuck, around that time, I was just running on dreams and aspirations because mentally and physically, I was already burnt out. I made sure Crystal got an email with pictures of my clothing along with me saying slick things about them. I managed to fling out my clothes on my bed and snap shot after shot, then uploaded everything to a file sharing site ready to send to her.

Fresh out of class and strolling the streets, I vividly remember making my way towards King Station around nine-forty-five p.m. Then I stopped and sent Crystal the email with all the pictures I took of my clothes along with catchy sayings. Then I got on the train heading back home. Weeks later, tossing and turning in bed was all I could do knowing that the day of our performance would be the next morning.

My stomach turned, and each time I was close to drifting off to sleep, I just couldn't. It was like I was getting jolts and surges going through my body with me not being able to process reality or make much sense of what I was hours away from doing. I stayed like that for the whole night going into the morning with my stomach retching. Luckily for me I didn't have anything in my system because if I had, I would have been throwing up all day. The thought of not going even crossed my mind and I thought of so many different excuses to use, but that spark got me again and when it gets you, it gets you...

When performing on the main stage, you have to dress up a bit. They just wanted us to look classy, so I went out and bought myself a black dress shirt which I actually got the day of our performance. With hardly any sleep and with a fucked-up stomach, I walked into my favorite store and purchased a black dress shirt with a smile, then left in the taxi and made my way downtown and waited in front of the Training Centre for the rest of my crew.

When we all finally came, we did some last-minute preparations before heading over to the main stage. This performance took place on December fourteenth, two-thousand-and-fourteen. I told my sister about it and my dad, but I don't even think I told anyone else. If I did, I never bothered to remind them about the fact my graduation performance was taking place that day.

When we *entered da stage*, we sat in the back and watched the crew that was on before us and I remember my feeling pretty clear... I had this not wanting to be on the stage feeling but with a sick comfort to it, like it was speaking to me, saying, "Well, where else would you be? Of course, you'd be here, you sick fuck!"

By the time the crew who were on stage finished up, we all assembled backstage in the main stage greenroom, which was inspiring because that was where we got to see all the pictures of the past famous performers who graced the stage, so it added even more of a sense of pride to it. While backstage, we hyped each other up and patted each other on the back while we screamed, getting as excited as we could before we were instructed to leave the room and hit the stage.

One by one as we hit the stage, it was insane, intense, and a beautiful feeling and I can't speak on behalf of everyone else, but for myself, it was an out of body experience! As usual we were all paired up for different games and scenes, and the partner I had was one of my VERY supportive classmates Terris Bueller, who was already doing his comedy and Improv thing over in another city a few hours southwest from Toronto called Hamilton.

Within the lineup and order of things, Terris and I were one of the last pairs to go up on stage to do scenes together. So as other pairs from our amazing team went up on stage, it felt like this twisted, happy, scared yet what am I doing with my life type of feeling. While watching my crew members on stage, I kept thinking about the simple fact that eventually I would have to go up on that stage just like them. As time went ticking down and as scenes finished up just as fast as they started, it finally came down to me and my homie Terris.

Once our names were announced for us to make our way towards the stage, I don't think I felt my body any more, but something came over me and I said, "Fuck it! This is what I do!"

"Let's go buddy!" Terris said as he got off his chair and ran towards the stage, and I went running up on stage in the same fashion.

"Fuck," I said to myself while on stage… then I also said to myself, "These show lights really are addictive and feel like nothing else in this world." The bright lights and the whole big giant stage to ourselves felt too good, and although it was nerve-wracking with everyone watching us, it was hard not to enjoy being in the spotlight at the same time.

With so much adrenaline pumping, scenes were just flying by with Terris and I. The very last scene we did together was this game called "Sounds like a song." Now with this game, you carry on with dialog back and forth, keeping things within the subject line and within the scene environment until someone from the crowd yells "sounds like a song." At that point, whatever your last sentence was, you, gotta sing about it.

I remember singing about Game of Thrones and being one of the characters, which was funny because I never watched that show a day in my fuckin' life so I just winged it. But that was my mentality on stage, just to wing it, and Frank always used to tell me even if you don't know what's going on within a scene to always own that bitch! Own it like your life depended on it and go all the way through!

We both sang, and then near the end I started to rap as the audio engineer cued up some beats for me to do my thing, and at the same time the bottom front stage lights went all funky with different colours (downstage). Then I got everyone to clap their hands as I rapped.

After all that was done, the whole crew hit the stage to do some long-form scenes.

Near the end of it all, I remember standing on stage with my crew and feeling so proud, and afterwards getting our Improvisational certificates. I then saw my teacher Cameron who came to support us, and I gave him a big hug as he hugged me back! Then we all headed over to a nearby pub to eat and celebrate until the late evening.

CHAPTER 15

Randomized

With the Christmas holidays over and me still being on a huge high from completing Second City's Improvisational short-form program, I was gearing myself up to start doing business with Crystal and the company. I emailed her to ask her if she received any of my emails with my sayings and shots of my clothing.

I finally heard back from her after emailing her, but she basically just let me know she got my emails and wished me a Merry Christmas since I had wished her one as well. I let her know that I was very eager to do business with her and the company, but beyond that point right there, our communication became fickle and nonexistent. I mean, a part of me was hurt while another part of me was still banking on this whole situation panning out, so I told myself I would only wait until the end of January or March to see what might happen.

When I had the meeting with Crystal and Nero, she had let me know that they wanted my help with rolling out their spring campaign and whatnot so I slowly found it to be odd that if they wanted me for something that was going to happen in the spring that I wasn't being contacted.

The less I heard from her or the company itself, I started to do my own research on how and when companies, especially clothing companies, rollout with their campaigns. Then I realized that spring campaigns usually take place in March, and months like January are pretty much the months for seeing how much had been made and selling off as much of the leftovers as possible.

"Okay, so you're either gonna work for them or not. Head back over to Second City for another course. Or head over to school to see if you can gain knowledge about starting up your own business to see if that can tie into public speaking at all."

Yup, that's what my plan was.

The burnout I felt from Second City, though, had me wanting to take a few months off, and with all these different things circulating around my mind, I never really knew which one I wanted to do first anymore. And with no company contacting me, that plan within all of my plans didn't seem like such a good... plan... anymore as the weeks went by. Most of January leading into March was just a lot of me sitting around, waiting and looking into school and at programs like academic upgrading, social work, public relations, and business workshops.

I had a shitload of ideas, but I wasn't really grounded with or in any of them, and out of everything I could have focused on, the idea that seemed the furthest away was the one I wanted the most. Maybe I felt passionate about that so much because I put a lot of time and effort into it with my books and all, plus after an interview at a head office, you kind of want to pursue that.

March two-thousand-and-fifteen.

Nothingness...

I wasn't doing much, my mood was fucked up, well, jacked up, and since it was cold with me getting little to no sunlight, I was kind of looking for excuses for me to think about taking myself out. Out of this world!

With me not hearing back from Crystal at ALL at this point, I casually went on to their website to see if anything had changed since remodeling a lot of their online presence was also something that was in the works. And to my surprise as I checked out what they had going on, all I saw is their spring campaign being rolled out nice and fresh. My eyes kind of popped out, and my heart started beating with me laughing at it all, and believe it or not, I said, "Oh fuck, I gotta write about this," to myself.

A few days later, I even got a little promotional telegram that came to my house since I was on their mailing list, with a similar promotional layout resembling what I saw online. Again, I just laughed, took some pictures, and sent them to a few of my friends through text on my phone and they tripped out. It was fucked up and funny at the same time because what this company did was rip off the whole presentation I had showed to them and rolled it out with their own shit, leaving me happy and stupid in the dark! But I played it cool and went into game mode, knowing damn well that I had to fire back with something as well as thinking up a strategy. I emailed Crystal directly as I always did, and to make sure that she got back to me, I made sure my email went to the HR department and the head of the company.

I let her know that I saw their campaign and that I liked it, and specifically let her know that I loved how much attention they paid to detail since one of the models they used looked like a slimmer version of myself, and again I found all this shit funny because it's damn good writing material, ha! After sending my professional yet cheeky email to her, she actually did write back to me and covered her ass once again. But I was fine with all of this. I learned a fine lesson with all of that, though, and some of those close to me told me to take heed as well.

Never give away your ideas! Speak less, and listen more!

smiles

Sigz/Shaking your Rump

In the middle of April, Sigz was gearing up to throw yet another one of his crazy parties that he got into the habit of doing even since we were going to Second City in two-thousand-and-fourteen. His humble beginnings with throwing parties gradually became bigger and bigger as he gained more experience, so it was only right that this epic party he was about to put on would be located a few blocks west of Queen and Spadina in a nice, chill and very lush velvety place.

The party was on a Saturday and I for sure wanted to make my way down to support him, and since I got enough sleep and felt up to it, I was ready to get it poppin'. Earlier that day, I was hanging out with my dad and ran some errands with him since Saturdays were the days my dad usually got out to take care of some personal business. Since it was so nice out, I said to my dad that we should walk in a nearby park path to get in some fresh air and to relax and chill, but being that it was too sunny outside, he said to me that maybe he'd wanna go later in the evening since it would be cooler than without the sun being so blistering.

When I finally arrived back home from following my dad around while he did his errands, I might have cleaned up my room a little bit, talked to Sigz, and kept looking at my phone to see what was going to be happening that night. By the time evening hit, I felt a mixture of anxiety and excitement since I was thinking about how crazy this party was going to be, so I took a shower, fixed myself up, then headed into my basement to work out for twenty minutes or so to feel on top of the world. Once I was done and came back upstairs, my dad screamed out to me from his room, "Aight, Andrew, soon come," in his chill Jamaican accent.

Whenever my dad is ready to do something, he'll usually just scream for me or say, "I'm ready," so at that point I got my shoes on, then waited for him to come downstairs to the main floor so that we could head to this conservation area I had been telling him about for a while.

Once we were up and about and on the road with my dad behind the wheel, we finally got to the conservation area which was really only a fifteen-minute drive away. My dad pulled up to a parking spot as we arrived then got out and walked down this steep road path with nothing but trees on both sides and with a huge hill directly in front of us.

"Where the fuck is dis, Andrew?" my dad said rapidly in a serious but funny way.

I said, "Well this is the damn area I've been meaning to show you, man!"

It was a goal of mine to get my dad out there because I wanted him to be relaxed and calm so that he wouldn't stress over the small things in life, and we even got to talk a bit about father and son stuff. After me and my dad made it all the way down and to the end of this path, there were train tracks. We crossed them and tried to make our way up towards where the hill was, but in doing so, we had to get past a few obstacles which we did before finally making it one fourth of the way up this hill, but it didn't take long for us to eventually turn back.

Heading down the hill then past all the obstacles, we crossed the train tracks again as I made a twisted joke about people wanting to lay themselves on the tracks in order to die... since I frequently used to think like that myself.

Passing the tracks and finally getting back onto the big path so that we could walk the whole stretch of it until we got back to my dad's car, we randomly bumped into some conservatory rangers, I guess you could say, and what were they doing? They were randomly barbequing so, being the person that I am, I ran over since they seemed friendly. They passed me over some chicken they were heating up along with a hot dog.

"Why you takin' dem food? Do you know them?" My dad said as I ran back over to him as we continued to walk this path. "Bwoy, you must be mad, not me...sir, mi nah take food from people mi nah know." But I laughed it off and said, "It's all good."

Reaching the middle of this path was strange because it was

basically in the middle of being somewhere and nowhere all at the same time. We were as far down as the path would go, then after a while, it curved back up. So while we kept walking, I noticed this older white dude behind us in the distance but he was gaining quickly so by the time we were halfway up this path, he actually caught up to us. We all started talking.

"Hey," I said to him so he smiled and said "hey" back.

We then started talking about the conservation area then he got into how he's been doing this same walk for years, plus would ride it with his bike, which I believed since he did have his bike with him. My dad asked him how old he was and this guy turned to us and said he was seventy years old! But he looked as though he was in his mid-to late fifties!

"Heh, these kids in the Olympics are a bunch ah pussies, they get scratched up and complain and stop playing after one little scrape," he said while laughing. He also disclosed that he was a farmer which made even more sense since he was in really good physical shape.

By the time we got to the top of the path, we shook hands and parted ways. Since I had to head to the train station for Sigz's jam, my dad gave me a ride over to the nearest station which was just fifteen to twenty minutes away from where we were. But that older farmer we crossed paths with really wasn't joking about him riding or walking that path at all because once we finally drove off, who did we see? The same farm dude and he was already one major intersection and a half ahead of us until we caught up with him!

Now, that's crazy.

When my dad finally dropped me off at the station, I gave him a dap aka a fist bump then got out of the car as he said, "You know, some sick fucks coulda came out them bushes we walked along, right?"

He laughed then I laughed as I waved and headed into the station as he drove off.

Doing the usual Scarborough to Downtown mission was the task at hand, and since I had to travel a bit further to the west this time, I made sure I had enough time. I mean, I somewhat always freak when it comes to making it somewhere on time but I was just wanting to make sure everything was okay.

Finally making it all the way Downtown, I didn't get off at Yonge Station, but I instead got off three stations later which brought me to Spadina Station. From there, I made my way off the train, then to the streetcars, but they were out of service so I freaked before reading a sign stating that streetcar services would be down for a while and directing people to the bus terminal, which was upstairs, so they could catch the detour bus, which is exactly what I did.

I kept watching my phone over and over just to make sure everything was still a go, and was also communicating with Rebel since I asked her to meet with me down at the party. When the detour bus finally came, me along with everyone else who waited for this alternative to the streetcars hopped on and just let the bus driver do his thing. Everything was nice and smooth and cool – that is, until this bus made a sharp, unpredictable right-turn which threw me off along with some others in the bus too!

Feeling confused and unsure about our route, I got out of my seat and ran up to the front of the bus to ask the driver what the hell he was doing? But this girl beat me to it and our driver reassured us that we were still headed towards the same section that the streetcar would have gone, and that the bus was a detour bus for a reason.

It wasn't exactly in the evening any more, it was nine something at night, and everything was dark all around so detours at night do look confusing as fuck and almost seem like you're headed into a psychotic episode. Being that I was jumpy and didn't want any more surprises, I figured I saw my stop right ahead so requested the bus to stop. Once I got out, I realized I was one major intersection away from where I really needed to be. I was in panic but played it cool all at once. I saw a cabbie so flagged him down as he semi-stopped for me asking me where I needed to go. But once I told him it was just down the street, this madman told me to go fuck myself as he sped off while coming inches away from running over my right foot!

"Fuck this shit," I said to myself and didn't let that stop me. I was at Spadina and Dundas so waited for another detour bus which didn't come, so I decided to speed walk south until I got to Queen and Spadina.

Along this walk, a detour bus did in fact pass me, but I didn't care. I kept speed walking, maneuvering myself around people bobbing and weaving until I got to that intersection. You'd figure that once I got to Spadina and Queen that everything would have been cool from that point on, but I had to walk a few blocks west bobbing and weaving through the night-time party crowd and I mean, what can I say? They were looking for their spot just like I was looking for mine.

When I finally got to where I needed to be, I saw Security outside, so I gave them my name checked myself in. Once I got in, I casually walked all the way to the back of this lounge and greeted my boy Sigz, and surprise, surprise, who else did I actually end up seeing? PARTY!

Seeing Party was a blessing since I never really saw him much being that we weren't doing Second City classes anymore.

Another person who I ended up seeing right when I got in was Kat. Kat was one of the DJs that were going to spin for the night, along with the headliner whose name was Plastician.

Plastician was a Bass, Grime, Dubstep and Juke DJ based out of the UK so I couldn't wait to hear him spin. Kat was a hometown favorite that all of us loved since she spins that raw House shit along with good Bass music so, waiting for her to do her thing was cool too. When everything was getting set up with last minute preparations, I saw this tiny but cute figure walk into the darkly lit lounge. It was Rebel, of course! She gave me a hug, I gave her a hug, and everyone else greeted her.

Shaking your Rump was the movement that Sigz started up to put on events along with putting out music as well. Little by little, when more people started coming into the lounge, it was a beautiful thing to see the venue get so packed up!

Rebel and I were dancing all crazy in the beginning since the DJ at that time was playing some pretty chill and sexy UK two-step songs that were fitting for dancing your backside off to, and I mean that's exactly what we did. We all did it! By the time this venue was nicely packed, Kat stepped onto the turntable decks to do her thing...

Kat has always been interesting to me since her playing style always seemed to cheer me the fuck up and get me hyper! While watching her spin, me along with everyone else fell into a euphoric trance... and the fact that she traditionally used two turntables and a mixer? That was a win right there!

By the time it was Plastician's time to head up on stage, the crowd was already twisted, so when he started to play the energy went even higher. What I'm trying to say is Kat killed it, and Plastcian murdered it. That's how Shaking your Rump does though.

A week later after experiencing that crazy night, I felt a bit more motivated but I also had all these different plans and ideas circulating throughout my head. By this point any hopes I had of working with that clothing company were dead. It was like beating a dead horse so I moved on and away from that for the time being. I realized that I was putting all of my talents in the wrong places and it didn't feel too good because I wasn't getting much back in return, so I decided to focus on stuff that would benefit me.

Once again, I looked into school programs and even workshops for people who would like to start up their own business. While researching on the net, I stumbled upon a few programs that were of interest to me so I started sending out emails and even started calling the direct lines for some of these programs so that I could speak to someone in regards to their programs and state what my situation was.

With all my calling around and emailing people, things naturally just seemed to go into this strange direction and I just took it for what it was, really. I ended up at a pretest at eight in the morning on a Tuesday or Wednesday to see if I was ready and the perfect fit for an Academic Upgrading program. I also enrolled myself into that business workshop.

Before going to any sort of pretest though, I attended an info session at the college to get a better understanding of what or how you even get into the Academic Upgrading program in the first place. With all of that going on, everything else was also going on with this business workshop and I don't know... I had a funny feeling about that workshop but I went head first into it anyhow, keeping in mind that if I actually got into both programs, I'd have to make my decision as to which one I would stick with since I couldn't do both at the same time.

The Academic Upgrading info session instructor was a bitch and figured she owned me after me coming to one session. She made comments on my phone saying she didn't think my greetings were professional and tried to intimidate me, forcing me to join the program, but not only did I not change my greeting to what she wanted, I made a new and improved version of the older one!

I ended up calling her back after she left a stern voice message on my phone asking whether or not I would like to be in the program? So, I called her back but only got her voice message saying to put everything on hold. It's crazy because based off my pretest, I actually got into the program too.

With me going the business workshop route, I don't really know what I expected. I guess I expected them to encourage me to do what was already there in my head. It was already all there... all the information and everything I generally wanted to do was already in my head. This program was located south of Yonge and King and started at nine-thirty in the morning.

Because of my crazy emails, the instructor for this workshop couldn't wait to see me and I couldn't wait to see her. When I finally made it on the first day, heading all the way up to the twenty-first floor of this undisclosed building, it was all love!

You know something, though? You know when you go into a class or situation and you damn well KNOW it's just not for you and that you won't really get much out of it? That's how I felt from the first day of class, and that feeling never left me nor could I shake it off.

I always considered myself an applied person, so sitting in class and listening to someone talk about how to run a business when I could simply get the fuck out there and do what I need to do regardless of if it works or not was how I saw things. When my instructor talked, I retained the information but hardly wrote anything down. Half the time when everyone was talking in class, I was already halfway zoned out thinking to myself about how I was actually going to execute my own ideas.

This program lasted for more than six weeks and it came with homework that I never really took seriously. Nearing the end of this workshop, it was mandatory that each and every person within our group do a presentation in front of the class. On the day of our presentation when it was finally my turn to go up, the instructor, she had a smirk on her face since she knew I was probably going to say something messed up.

I slowly made my way up to the front of the class with nothing in my hands and with my back pressed to the wall in this brightly lit office meeting room, and I took a deep breath and said,

"I would like to get into public speaking in order to stop people from wanting to blow their brains out and so that I can get hot chicks."

The class went dead. Then one of my classmates, Ashley, broke down and started laughing all crazy and she blurted out, "I don't care what you guys think! That shit was funny! I can relate to that shit right there! That's some reality!"

Some in class were shocked that I said all that but I let people know that I wouldn't be saying' all this crazy shit if I didn't come from that type of background. I mean, to me it was obvious that someone talking about all that would without a doubt know a thing or two about it.

Then I went on to say, "Why do you think I went to Second City? This crazy shit can be funny, man!"

I was glad when that workshop was done, though, because I didn't see it doing anything significant for me.

Right after that, I headed back into the direction of conventional school and right back to the college I wanted to go to in the first place, except this time I said "fuck you" to Academic Upgrading and went straight for the English assessment for them to grade me to see if I would be capable of performing at a college level and if I would be eligible for the program I actually wanted to get into, which was Graphic Design and also Art and Design Foundation.

I moved in that direction because I was making all these crazy booklets for these companies, and figured I might as well go to school for this, see if I could network and try to get myself a job working at a marketing firm.

Heading back to this college at around nine in the morning to do an assessment was what ended up happening, and that morning was interesting because I ended up complimenting a girl, then got her number at Kennedy Station. Then By the time I got above ground and towards the school, she sent me a message saying, "Thank you for the sweet compliments, you have a lot of balls." That alone right there gave me enough motivation to want to make sure I passed my assessment!

When I got to the waiting room, I saw a white room filled with others similar to myself and everyone seemed to be shitting bricks since they were thinking the same thing as me: "I just wanna get this over with!"

Once everything was more settled and organized, someone came into this waiting room to get us, and I was glad because they had some fucked-up cartoon playing on this small TV which was situated right dead Centre in the room while we all watched in silence with a few laughs here and there. One by one, they started to get people and sort us by what types of tests we were assigned to do based off the requirements for the programs we were trying to get into. There was this cute Asian girl and this stylish chill black kid that I ended up standing with before I was called into do my test. I asked what their names were, wished them luck and gave both of them daps and smiled before walking away since I was called in, to do my assessment test.

"Okay...come with me Andrew," one of the assessment assistants said as I let them lead the way to my test room.

The test that I did required a lot of reading and dissection of grammar with a bit of mind fuckery ... Then there was a five-hundred-word essay that had to be done on whichever subject you wanted to write about.

I chose to write about Hip Hop and how it started. Since I spent so much time writing and putting together all these booklets, I felt more than confident that I could write an okay essay.

"Andrew? Andrew?" the same assistant said to me.

I said, "Yes?"

I had an hour and some more extra time to finish up the test they had me do, which was done on a computer, then right after that I started doing the essay portion of this English assessment, which was all done within a room with nothing to really help or guide me except for a dictionary booklet as their camera looked down on me to see if I was cheating.

Then she said, "Congratulations, you passed!"

"The hell!? Are you serious!? I said to the assistant and she smiled and said, "Yes, you passed!"

I was all happy, she was happy and we were happy!

After seeing my results, I realized that I was actually getting marked for certain sections within the test which I figured I wasn't even going to be marked on, and with the essay, I got seventy-five percent if I remember correctly. I remember strutting out of the assessment Centre like I was hot shit and past a few students feeling like I was just like them if not better since I knocked my test out of the park.

I also got a flashback about how hard it was to actually get to this school in the first place ... before I wouldn't dare step foot in front or past this school, but now? I was walking through the hallways feeling like myself because I just finished a test that I passed for one of the programs offered at their school! It all felt good. But one thing was for sure... none of this would have been possible if I didn't first confront riding on the train, and also heading over to The Second City Training Centre in order for me to feel a bit more confident about doing things like this.

Taking the test didn't even seem that intimidating as how I viewed it in the past, and when I finally made my way out of the front entrance of the college, I made sure to strut my shit down the street while looking at my phone so I could reply to that girl I picked up earlier that day.

With a big smile, I sent her a text saying, "Hey, I finished up my assessment and I passed! I feel damn good! Well, I'll talk to you tonight... peace *with a smile*."

I think I may have hung around the area for a bit just to collect myself and to analyze the last few months of my life up to that point because for as real as it was, some of it didn't seem real because I couldn't believe that I was confronting something that was so bothersome to me in the past. I actually attempted to head into this same school in the past... but once I walked along the hallways and saw the lockers, that was enough to trigger me into saying, "fuck this place!"

Then I had walked out. But not this time, since I was beyond victorious!

With my assessment done, I kind of felt like that was all I really had to do in order to get into my programs of choice, but I was terribly mistaken since there would be a hell of a lot more that I would experience. Every other day I was getting letters in the mail from this college and they were giving me codes, passwords, and just keeping me up to date on my progress in regards to whether I got into my programs. I had to sign in here, sign in there, and I had a couple of passwords along with me coughing up five hundred dollars to reserve my spot for my programs.

When I finally figured out how to work my passwords and how to accept an offer into the program of my choice that actually accepted me, it made things a bit smoother. Oh, and sorry... we just went through March, April, May, June, and July and getting into August... and that cute girl that I picked up on the day of my assessment? She never really responded back to my text reply, but I didn't care since my mind was on school.

Since I got into the Art and Design Foundation program, I started thinking about how I was going to fund all of this financially, so I ended up going to the financial department at this school which depressed me because I waited for quite a while and had some time to reassess my life.

Because of a situation I got myself into and thankfully out of, I later found out that I couldn't take the financial aid route. And that was okay with me because waiting long hours in an office wasn't my thing. I didn't let any of that stop me, though. From that moment on, I made up my mind that I would attempt to pay for school on my own, so I contacted that same office and tried to work out payments in installments.

Going through so many hoops and continuously signing into my school account, I don't really know how I felt. My thought process was like, "Yeah, you can do this!" with a mixture of, "Let's try this out and see what happens."

One thing that put me at ease was the fact that I enrolled myself into their disability services office so that I could get some type of support along my journey, be it some sort of encouragement or more time for assignments. I was assigned to a support worker, too, and I got to sit down and talk with her a week before school started. The worker I had was this really caring female who I will just call "Care."

Care really put me at ease, and she was one of those people that really were born to be compassionate. It's a true gift and she had it without a doubt! On my first day of class, I had remembered to prep myself the day before and to make sure that anything and everything I would need would be in my trusty messenger bag. Doing my usual commute, I made it down to my class but was ten to twenty minutes late from what I remember.

I already knew my way around this school, though, since I made damn sure I knew where everything was since not knowing sometimes would make me feel uneasy.

Because I was doing an Art and Design Foundation program which was related to and actually connected with getting into the Graphic Design program, most of my classes would be taking place in the artsy building, and I loved that.

When I arrived, and walked right into my class, everyone was already seated. I casually walked across the front of this room, then speed walked while ducking my head, then just stood there in front of two kids looking down at them as they looked up.

"Here you go," one of them said to me while passing me a chair so I could sit down. I thanked him then ran back to the other side of the room, placing my chair down since there was more room there, then I just sat with this painting stand with a big sheet of paper right in front of me.

While our teacher was talking, I scanned the room a couple of times to scope out who was in this program with me, and I don't know... I just didn't feel like I fit in.

Again, I started zoning out and thinking about my life.

"And now, class, we are going to learn how to draw a pear."

Once I heard those words and her sentence, it impacted me and caused a chain reaction of thought and I knew that I might not be lasting long within this program.

Once class ended, I walked around, checking out some of the art in this classroom before I left.

I set up a session with my support worker within the week that same day, too, since I didn't really feel like staying around anymore.

Within a couple of days, I finally met up with Care and told her how class was and how I felt. I gave her a brief rundown of my history and she understood where I was coming from and hinted at the fact that maybe I was a creative, caring person and doing things that were creative yet helpful might be the direction for me.

The more I talked to her and especially about school, the more I realized I didn't want to be there, and she seemed to understand what or where my direction was more than I did.

My second ever class was on a Thursday within this same week, but after arriving thirty minutes late, I basically stood by the front doors of my school's building. Then saw one of my classmates and we both walked in, but I separated from him and shrugged my shoulders and left the school to walk the streets.

Leaving school, I headed down this side street and had this mindset of saying "fuck it" to school and all that shit, which really didn't seem natural to me. As I walked I also remember reaching into my bag for my phone and calling up Rebel and telling her how I didn't think this was the right decision.

She basically agreed with me and said that she knew I wasn't going to last long there because it wasn't my personality, which is funny and it seemed like most people that really knew me knew I wasn't going to be around there for long. Walking along the streets, I kept talking to Rebel about how I felt about school and me being stuck inside of a fuckin' class just to learn how to draw a pear.

When I finally got off the phone with her, I strolled along the street slowly and just watched and looked at everyone. I looked at businessmen, I saw one guy cleaning the street, and I watched another dumping out garbage, and everyone else in between.

I thought about my life and where I fit within all this and asked myself if I had just fucked myself by not attending class? By the time I got to this highly populated intersection, I got bombarded by this guy trying to sell me into a phone contract but I declined, but not before saying, "I feel your pain, yo, keep trying and get dat money!" Then I walked off and calmly sat on a ledge right across the street.

I was just zoned out, looking at the city, the people, and thinking about my life and thinking about what means what? Then this really cute girl in black tights with a long ponytail and a beautiful skin complexion two shade darker than myself appeared.

She went towards one of the trees and unlocked what seemed to be her bike, so I said to myself, "If she comes in my direction, I'm gonna ask her what she thinks about my situation." And what do you know? She did come in my direction.

"Oh, excuse me," I said to her, and she smiled and said, "Hey, what's up?"

I said to her, "I wanna ask you something if I could, see, I just walked out from my class and I really don't feel like going back. I actually feel like I'm better off just doing things the way I want to do them."

With this really concerned and analytical look on her face, she paused, then said, "Yup! I feel you. See, school isn't for everyone, and if you're going to do it? You've got to be dedicated, but even with that being said, if you go off and do your own thing, that requires hard work as well."

"True dat," I said to her as we both nodded our heads.

She went on to say to me, "I mean, hey, I'm studying to become a lawyer, but I LOVE IT!"

I said, "Well, see? That's the thing! You LOVE it! I don't give a shit about any of this, I'm not a classroom person and never was. You gotta love what you do, right?"

She agreed, then I thanked her for chatting with me before she peddled off on her bike.

You know what was funny?

Around the time that I was setting up to head to school, I actually met with Marjorie briefly and told her that I would be going to school, and the look her face had been priceless. Not only did she have a concerned look on her face, but she went on to ask me if Graphic Design was something I really wanted to do with my life? And at the time I said "yes!"

Marjorie's body language at that time seemed as though she wanted to say a bit more to me, but at the same time I think she just wanted to see me figure this out on my own, I guess.

Now with that business workshop I attended, I guess I can say that I did get at least a few good things from it. Whichever field everyone in class wanted to get into, we actually had to research a bit on it and find out as much information as possible, which is what I had done.

I mean, when it comes to research or finding out more about something, I eventually will learn and will find out. It's like a favorite pastime of mine or something since knowledge is power, as they say.

Before ever enrolling in this workshop, I looked up public speakers and messaged a few of them as well but none of them got back to me, except for this really cool dude named Joshua Walters who lives out on the west coast in California.

I gravitated towards him because he was like me in many ways. We got close as we both disclosed our goals in life, our struggles in life, and what we wanted to do with our lives. He came from a performing arts background too and he also liked the same music as I did which seems to be the pattern for people I become cool with.

Through Skype, he offered to Life Coach me once a week for a full month or so, and although it was scary to do for the first few couple of times, it sure as hell helped!

My love and my family Susan Stuart was another speaker I happened to discover via the internet just by simply searching up Public Speakers in Toronto.

She offered to meet up with me and we hit it off immediately.

I had the chance to meet up with her before I went to school and even asked her if she thought I was making the right decision? But like Marjorie, she kind of wanted me to figure it out. What strikes me to this day is that in the past when I looked up Public Speakers from Toronto, Susan never came up in the search engine, and the day I decided to search Speakers up and found her, I was pretty pessimistic about finding anyone out there from Toronto that was similar to myself.

She changed all that, though.

Since my mind wasn't really in school mode and with my mind swaying back and forth with me trying to figure out if I wanted to at least see how things worked out for the first semester, I already missed a whole bunch of classes and I increasingly became turned off from the whole experience.

What really did it was we only had until the end of the month to put down a hefty payment if we would have liked to stick around for school and still be allowed to attend classes. I think that made it easier for me to separate from school completely. Plus I knew I wasn't committed.

I marched in one morning and went into the head office of the arts building and stated my case to the coordinator that I simply wanted a clear-cut removal from my program, but they let me know that if I changed my mind I could always come back. But "nah," I knew I never wanted to. After all that was said and done, I actually got to see Care a couple of times since it takes them a while to out you from their system.

I really connected with Care, and we talked about what my journey looked like from that point on, and I even showed her some of the damn booklets I worked on before ever coming into the school.

My last visit seeing Care was an emotional one because I knew I wouldn't be seeing her anymore, but she did connect me with a like-minded individual who I did talk to a few times through email. But we never actually met up because I never really replied back since I felt like she was more about academics than I was.

Care kind of wanted me to became a Support Worker at the school, but in order to become a worker, you have to be an attending student, which I guess is fair in a sense, but doesn't make much sense to me at the same time.

When I was finally out of their school system, I met up with Susan again and told her the whole ordeal. She basically looked at me with this passionate look on her face and in her eyes and said, "Andrew, you're not the guy to be sitting in front of a computer for hours, that's not you, man, ... it's not you, you have too much passion for speaking with people!"

It got emotional and I understood what she was saying. She told me not to do anything too drastic, but for me to know and realize what I was put on this earth to do. Take six months to think about what it was I would like to do and then get started with it... I believe in life we meet people when we are supposed to meet them, and it also comes down to where we meet them.

It's like she was one of my guardian angels sent down to help me, and she did and still does.

Friends and Thinking about my Life...

While in the worst stages of my life when all my life consisted of was just going on the computer and heading back into my room, if and when I was lucky enough to break the rhythm of things, I would find myself heading back up to my room so I could sit on the edge of my bed to look outside at the sky to witness the afternoon transition into the evening.

It was beautiful and it always gave me some sort of inspiration, you know? Like seeing the blue sky get darker with fading light, which made half of the sky appear to be mixed-in with purple... it all looked so seductive.

When I sat on my bed looking at all this, it usually made me think about how I wanted my life to be, and it made me think about what I really wanted to do. It's like the sky spoke to me and kept telling me that my true self was beyond my room, and the wood and insulation and windows that at the time felt like it was locking me in, would vanish.

Sitting looking at the sky, I felt this natural high, and portions of how I wanted my life to be were picture perfect and clear.

I envisioned myself taking pictures in and around the city and I thought of exploring my city too, finding new and exciting places to take pictures of all that I saw.

Going out and having a blast with friends was something I thought about a hell of a lot, and it was a bittersweet feeling because I wanted to go out so badly, but there I was within my house feeling like I didn't have the ability to put on my clothes and open up my door to venture out.

I could have had the worst day, I could have been suicidal or in a self-harm state, but if I had the chance or remembered to just look out of my window around that transitional time where the evening was about to come in, half of my problems went away. That whole setting made me think about everything I had to work towards and that there was still some sort of hope out there somewhere.

Something! Anything!

And I mean, I wanted to reach far and high for everything that I was thinking about while in this setting, but as inspiring as it got, I would sometimes snap out of it and come back to my reality. This kept happening repeatedly. Until I was looking up at the sky one day and the question that popped up in my mind was, "Well, why are you wishing for all of this good shit when you can just make it happen?

Wishing don't mean shit! But actions mean a whole hell of a lot! Drew, it's time to act!"

That was when I stopped wishing and when my feet hit the pavement for all my dreams, and half of most of everything I have dreamed for has and is coming true right now, but it's all about making it happen!

Perspective

In two-thousand-and-eight and nine, I became pretty sick with my blood pressure going up and down all over the place, and it didn't make much sense to me at the time. I later found out that it was because of bad eating habits, and the medicines I was putting into my body. Which put me in bad shape.

My life was in complete chaos, I wasn't sleeping, and happiness didn't exist in my life at all in any sense of the word.

I wasn't going to write about this, but I'm just going with the flow right now and I would like to give anyone and everyone some type of hope. At this period in my life, I didn't really know what was going on, and I had doctor appointments every other day, and after my doctor visits, I would wait on the corner with a regular-sized bag of Cheetos and a drink of apple juice.

I was hooked up to a sleep apnea machine, in bed or for whenever I tried to rest and I had no energy…Most people who were around me at that point in my life never thought that I would make it, including my loving mother who expected me to be lifeless eventually while walking into my room in the mornings.

I myself never even thought that I would make it to see Christmas or two-thousand-and-nine. When I would lie in my bed at night waiting to fall asleep, I would put my headphones on and would listen to feel good music, like *Common*, or some *Alicia Keys* and *Jully Black*. I wanted to die happy, so I figured that I'd have some damn good music bumping if and when the world would take me away.

During this time, I also thought about the afterlife a lot and what it might be like. This also made me disconnect with and not be so attached to worldly or material possessions as much as I used to be.

But fuck! Again, once the dreaming and fantasizing was something I didn't want to do anymore, a lot of these issues went away and/or were manageable. Fighting for myself was anything other than easy, but it was well worth it! Over on the other side, the living side where you're doing more than just surviving, things really do seem more hopeful.

Life also seems more colourful as well once you get yourself to that point where you'll have a shitload of new and improved goals and aspirations.

The People

Thank you so much for reading about this crazy up and down portion of my life. It has always been my dream to share with others how interesting things got with me to say the least!

There are a lot, and I mean a lot, of people out there who are similar to me who are trying to find their way in this world, and some of them might even have crazier stories than I do.

I hope all that you have read was entertaining as well as motivational and inspiring to you. Sometimes when people are far, really far, "yeah," that far down the hole, all that person wants to hear from someone else is that, "Yes, it is possible to change and get better." That's all people want to hear because when one is way far down the dark hole like that, they've already given up hope so all they constantly do is look up every now and then to see if they hear anyone passing by to offer some encouraging words.

The person I was while starting out writing this book is not the same person I am now on the verge of finishing it. I have grown a lot, and this book itself has helped me to grow and was a healing process as well.

Half of the things I chose to write about were things I never even really addressed to myself, and I myself laughed while writing about some of these situations.

I wrote while tired, depressed, dead-like tired, feeling like a zombie, feeling very happy and hopeful, being VERY busy, and having blocks where I didn't even remember what to write, but regardless I pushed through.

Everything that I wrote here was from the heart, and when it comes to someone's life, why would someone want to sugarcoat that?

There are a lot of people out there who don't have picture-perfect lives and that needs to be shown, expressed, and talked about.

Within our society, we all try to be too perfect. Meanwhile, we really aren't, but we feel we have to live up to this image, which really isn't realistic, which is why so many people probably crack and do themselves in or fall into a very deep depression.

We're all real people, man, and one of my good friends that I actually spoke to the night before finishing this book had a really good convo with me, and we both reminded each other that everyone deals with their own personal demons. Some talk about it, and some don't.

In the end? We're all the same and we're just trying to figure out the right and proper balance to life, a balance that works for us.

So, in closing, I would like to say, whatever this book means to you and whatever you got out of it, I hope it is of some sort of good substance... and I hope to meet you on the other side, living life and achieving goals.

Drew signing off
Peace <3

P.S. Thank you so much for putting up with, and accepting my to-the-point, and, non-conventional writing style.

"Ha!"

Shout-Outs

This is in no particular order so... yeah...
Miss Alethea Spiridon, Soul, P, Funky, Rebel, Dani, Nicole,
my Second City Crew, the Secret Social, SIGZ! Everyone who
bought this damn book! My loving sister Natasha Marshall! She
always encouraged me to write as well as finish this book!

The people who are struggling, in a struggle, and those lost
within a struggle, Jobim, Big-ups to Baltimore, Maryland, Philly,
Edmonton, California, Jersey, NYC and of course my home
always and forever TORONTO, ONTARIO! People who are
contemplating suicide, and those who have lost their lives by
way of suicide, loved ones who might have a family member or a
friend who is in need of some help, all cities and towns in South,
Central and North America, Africa and around the world!

Big-up my loving Taxi crew! Keep your heads up! Shout out to that
girl from Michigan and Christa from Miami, Florida — girl you're a
lifeline! Heart, you already know what it is... *hearts* Jessica? I hope
I'm making you smile... and _____ thank you so much, you got
my back so without a doubt I got yours, and any and every one else
that I mentioned directly or indirectly within this book and those
who I did not get the chance to mention, oh and to those I crossed
paths with and to new friends as well, one love plus a big shout to
Ashley Clyke, with her talented writing self! Matt Baxter and Danny
Adhim, DIANNE STUART, Jeff D Stevens, and Blake Slinkard!
And a very, very, VERY special love and appreciation
to the people I did not and could not place within
the confines of this book! One LOVE!

A big special thanks also, to rapper AZ straight out of Brooklyn, NYC!
I say this because his music was often playing while my life was
playing out. His music was and still is an important part of my life
since it naturally became the soundtrack to my life and helped me
persevere during some very dark times. So, to you Mr. Anthony Cruz
I say love and respect! You helped to balance out the not so great
times and encouraged me to believe in myself and to strive for better.

ABOUT THE AUTHOR

Andrew Marshall, aka Drew M., is a wacky, quirky, loving, and creative individual who can be outspoken when it comes to specific topics such as mental health, creation, motivation, and innovation. He currently resides in Toronto, Canada. My Experience: Climbing Out the Hole is his first book.

Bookings

If you would like for me to talk more about my
book or my experience in person, please do not
hesitate to contact me through my channels!
I look forward to connecting with you all...
With lots of love...

Drew.

Cr8tv Design

Web: www.cr8tv.design
Email: drewcr8tv@gmail.com
Instagram: @drew_cr8tv

Printed in the United States
By Bookmasters